TENNIS AND PHILOSOPHY

The Philosophy of Popular Culture

The books published in the Philosophy of Popular Culture series will illuminate and explore philosophical themes and ideas that occur in popular culture. The goal of this series is to demonstrate how philosophical inquiry has been reinvigorated by increased scholarly interest in the intersection of popular culture and philosophy, as well as to explore through philosophical analysis beloved modes of entertainment, such as movies, TV shows, and music. Philosophical concepts will be made accessible to the general reader through examples in popular culture. This series seeks to publish both established and emerging scholars who will engage a major area of popular culture for philosophical interpretation and examine the philosophical underpinnings of its themes. Eschewing ephemeral trends of philosophical and cultural theory, authors will establish and elaborate on connections between traditional philosophical ideas from important thinkers and the ever-expanding world of popular culture.

Series Editor

Mark T. Conard, Marymount Manhattan College, NY

Books in the Series

The Philosophy of Stanley Kubrick, edited by Jerold J. Abrams
Football and Philosophy, edited by Michael W. Austin
The Philosophy of the Coen Brothers, edited by Mark T. Conard
The Philosophy of Film Noir, edited by Mark T. Conard
The Philosophy of Martin Scorsese, edited by Mark T. Conard
The Philosophy of Neo-Noir, edited by Mark T. Conard
The Philosophy of Horror, edited by Thomas Fahy
The Philosophy of The X-Files, edited by Dean A. Kowalski
Steven Spielberg and Philosophy, edited by Dean A. Kowalski
The Philosophy of Science Fiction Film, edited by Steven M. Sanders
The Philosophy of TV Noir, edited by Steven M. Sanders and Aeon J. Skoble
Basketball and Philosophy, edited by Jerry L. Walls and Gregory Bassham

TENNIS AND PHILOSOPHY

WHAT THE RACKET IS ALL ABOUT

EDITED BY **DAVID BAGGETT**

THE UNIVERSITY PRESS OF KENTUCKY

Copyright © 2010 by The University Press of Kentucky

Scholarly publisher for the Commonwealth,
serving Bellarmine University, Berea College, Centre
College of Kentucky, Eastern Kentucky University,
The Filson Historical Society, Georgetown College,
Kentucky Historical Society, Kentucky State University,
Morehead State University, Murray State University,
Northern Kentucky University, Transylvania University,
University of Kentucky, University of Louisville,
and Western Kentucky University.
All rights reserved.

Editorial and Sales Offices: The University Press of Kentucky
663 South Limestone Street, Lexington, Kentucky 40508-4008
www.kentuckypress.com

14 13 12 11 10   5 4 3 2 1

Library of Congress Cataloging-in-Publication Data

Tennis and philosophy : what the racket is all about / edited by David
Baggett.
        p.   cm.— (The philosophy of popular culture)
    Includes bibliographical references and index.
    ISBN 978-0-8131-2574-9 (hardcover : alk. paper)
    1. Tennis. 2. Tennis—Philosophy. I. Baggett, David.
    GV995.T414 2010
    796.34201—dc22

                                    2010006311

This book is printed on acid-free recycled paper meeting
the requirements of the American National Standard
for Permanence in Paper for Printed Library Materials.

Manufactured in the United States of America.

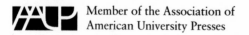 Member of the Association of
American University Presses

To Arthur Ashe

It's no accident . . . that tennis uses the language of life. Advantage, service, fault, break, love, the basic elements of tennis are those of everyday existence, because every match is a life in miniature. Even the structure of tennis, the way the pieces fit inside one another like Russian nesting dolls, mimics the structure of our days. Points become games become sets become tournaments, and it's all so tightly connected that any point can become the turning point. It reminds me of the way seconds become minutes become hours, and any hour can be our finest. Or darkest. It's our choice.

—Andre Agassi, *Open: An Autobiography*

CONTENTS

ACKNOWLEDGMENTS

My sincerest thanks to Joshua Walker, Laura Jones, JohnMark Slothower, Joshua Tomlinson, David Lahm, Steve Hudson, and Ryan Andrews for each of their valuable contributions to this book. Many thanks to my copyeditor, Erin Holman, and to all the good folks at the University Press of Kentucky, especially Anne Dean Watkins and David Cobb, for believing in the project, seeing it through to completion, and for being such a joy to work with. And thanks most of all to my contributors for their tireless and patient efforts to make the book all it could be.

Thanks as well to Steve Archibald, Ginger Asel, Pete Oleksiak, Rusty Wallace, and my Kingston bunch for all the tennis memories.

David Baggett

INTRODUCTION

The Love of Wisdom

From the Red Wings to the Tigers, Michigan is an ideal place for a kid to enjoy sports. It was there that I fell in love with tennis one summer, after my parents had given me and my siblings tennis rackets the Christmas before. I soon played with whomever I could find, usually a hapless neighbor or friend, though one particular friend and I got to enjoy imagining ourselves as Björn Borg and Vitas Gerulaitis, respectively, envisioning throngs of admiring spectators relishing every moment of our little matches.

Something about the game captured my attention right from the start, and I have grown only more and more fond of it through the years. I never played on a tennis team; my high school didn't have one, and in college I was too busy falling in love with philosophy. Tennis always remained a passion for me, even though I was never more than a recreational player—my one personal brush with tennis greatness was a group lesson with Eddie Dibbs, who reached #5 in the world in 1978 (Borg considers his 1977 win over Dibbs in Barcelona one of his ten biggest victories). The sport still mesmerizes me. I love the strategy, the angles, the power, the challenge of it all. The thousand variables, the need for mental resilience, the rugged individualism of it, the back and forth and side to side, the spins and slices and serves—everything about the game enthralls me as a player. Its sheer beauty, and the occasions it affords for excellence, at times have seemed to me nothing less than sublime and not infrequently have brought to mind the way Plato thought that instances of beauty in this world make our hearts ache for its truest source. When anyone ever says it's just a game, I have to smile.

As fanatical as I have been as a player for the last twenty-five years, I am an even bigger fan. Little did I know how magical was the time of professional tennis when I started watching it on television—it wasn't until I went in person to a professional tournament years later and saw the likes of Connors and Vilas that I had the slightest clue how hard these guys hit. I sat spellbound for four hours watching Borg and McEnroe in their classic Wimbledon match in 1980, and I was hooked. More than that, I was enthralled all over again—this time by the way these two polar opposites, fire and ice, could equally arrive at such lofty peaks by such utterly different routes. This dazzling demonstration of tennis brilliance didn't discourage me from ever aspiring to such greatness; rather, I could hardly wait to get out and play afterward. And inspiration to play and improve came not just from the Ice Man and Johnny Mac. I got to watch the Evert-Navratilova rivalry, and the Borg-Connors matchup, and the McEnroe-Lendl challenge. Later came Sampras and Agassi, Graf and Seles, Federer and Nadal, Serena and Venus. I'm still fourteen years old when I watch a match.

A third element added to my love of sports, and tennis in particular, and this one was a direct function of living in Michigan. I still remember the morning, as a teenager, I sat and ate breakfast while I enjoyed the sports section of the newspaper, like I always did growing up, and read an article by a fresh new writer in town. Halfway through the piece I forgot I was reading an article; I was that caught up in it. I knew after reading it that I would start every morning reading this fellow, and immediately I started telling everyone that this guy was special. (When I was in graduate school a few years later, my parents clipped out his articles and mailed them to me.) Indeed he was special, and still is. Soon after arriving in Detroit, he went up for a prestigious sportswriting award and won it, and the next year he was in the running for it again. Nobody had ever won it twice. He did. He's now been named the best sports columnist in the nation a record thirteen times by the Associated Press Sports Edition and won best feature-writing honors from that same outfit seven times, also a record. In fact, no other writer has received the award more than once. So it wasn't long before the whole world knew what Michiganders already did: Mitch Albom was no ordinary sportswriter. His *Tuesdays with Morrie* would show the nation and the world what a remarkable writer he is. Perhaps more than anyone, Mitch developed within me a love for analyzing sport, for "peeling back the human side of sports"—as he put it in that first article I read. Later, after I trained to become a philosopher, it was only a matter of time before I would do some work in the philosophy of sport, tennis in particular, in no small part thanks to him. That's why I wanted to edit this book.

It's been thirty years since I started playing the game, and my love for tennis has only grown. Although I eventually reconciled myself never to even begin attaining the heights of my childhood heroes, tennis was an endless source of delight for me as I played through my twenties and thirties. Tennis has never stopped being a cherished companion along life's way, and I never stopped being a fan of the tennis greats. The older I have grown, the more zealous I have become as a lover of tennis and its history, of those who showed what tennis at its best could be, and of those seminal defining moments when we can't help but marvel at the excellence displayed, the humanness revealed, the beauty exemplified.

Like you, we are aware of swirling allegations of the occasional betting, tanking, or drug issue; the peculiar pitfalls an individualistic sport like tennis is vulnerable to; the way televised tennis, with its ubiquitous microphones, can lay bare a player's psyche for all of us to see and hear— and then either recoil from such displays, recognize our own worst selves at those moments, or both. We're all too aware of the way image can replace substance and advertisers can reward a pretty player or colorful personality more than a more accomplished or quieter player with a stronger character. Such realities are part of the world of tennis as well.

Tennis remains, however, indelibly defined in my mind by its best moments—youngsters shaking hands after a match and remaining friends; partisans acknowledging the brilliant shots of the players they're rooting against; a player correcting a line call in favor of his opponent; children of apartheid seeing a black man win a tournament and feeling hope; a girl's eyes brightening watching the likes of a Steffi Graf or Serena Williams win Wimbledon; an Andre Agassi using his earnings to start a school for underprivileged kids; a Billie Jean King showing the world a woman could beat a man; a Pete Sampras courageously fighting on while losing his best friend to cancer; the artistry of a Roger Federer or John McEnroe; the dignity of a Rod Laver or Arthur Ashe; the tenacity and talent of a Martina Navratilova or Venus Williams; the resilience of a Monica Seles, James Blake, or Justine Henin.

As a philosopher, I have long thought that tennis provides a practically ideal springboard to discuss issues that matter. Philosophy, etymologically, is the "love of wisdom," and tennis can help us glean insights into wisdom—perhaps more than you might imagine. David Foster Wallace's blurb for the book *Tennis and the Meaning of Life* was perfect: "My only complaint is the title's redundant." Our book aims to allow even longtime lovers of tennis to remember what drew them into the game, what about this dance of serves and volleys is so exciting, and how tennis can perhaps indeed shed a little light on the meaning of life.

Our goal in this book is to use tennis for discussing philosophy, but we are equally aiming, in our discussion, to accord tennis the pride of place it deserves as a worthwhile and valuable end in itself, a showcase of intrinsic goods like excellence, sportsmanship, and beauty. All of the contributors, in addition to being philosophers, are lovers of the game who have no intention to downplay the elegance or importance of tennis itself. In each chapter we strive to share knowledge of the game while showing a heartfelt respect for its history and inherent worth. Even when we are critical of the behaviors of certain players, we tend to craft sufficiently nuanced analyses in order that we never come across as categorically critical. Moreover, as philosophers and fans, we aim to highlight distinctive features of tennis itself, rather than aspects of sports more generally, and in this way too, we hope to draw in readers who are lovers of the game. In the process we strive to offer substantive philosophical analyses, with ample tennis examples to make the medicine go down smoothly, along with plenty of practical wisdom and fun along the way.

There's something for everyone here, even an interview with Brad Gilbert! We're delighted to start off the fun with the legendary David Foster Wallace piece, "Federer as Religious Experience." In the Tennis Hall of Fame in Newport, Rhode Island, a whole room is devoted to the famous King versus Riggs Battle of the Sexes, perhaps the most important tennis match ever played. We devote a chapter to it here. We also discuss race and gender, beauty and virtue, excellence and sportsmanship. We explore temper tantrums and the ugly aspects of competition, pushy tennis parents, and improper behavior of fans. We delve into the artistic and aesthetic aspects of tennis, the intrinsic goods of the game, and its social relevance. We ask and try to answer the question of who was the all-time greatest tennis player, whether there will ever be a great tennis movie, the infamous and tragic Seles stabbing; we look at the impact of technology, the evolution of the game, the ethics and etiquette of rage, the vice of gamesmanship. We peel back the personal dimension of the game, focus our attention on some moments when tennis transcended sport, and other moments when it revealed both the potential and pitfalls of the human condition, and generally use tennis as a springboard to consider questions that matter. As lovers of philosophy and tennis, it was our pleasure to write such a book, and we hope you derive as much enjoyment from reading it.

David Foster Wallace

FEDERER AS RELIGIOUS EXPERIENCE

Almost anyone who loves tennis and follows the men's tour on television has, over the last few years, had what might be termed Federer Moments. These are times, as you watch the young Swiss play, when the jaw drops and eyes protrude and sounds are made that bring spouses in from other rooms to see if you're O.K.

The Moments are more intense if you've played enough tennis to understand the impossibility of what you just saw him do. We've all got our examples. Here is one. It's the finals of the 2005 U.S. Open, Federer serving to Andre Agassi early in the fourth set. There's a medium-long exchange of groundstrokes, one with the distinctive butterfly shape of today's power-baseline game, Federer and Agassi yanking each other from side to side, each trying to set up the baseline winner . . . until suddenly Agassi hits a hard heavy cross-court backhand that pulls Federer way out wide to his ad (=left) side, and Federer gets to it but slices the stretch backhand short, a couple feet past the service line, which of course is the sort of thing Agassi dines out on, and as Federer's scrambling to reverse and get back to center, Agassi's moving in to take the short ball on the rise, and he smacks it hard right back into the same ad corner, trying to wrong-foot Federer, which in fact he does—Federer's still near the corner but running toward the centerline, and the ball's heading to a point behind him now, where he just was, and there's no time to turn his body around, and Agassi's following the shot in to the net at an angle from the backhand side . . . and what Federer now does is somehow instantly reverse thrust and sort of skip backward three or four steps, impossibly fast, to hit a forehand out of his backhand corner, all his weight moving backward, and the forehand is a topspin screamer down the line past Agassi at net, who lunges for it but the ball's past him, and it flies straight down the sideline and lands exactly in the deuce corner of Agassi's side, a winner—Federer's still dancing backward as it lands. And there's that familiar little second of shocked silence from the New York crowd before it erupts, and John McEnroe with his color man's headset on TV says (mostly to himself, it sounds like), "How do you hit a winner from that position?" And he's right: given Agassi's position and world-class quickness, Federer had to send that ball down a two-inch pipe of space in order to pass him, which he did, moving backwards, with no setup time and none of his weight behind the shot. It was impossible. It was like something out of *The Matrix*. I don't know what-all sounds were involved, but my spouse says she hurried in and there was popcorn all over the couch and I was down on one knee and my eyeballs looked like novelty-shop eyeballs.

Anyway, that's one example of a Federer Moment, and that was merely on TV—and the truth is that TV tennis is to live tennis pretty much as video porn is to the felt reality of human love.

Journalistically speaking, there is no hot news to offer you about Roger Federer. He is, at 25, the best tennis player currently alive. Maybe the best ever. Bios and profiles abound. *60 Minutes* did a feature on him just last year. Anything you want to know about Mr. Roger N.M.I. Federer—his background, his home town of Basel, Switzerland, his parents' sane and unexploitative support of his talent, his junior tennis career, his early problems with fragility and temper, his beloved junior coach, how that coach's accidental death in 2002 both shattered and annealed Federer and helped make him what he now is, Federer's 39 career singles titles, his eight Grand Slams, his unusually steady and mature commitment to the girlfriend who travels with him (which on the men's tour is rare) and handles his affairs (which on the men's tour is unheard of), his old-school stoicism and mental toughness and good sportsmanship and evident overall decency and thoughtfulness and charitable largess—it's all just a Google search away. Knock yourself out.

This present article is more about a spectator's experience of Federer, and its context. The specific thesis here is that if you've never seen the young man play live, and then do, in person, on the sacred grass of Wimbledon, through the literally withering heat and then wind and rain of the '06 fortnight, then you are apt to have what one of the tournament's press bus drivers describes as a "bloody near-religious experience." It may be tempting, at first, to hear a phrase like this as just one more of the overheated tropes that people resort to to describe the feeling of Federer Moments. But the driver's phrase turns out to be true—literally, for an instant ecstatically—though it takes some time and serious watching to see this truth emerge.

Beauty is not the goal of competitive sports, but high-level sports are a prime venue for the expression of human beauty. The relation is roughly that of courage to war.

The human beauty we're talking about here is beauty of a particular type; it might be called kinetic beauty. Its power and appeal are universal. It has nothing to do with sex or cultural norms. What it seems to have to do with, really, is human beings' reconciliation with the fact of having a body.[1]

Of course, in men's sports no one ever talks about beauty or grace or the body. Men may profess their "love" of sports, but that love must always be cast and enacted in the symbology of war: elimination vs. advance, hierarchy of rank and standing, obsessive statistics, technical analysis, tribal and/or nationalist fervor, uniforms, mass noise, banners, chest-thumping, face-painting, etc. For reasons that are not well understood, war's codes are safer for most of us than love's. You too may find them so, in which case Spain's mesomorphic and totally martial Rafael Nadal is the man's man for you—he of the unsleeved biceps and Kabuki self-exhortations. Plus Nadal is also Federer's nemesis and the big surprise of this year's Wimbledon, since he's a clay-court specialist and no one expected him to make it past the first few rounds here. Whereas Federer, through the semifinals, has provided no surprise or competitive drama at all. He's outplayed each opponent so completely that the TV and print press are worried his matches are dull and can't compete effectively with the nationalist fervor of the World Cup.[2]

July 9's men's final, though, is everyone's dream. Nadal vs. Federer is a replay of last month's French Open final, which Nadal won. Federer has so far lost only four matches all year, but they've all been to Nadal. Still, most of these matches have been on slow clay, Nadal's best surface.

Grass is Federer's best. On the other hand, the first week's heat has baked out some of the Wimbledon courts' slickness and made them slower. There's also the fact that Nadal has adjusted his clay-based game to grass—moving in closer to the baseline on his groundstrokes, amping up his serve, overcoming his allergy to the net. He just about disemboweled Agassi in the third round. The networks are in ecstasies. Before the match, on Centre Court, behind the glass slits above the south backstop, as the linesmen are coming out on court in their new *Ralph Lauren* uniforms that look so much like children's navalwear, the broadcast commentators can be seen practically bouncing up and down in their chairs. This Wimbledon final's got the revenge narrative, the king-versus-regicide dynamic, the stark character contrasts. It's the passionate machismo of southern Europe versus the intricate clinical artistry of the north. Apollo and Dionysus. Scalpel and cleaver. Righty and southpaw. Nos. 1 and 2 in the world. Nadal, the man who's taken the modern power-baseline game just as far as it goes, versus a man who's transfigured that modern game, whose precision and variety are as big a deal as his pace and foot-speed, but who may be peculiarly vulnerable to, or psyched out by, that first man. A British sportswriter, exulting with his mates in the press section, says, twice, "It's going to be a war."

Plus it's in the cathedral of Centre Court. And the men's final is always on the fortnight's second Sunday, the symbolism of which Wimbledon emphasizes by always omitting play on the first Sunday. And the spattery gale that has knocked over parking signs and everted umbrellas all morning suddenly quits an hour before match time, the sun emerging just as Centre Court's tarp is rolled back and the net posts driven home.

Federer and Nadal come out to applause, make their ritual bows to the nobles' box. The Swiss is in the buttermilk-colored sport coat that Nike's gotten him to wear for Wimbledon this year. On Federer, and perhaps on him alone, it doesn't look absurd with shorts and sneakers. The Spaniard eschews all warm-up clothing, so you have to look at his muscles right away. He and the Swiss are both in all-Nike, up to the very same kind of tied white Nike hankie with the swoosh positioned above the third eye. Nadal tucks his hair under his hankie, but Federer doesn't, and smoothing and fussing with the bits of hair that fall over the hankie is the main Federer tic TV viewers get to see; likewise Nadal's obsessive retreat to the ballboy's towel between points. There happen to be other tics and habits, though, tiny perks of live viewing. There's the great care Roger Federer takes to hang the sport coat over his spare courtside chair's back, just so, to keep it from wrinkling—he's done this before each match here, and something about it seems childlike and weirdly sweet. Or the way he inevitably changes out his racket sometime in the second set, the new one always in the same clear plastic bag closed with blue tape, which he takes off carefully and always hands to a ballboy to dispose of. There's Nadal's habit of constantly picking his long shorts out of his bottom as he bounces the ball before serving, his way of always cutting his eyes warily from side to side as he walks the baseline, like a convict expecting to be shanked. And something odd on the Swiss's serve, if you look very closely. Holding ball and racket out in front, just before starting the motion, Federer always places the ball precisely in the V-shaped gap of the racket's throat, just below the head, just for an instant. If the fit isn't perfect, he adjusts the ball until it is. It happens very fast, but also every time, on both first serves and second.

Nadal and Federer now warm each other up for precisely five minutes; the umpire keeps time. There's a very definite order and etiquette to these pro warm-ups, which is something that television has decided you're not interested in seeing. Centre Court holds 13,000 and change. Another several thousand have done what people here do willingly every year, which is to pay a stiff general admission at the gate and then gather, with hampers and mosquito spray, to watch the match on an enormous TV screen outside Court 1. Your guess here is probably as good as anyone's.

Right before play, up at the net, there's a ceremonial coin-toss to see who'll serve first. It's another Wimbledon ritual. The honorary coin-tosser this year is William Caines, assisted by the umpire and tournament referee. William Caines is a 7-year-old from Kent who contracted liver cancer at age 2 and somehow survived after surgery and horrific chemo. He's here representing Cancer Research UK. He's blond and pink-cheeked and comes up to about Federer's waist. The crowd roars its approval of the reenacted toss. Federer smiles distantly the whole time. Nadal, just across the net, keeps dancing in place like a boxer, swinging his arms from side to side. I'm not sure whether the U.S. networks show the coin-toss or not, whether this ceremony's part of their contractual obligation or whether they get to cut to commercial. As William's ushered off, there's more cheering, but it's scattered and disorganized; most of the crowd can't quite tell what to do. It's like once the ritual's over, the reality of why this child was part of it sinks in. There's a feeling of something important, something both uncomfortable and not, about a child with cancer tossing this dream-final's coin. The feeling, what-all it might mean, has a tip-of-the-tongue-type quality that remains elusive for at least the first two sets.[3]

A top athlete's beauty is next to impossible to describe directly. Or to evoke. Federer's forehand is a great liquid whip, his backhand a one-hander that he can drive flat, load with topspin, or slice—the slice with such snap that the ball turns shapes in the air and skids on the grass to maybe ankle height. His serve has world-class pace and a degree of placement and variety no one else comes close to; the service motion is lithe and uneccentric, distinctive (on TV) only in a certain eel-like all-body snap at the moment of impact. His anticipation and court sense are otherworldly, and his footwork is the best in the game—as a child, he was also a soccer prodigy. All this is true, and yet none of it really explains anything or evokes the experience of watching this man play. Of witnessing, firsthand, the beauty and genius of his game. You more have to come at the aesthetic stuff obliquely, to talk around it, or—as Aquinas did with his own ineffable subject—to try to define it in terms of what it is not.

One thing it is not is televisable. At least not entirely. TV tennis has its advantages, but these advantages have disadvantages, and chief among them is a certain illusion of intimacy. Television's slow-mo replays, its close-ups and graphics, all so privilege viewers that we're not even aware of how much is lost in broadcast. And a large part of what's lost is the sheer physicality of top tennis, a sense of the speeds at which the ball is moving and the players are reacting. This loss is simple to explain. TV's priority, during a point, is coverage of the whole court, a comprehensive view, so that viewers can see both players and the overall geometry of the exchange. Television therefore chooses a specular vantage that is overhead and behind one baseline. You, the viewer, are above and looking down from behind the court. This perspective, as any art student will tell you, "foreshortens" the court. Real tennis, after all, is three-dimensional, but a TV screen's image is only 2-D. The dimension that's lost (or rather distorted) on the screen is the real court's length, the 78 feet between baselines; and the speed with which the ball traverses this length is a shot's pace, which on TV is obscured, and in person is fearsome to behold. That may sound abstract or overblown, in which case by all means go in person to some professional tournament—especially to the outer courts in early rounds, where you can sit 20 feet from the sideline—and sample the difference for yourself. If you've watched tennis only on television, you simply have no idea how hard these pros are hitting the ball, how fast the ball is moving,[4] how little time the players have to get to it, and how quickly they're able to move and rotate and strike and recover. And none are faster, or more deceptively effortless about it, than Roger Federer.

Interestingly, what is less obscured in TV coverage is Federer's intelligence, since this intelligence often manifests as angle. Federer is able to see, or create, gaps and angles for winners that no one else can envision, and television's perspective is perfect for viewing and reviewing these Federer Moments. What's harder to appreciate on TV is that these spectacular-looking angles and winners are not coming from nowhere—they're often set up several shots ahead, and depend as much on Federer's manipulation of opponents' positions as they do on the pace or placement of the coup de grâce. And understanding how and why Federer is able to move other world-class athletes around this way requires, in turn, a better technical understanding of the modern power-baseline game than TV—again—is set up to provide.

Wimbledon is strange. Verily it is the game's Mecca, the cathedral of tennis; but it would be easier to sustain the appropriate level of on-site veneration if the tournament weren't so intent on reminding you over and over that it's the cathedral of tennis. There's a peculiar mix of stodgy self-satisfaction and relentless self-promotion and -branding. It's a bit like the sort of authority figure whose office wall has every last plaque, diploma, and award he's ever gotten, and every time you come into the office you're forced to look at the wall and say something to indicate that you're impressed. Wimbledon's own walls, along nearly every significant corridor and passage, are lined with posters and signs featuring shots of past champions, lists of Wimbledon facts and trivia, historic lore, and so on. Some of this stuff is interesting; some is just odd. The Wimbledon Lawn Tennis Museum, for instance, has a collection of all the various kinds of rackets used here through the decades, and one of the many signs along the Level 2 passage of the Millennium Building[5] promotes this exhibition with both photos and didactic text, a kind of History of the Racket. Here, *sic,* is the climactic end of this text:

> Today's lightweight frames made of space-age materials like graphite, boron, titanium and ceramics, with larger heads—mid-size (90–95 square inches) and over-size (110 square inches)—have totally transformed the character of the game. Nowadays it is the powerful hitters who dominate with heavy topspin. Serve-and-volley players and those who rely on subtlety and touch have virtually disappeared.

It seems odd, to say the least, that such a diagnosis continues to hang here so prominently in the fourth year of Federer's reign over Wimbledon, since the Swiss has brought to men's tennis degrees of touch and subtlety unseen since (at least) the days of McEnroe's prime. But the sign's really just a testament to the power of dogma. For almost two decades, the party line's been that certain advances in racket technology, conditioning, and weight training have transformed pro tennis from a game of quickness and finesse into one of athleticism and brute power. And as an etiology of today's power-baseline game, this party line is broadly accurate. Today's pros truly are measurably bigger, stronger, and better conditioned,[6] and high-tech composite rackets really have increased their capacities for pace and spin. How, then, someone of Federer's consummate finesse has come to dominate the men's tour is a source of wide and dogmatic confusion.

There are three kinds of valid explanation for Federer's ascendancy. One kind involves mystery and metaphysics and is, I think, closest to the real truth. The others are more technical and make for better journalism.

The metaphysical explanation is that Roger Federer is one of those rare, preternatural athletes who appear to be exempt, at least in part, from certain physical laws. Good analogues here include Michael Jordan,[7] who could not only jump inhumanly high but actually hang there a beat or two longer than gravity allows, and Muhammed Ali, who really could "float" across the canvas and land two or three jabs in the clock-time required for one. There are probably a half-dozen other examples since 1960. And Federer is of this type—a type that one could call genius, or mutant, or avatar. He is never hurried or off-balance. The approaching ball hangs, for him, a split-second longer than it ought to. His movements are lithe rather than athletic. Like Ali, Jordan, Maradona, and

Gretzky, he seems both less and more substantial than the men he faces. Particularly in the all-white that Wimbledon enjoys getting away with still requiring, he looks like what he may well (I think) be: a creature whose body is both flesh and, somehow, light.

This thing about the ball cooperatively hanging there, slowing down, as if susceptible to the Swiss's will—there's real metaphysical truth here. And in the following anecdote. After a July 7 semifinal in which Federer destroyed Jonas Bjorkman—not just beat him, destroyed him—and just before a requisite postmatch news conference in which Bjorkman, who's friendly with Federer, says he was pleased to "have the best seat in the house" to watch the Swiss "play the nearest to perfection you can play tennis," Federer and Bjorkman are chatting and joking around, and Bjorkman asks him just how unnaturally big the ball was looking to him out there, and Federer confirms that it was "like a bowling ball or basketball." He means it just as a bantery, modest way to make Bjorkman feel better, to confirm that he's surprised by how unusually well he played today; but he's also revealing something about what tennis is like for him. Imagine that you're a person with preternaturally good reflexes and co-ordination and speed, and that you're playing high-level tennis. Your experience, in play, will not be that you possess phenomenal reflexes and speed; rather, it will seem to you that the tennis ball is quite large and slow-moving, and that you always have plenty of time to hit it. That is, you won't experience anything like the (empirically real) quickness and skill that the live audience, watching tennis balls move so fast they hiss and blur, will attribute to you.[8]

Velocity's just one part of it. Now we're getting technical. Tennis is often called a "game of inches," but the cliché is mostly referring to where a shot lands. In terms of a player's hitting an incoming ball, tennis is actually more a game of micrometers: vanishingly tiny changes around the moment of impact will have large effects on how and where the ball travels. The same principle explains why even the smallest imprecision in aiming a rifle will still cause a miss if the target's far enough away.

By way of illustration, let's slow things way down. Imagine that you, a tennis player, are standing just behind your deuce corner's baseline. A ball is served to your forehand—you pivot (or rotate) so that your side is to the ball's incoming path and start to take your racket back for the forehand return. Keep visualizing up to where you're about halfway into the stroke's forward motion; the incoming ball is now just off your front hip, maybe six inches from point of impact. Consider some of the variables involved here. On the vertical plane, angling your racket face just a couple degrees forward or back will create topspin or slice, respectively; keeping it perpendicular will produce a flat, spinless drive. Horizontally, adjusting the racket face ever so slightly to the left or right, and hitting the ball maybe a millisecond early or late, will result in a cross-court versus down-the-line return. Further slight changes in the curves of your groundstroke's motion and follow-through will help determine how high your return passes over the net, which, together with the speed at which you're swinging (along with certain characteristics of the spin you impart), will affect how deep or shallow in the opponent's court your return lands, how high it bounces, etc. These are just the broadest distinctions, of course—like, there's heavy topspin vs. light topspin, or sharply cross-court vs. only slightly cross-court, etc. There are also the issues of how close you're allowing the ball to get to your body, what grip you're using, the extent to which your knees are bent and/or weight's moving forward, and whether you're able simultaneously to watch the ball and to see what your opponent's doing after he serves. These all matter, too. Plus there's the fact that you're not putting a static object into motion here but rather reversing the flight and (to a varying extent) spin of a projectile coming toward you—coming, in the case of pro tennis, at speeds that make conscious thought impossible. Mario Ancic's first serve, for instance, often comes in around 130 m.p.h. Since it's 78 feet from Ancic's baseline to yours, that means it takes 0.41 seconds for his serve to reach you.[9] This is less than the time it takes to blink quickly, twice.

The upshot is that pro tennis involves intervals of time too brief for deliberate action. Temporally, we're more in the operative range of reflexes, purely physical reactions that bypass conscious thought. And yet an effective return of serve depends on a large set of decisions and physical adjustments that are a whole lot more involved and intentional than blinking, jumping when startled, etc.

Successfully returning a hard-served tennis ball requires what's sometimes called "the kinesthetic sense," meaning the ability to control the body and its artificial extensions through complex and very quick systems of tasks. English has a whole cloud of terms for various parts of this ability: feel, touch, form, proprioception, coordination, hand-eye coordination, kinesthesia, grace, control, reflexes, and so on. For promising junior players, refining the kinesthetic sense is the main goal of the extreme daily practice regimens we often hear about.[10] The training here is both muscular and neurological. Hitting thousands of strokes, day after day, develops the ability to do by "feel" what cannot be done by regular conscious thought. Repetitive practice like this often looks tedious or even cruel to an outsider, but the outsider can't feel what's going on inside the player—tiny adjustments, over and over, and a sense of each change's effects that gets more and more acute even as it recedes from normal consciousness.[11]

The time and discipline required for serious kinesthetic training are one reason why top pros are usually people who've devoted most of their waking lives to tennis, starting (at the very latest) in their early teens. It was, for example, at age 13 that Roger Federer finally gave up soccer, and a recognizable childhood, and entered Switzerland's national tennis training center in Ecublens. At 16, he dropped out of classroom studies and started serious international competition.

It was only weeks after quitting school that Federer won Junior Wimbledon. Obviously, this is something that not every junior who devotes himself to tennis can do. Just as obviously, then, there is more than time and training involved—there is also sheer talent, and degrees of it. Extraordinary kinesthetic ability must be present (and measurable) in a kid just to make the years of practice and training worthwhile . . . but from there, over time, the cream starts to rise and separate. So one type of technical explanation for Federer's dominion is that he's just a bit more kinesthetically talented than the other male pros. Only a little bit, since everyone in the Top 100 is himself kinesthetically gifted—but then, tennis is a game of inches.

This answer is plausible but incomplete. It would probably not have been incomplete in 1980. In 2006, though, it's fair to ask why this kind of talent still matters so much. Recall what is true about dogma and Wimbledon's sign. Kinesthetic virtuoso or no, Roger Federer is now dominating the largest, strongest, fittest, best-trained and -coached field of male pros who've ever existed, with everyone using a kind of nuclear racket that's said to have made the finer calibrations of kinesthetic sense irrelevant, like trying to whistle Mozart during a Metallica concert.

According to reliable sources, honorary coin-tosser William Caines's backstory is that one day, when he was 2½, his mother found a lump in his tummy, and took him to the doctor, and the lump was diagnosed as a malignant liver tumor. At which point one cannot, of course, imagine . . . a tiny child undergoing chemo, serious chemo, his mother having to watch, carry him home, nurse him, then bring him back to that place for more chemo. How did she answer her child's question—the big one, the obvious one? And who could answer hers? What could any priest or pastor say that wouldn't be grotesque?

It's 2–1 Nadal in the final's second set, and he's serving. Federer won the first set at love but then flagged a bit, as he sometimes does, and is quickly down a break. Now, on Nadal's ad, there's a 16-stroke point. Nadal is serving a lot faster than he did in Paris, and this one's down the center. Federer floats a soft forehand high over the net, which he can get away with because Nadal never comes in behind his serve. The Spaniard now hits a characteristically heavy topspin forehand deep to Federer's backhand; Federer comes back with an even heavier topspin backhand, almost a clay-court shot. It's unexpected and backs Nadal up, slightly, and his response is a low hard short ball that lands just past the service line's T on Federer's forehand side. Against most other opponents, Federer could simply end the point on a ball like this, but one reason Nadal gives him trouble is that he's faster than the others, can get to stuff they can't; and so Federer here just hits a flat, medium-hard cross-court forehand, going not for a winner but for a low, shallowly angled ball that forces Nadal up and out to the deuce side, his backhand. Nadal, on the run, backhands it hard down the line to Federer's backhand; Federer slices it right back down the same line, slow and floaty with backspin, making Nadal come back to the same spot. Nadal slices the ball right back—three shots now all down the same line—and Federer slices the ball back to the same spot yet again, this one even slower and floatier, and Nadal gets planted and hits a big two-hander back down the same line—it's like Nadal's camped out now on his deuce side; he's no longer moving all the way back to the baseline's center between shots; Federer's hypnotized him a little. Federer now hits a very hard, deep topspin backhand, the kind that hisses, to a point just slightly on the ad side of Nadal's baseline, which Nadal gets to and forehands cross-court; and Federer responds with an even harder, heavier cross-court backhand, baseline-deep and moving so fast that Nadal has to hit the forehand off his back foot and then scramble to get back to center as the shot lands maybe two feet short on Federer's backhand side again. Federer steps to this ball and now hits a totally different cross-court backhand, this one much shorter and sharper-angled, an angle no one would anticipate, and so heavy and blurred with topspin that it lands shallow and just inside the sideline and takes off hard after the bounce, and Nadal can't move in to cut it off and can't get to it laterally along the baseline, because of all the angle and topspin—end of point. It's a spectacular winner, a Federer Moment; but watching it live, you can see that it's also a winner that Federer started setting up four or even five shots earlier. Everything after that first down-the-line slice was designed by the Swiss to maneuver Nadal and lull him and then disrupt his rhythm and balance and open up that last, unimaginable angle—an angle that would have been impossible without extreme topspin.

Extreme topspin is the hallmark of today's power-baseline game. This is something that Wimbledon's sign gets right.[12] Why topspin is so key, though, is not commonly understood. What's commonly understood is that high-tech composite rackets impart much more pace to the ball, rather like aluminum baseball bats as opposed to good old lumber. But that dogma is false. The truth is that, at the same tensile strength, carbon-based composites are lighter than wood, and this allows modern rackets to be a couple ounces lighter and at least an inch wider across the face than the vintage Kramer and Maxply. It's the width of the face that's vital. A wider face means there's more total string area, which means the sweet spot's bigger. With a composite racket, you don't have to meet the ball in the precise geometric center of the strings in order to generate good pace. Nor must you be spot-on to generate topspin, a spin that (recall) requires a tilted face and upwardly curved stroke, brushing over the ball rather than hitting flat through it—this was quite hard to do with wood rackets, because of their smaller face and niggardly sweet spot. Composites' lighter, wider heads and more generous centers let players swing faster and put way more topspin on the ball . . . and, in turn, the more topspin you put on the ball, the harder you can hit it, because there's more margin for error. Topspin causes the ball to pass high over the net, describe a sharp arc, and come down fast into the opponent's court (instead of maybe soaring out).

So the basic formula here is that composite rackets enable topspin, which in turn enables groundstrokes vastly faster and harder than 20 years ago—it's common now to see male pros pulled up off the ground and halfway around in the air by the force of their strokes, which in the old days was something one saw only in Jimmy Connors.

Connors was not, by the way, the father of the power-baseline game. He whaled mightily from the baseline, true, but his groundstrokes were flat and spinless and had to pass very low over the net. Nor was Björn Borg a true power-baseliner. Both Borg and Connors played specialized versions of the classic baseline game, which had evolved as a counterforce to the even more classic serve-and-volley game, which was itself the dominant form of men's power tennis for decades, and of which John McEnroe was the greatest modern exponent. You probably know all this, and may also know that McEnroe toppled Borg and then more or less ruled the men's game until the appearance, around the mid-1980s, of (a) modern composite rackets[13] and (b) Ivan Lendl, who played with an early form of composite and was the true progenitor of power-baseline tennis.[14]

Ivan Lendl was the first top pro whose strokes and tactics appeared to be designed around the special capacities of the composite racket. His goal was to win points from the baseline, via either passing shots or outright winners. His weapon was his groundstrokes, especially his forehand, which he could hit with overwhelming pace because of the amount of topspin he put on the ball. The blend of pace and topspin also allowed Lendl to do something that proved crucial to the advent of the power-baseline game. He could pull off radical, extraordinary angles on hard-hit groundstrokes, mainly because of the speed with which heavy topspin makes the ball dip and land without going wide. In retrospect, this changed the whole physics of aggressive tennis. For decades, it had been angle that made the serve-and-volley game so lethal. The closer one is to the net, the more of the opponent's court is open—the classic advantage of volleying was that you could hit angles that would go way wide if attempted from the baseline or midcourt. But topspin on a groundstroke, if it's really extreme, can bring the ball down fast and shallow enough to exploit many of these same angles. Especially if the groundstroke you're hitting is off a somewhat short ball—the shorter the ball, the more angles are possible. Pace, topspin, and aggressive baseline angles: and lo, it's the power-baseline game.

It wasn't that Ivan Lendl was an immortally great tennis player. He was simply the first top pro to demonstrate what heavy topspin and raw power could achieve from the baseline. And, most important, the achievement was replicable, just like the composite racket. Past a certain threshold of physical talent and training, the main requirements were athleticism, aggression, and superior strength and conditioning. The result (omitting various complications and subspecialties[15]) has been men's pro tennis for the last 20 years: ever bigger, stronger, fitter players generating unprecedented pace and topspin off the ground, trying to force the short or weak ball that they can put away.

Illustrative stat: When Lleyton Hewitt defeated David Nalbandian in the 2002 Wimbledon men's final, there was not one single serve-and-volley point.[16]

The generic power-baseline game is not boring—certainly not compared with the two-second points of old-time serve-and-volley or the moon-ball tedium of classic baseline attrition. But it is somewhat static and limited; it is not, as pundits have publicly feared for years, the evolutionary endpoint of tennis. The player who's shown this to be true is Roger Federer. And he's shown it from within the modern game.

This within is what's important here; this is what a purely neural account leaves out. And it is why sexy attributions like touch and subtlety must not be misunderstood. With Federer, it's not either/or. The Swiss has every bit of Lendl and Agassi's pace on his groundstrokes, and leaves the ground when he swings, and can out-hit even Nadal from the backcourt.[17] What's strange and wrong about Wimbledon's sign, really, is its overall dolorous tone. Subtlety, touch, and finesse are not dead in the power-baseline era. For it is, still, in 2006, very much the power-baseline era: Roger Federer is a first-rate, kick-ass power-baseliner. It's just that that's not all he is. There's also his intelligence, his occult anticipation, his court sense, his ability to read and manipulate opponents, to mix spins and speeds, to misdirect and disguise, to use tactical foresight and peripheral vision and kinesthetic range instead of just rote pace—all this has exposed the limits, and possibilities, of men's tennis as it's now played.

Which sounds very high-flown and nice, of course, but please understand that with this guy it's not high-flown or abstract. Or nice. In the same emphatic, empirical, dominating way that Lendl drove home his own lesson, Roger Federer is showing that the speed and strength of today's pro game are merely its skeleton, not its flesh. He has, figuratively and literally, reembodied men's tennis, and for the first time in years the game's future is unpredictable. You should have seen, on the grounds' outside courts, the variegated ballet that was this year's Junior Wimbledon. Drop volleys and mixed spins, off-speed serves, gambits planned three shots ahead—all as well as the standard-issue grunts and booming balls. Whether anything like a nascent Federer was here among these juniors can't be known, of course. Genius is not replicable. Inspiration, though, is contagious, and multiform—and even just to see, close up, power and aggression made vulnerable to beauty is to feel inspired and (in a fleeting, mortal way) reconciled.

Notes

This correction was in the August 27, 2006, edition of the *New York Times:* An article in *PLAY* magazine last Sunday about the tennis player Roger Federer referred incompletely to a point between Federer and Andre Agassi in the 2005 United States Open final and incorrectly described Agassi's position on the final shot of the point. There was an exchange of groundstrokes in the middle of the point that was not described. And Agassi remained at the baseline on Federer's winning shot; he did not go to the net.

1. There's a great deal that's bad about having a body. If this is not so obviously true that no one needs examples, we can just quickly mention pain, sores, odors, nausea, aging, gravity, sepsis, clumsiness, illness, limits—every last schism between our physical wills and our actual capacities. Can anyone doubt we need help being reconciled? Crave it? It's your body that dies, after all.

There are wonderful things about having a body, too, obviously—it's just that these things are much harder to feel and appreciate in real time. Rather like certain kinds of rare, peak-type sensuous epiphanies ("I'm so glad I have eyes to see this sunrise!" etc.), great athletes seem to catalyze our awareness of how glorious it is to touch and perceive, move through space, interact with matter. Granted, what great athletes can do with their bodies are things that the rest of us can only dream of. But these dreams are important—they make up for a lot.

2. The U.S. media here are especially worried because no Americans of either sex survived into even the quarterfinals this year. (If you're into obscure statistics, it's the first time this has happened at Wimbledon since 1911.)

3. Actually, this is not the only Federer-and-sick-child incident of Wimbledon's second week. Three days prior to the men's final, a Special One-on-One Interview with Mr. Roger Federer[†] takes place in a small, crowded International Tennis Federation office just off the third floor of the Press Center. Right afterward, as the ATP player-rep is ushering Federer out the back door for his next scheduled obligation, one of the I.T.F. guys (who's been talking loudly on the telephone through the whole Special Interview) now comes up and asks for a moment of Roger's time. The man, who has the same slight, generically foreign accent as all I.T.F. guys, says: "Listen, I hate doing this. I don't do this, normally. It's for my neighbor. His kid has a disease. They will do a fund-raiser, it's planned, and I'm asking can you sign a shirt or something, you know—something." He looks mortified. The ATP rep is glaring at him. Federer, though, just nods, shrugs: "No problem. I'll bring it tomorrow." Tomorrow's the men's semifinal. Evidently the I.T.F. guy has meant one of Federer's own shirts, maybe from the match, with Federer's actual sweat on it. (Federer throws his used wristbands into the crowd after matches, and the people they land on seem pleased rather than grossed out.) The I.T.F. guy, after thanking Federer three times very fast, shakes his head: "I hate doing this." Federer, still halfway out the door: "It's no problem." And it isn't. Like all pros, Federer changes his shirt during matches, and he can just have somebody save one, and then he'll sign it. It's not like Federer's being Gandhi here—he doesn't stop and ask for details about the kid or his illness. He doesn't pretend to care more than he does. The request is just one more small, mildly distracting obligation he has to deal with. But he does say yes, and he will remember—you can tell. And it won't distract him; he won't permit it. He's good at this kind of stuff, too.

4. Top men's serves often reach speeds of 125–135 m.p.h., true, but what all the radar signs and graphics neglect to tell you is that male power-baseliners' groundstrokes themselves are often traveling at over 90 m.p.h., which is the speed of a big-league fastball. If you get down close enough to a pro court, you can hear an actual *sound* coming off the ball in flight, a kind of liquid hiss, from the combination of pace and spin. Close up and live, you'll also understand better the "open stance" that's become such an emblem of the power-baseline game. The term, after all, just means not turning one's side all the way to the net before hitting a groundstroke, and one reason why so many power-baseliners hit from the open stance is that the ball is now coming too fast for them to get turned all the way.

5. This is the large (and presumably six-year-old) structure where Wimbledon's administration, players, and media all have their respective areas and HQs.

6. (Some, like Nadal or Serena Williams, look more like cartoon superheroes than people.)

[†] (Only considerations of space and basic believability prevent a full description of the hassles involved in securing such a One-on-One. In brief, it's rather like the old story of someone climbing an enormous mountain to talk to the man seated lotus on top, except in this case the mountain is composed entirely of sports-bureaucrats.)

7. When asked, during the aforementioned Special One-on-One Interview, for examples of other athletes whose performances might seem beautiful to him, Federer mentions Jordan first, then Kobe Bryant, then "a soccer player like—guys who play very relaxed, like a Zinédine Zidane or something: he does great effort, but he seems like he doesn't need to try hard to get the results."

Federer's response to the subsequent question, which is what-all he makes of it when pundits and other players describe his own game as "beautiful," is interesting mainly because the response is pleasant, intelligent, and cooperative—as is Federer himself—without ever really saying anything (because, in fairness, what could one say about others' descriptions of him as beautiful? What would you say? It's ultimately a stupid question): "It's always what people see first—for them, that's what you are 'best at.' When you used to watch John McEnroe, you know, the first time, what would you see? You would see a guy with incredible talent, because the way he played, nobody played like this. The way he played the ball, it was just all about feel. And then you go over to Boris Becker, and right away you saw a *powerful* player, you know?[†] When you see me play, you see a 'beautiful' player—and maybe after that you maybe see that he's fast, maybe you see that he's got a good forehand, maybe then you see that he has a good serve. First, you know, you have a base, and to me, I think it's great, you know, and I'm very lucky to be called basically 'beautiful,' you know, for style of play. . . . With me it's, like, 'the beautiful player,' and that's really cool."

8. Special One-on-One support from the man himself for this claim: "It's interesting, because this week, actually, Ancic [comma Mario, the towering Top-10 Croatian whom Federer beat in Wednesday's quarterfinal] played on Centre Court against my friend, you know, the Swiss player Wawrinka [comma Stanislas, Federer's Davis Cup teammate], and I went to see it out where, you know, my girlfriend Mirka [Vavrinec, a former women's Top-100 player, knocked out by injury, who now basically functions as Federer's Alice B. Toklas] usually sits, and I went to see—for the first time since I have come here to Wimbledon, I went to see a match on Centre Court, and I was also surprised, actually, how fast, you know, the serve is and how fast you have to react to be able to get the ball back, especially when a guy like Mario [Ancic, who's known for his vicious serve] serves, you know? But then once you're on the court

---

[†] N.B. Federer's big conversational tics are "maybe" and "you know." Ultimately, these tics are helpful because they serve as reminders of how appallingly young he really is. If you're interested, the world's best tennis player is wearing white warm-up pants and a long-sleeved white microfiber shirt, possibly Nike. No sport coat, though. His handshake is only moderately firm, though the hand itself is like a carpentry rasp (for obvious reasons, tennis players tend to be very callusy). He's a bit bigger than TV makes him seem—broader-shouldered, deeper in the chest. He's next to a table that's covered with visors and headbands, which he's been autographing with a Sharpie. He sits with his legs crossed and smiles pleasantly and seems very relaxed; he never fidgets with the Sharpie. One's overall impression is that Federer is either a very nice guy or a guy who's very good at dealing with the media—or (most likely) both.

yourself, it's totally different, you know, because all you see is the ball, really, and you don't see the speed of the ball. . . ."

9. We're doing the math here with the ball traveling as the crow flies, for simplicity. Please do not write in with corrections. If you want to factor in the serve's bounce and so compute the total distance traveled by the ball as the sum of an oblique triangle's[†] two shorter legs, then by all means go ahead—you'll end up with between two and five additional hundredths of a second, which is not significant.

10. Conditioning is also important, but this is mainly because the first thing that physical fatigue attacks is the kinesthetic sense. (Other antagonists are fear, self-consciousness, and extreme upset—which is why fragile psyches are rare in pro tennis.)

11. The best lay analogy is probably to the way an experienced driver can make all of good driving's myriad little decisions and adjustments without having to pay attention to them.

12. (. . . assuming, that is, that the sign's "with heavy topspin" is modifying "dominate" rather than "powerful hitters," which actually it might or might not— British grammar is a bit dodgy.)

13. (which neither Connors nor McEnroe could switch to with much success— their games were fixed around pre-modern rackets.)

14. Formwise, with his whippy forehand, lethal one-hander, and merciless treatment of short balls, Lendl somewhat anticipated Federer. But the Czech was also stiff, cold, and brutal; his game was awesome but not beautiful. (My college doubles partner used to describe watching Lendl as like getting to see *Triumph of the Will* in 3-D.)

15. See, for one example, the continued effectiveness of some serve-and-volley (mainly in the adapted, heavily ace- and quickness-dependent form of a Sampras or Rafter) on fast courts through the 1990's.

16. It's also illustrative that 2002 was Wimbledon's last pre-Federer final.

17. In the third set of the '06 final, at three games all and 30–15, Nadal kicks his second serve high to Federer's backhand. Nadal's clearly been coached to go high and heavy to Federer's backhand, and that's what he does, point after point. Federer slices the return back to Nadal's center and two feet short—not short enough to let the Spaniard hit a winner, but short enough to draw him slightly into the court, whence Nadal winds up and puts all his forehand's strength into a hard heavy shot to (again) Federer's backhand. The pace he's put on the ball means that Nadal is still backpedaling to the baseline as Federer leaves his feet and cranks a very hard topspin backhand down the line to Nadal's deuce side, which Nadal—out of position but world-class fast—reaches and manages to one-hand back deep to (again) Federer's backhand side, but this ball's floaty and slow, and Federer has time to step around and hit an inside-out forehand, a forehand as hard as anyone's hit all tournament, with just enough topspin to bring it down in Nadal's ad corner, and the Spaniard gets there but can't

---

[†] (The slower a tennis court's surface, the closer to a right triangle you're going to have. On fast grass, the bounce's angle is always oblique.)

return it. Big ovation. Again, what looks like an overwhelming baseline winner was actually set up by that first clever semi-short slice and Nadal's own predictability about where and how hard he'll hit every ball. Federer sure whaled that last forehand, though. People are looking at each other and applauding. The thing with Federer is that he's Mozart and Metallica at the same time, and the harmony's somehow exquisite.

By the way, it's right around here, or the next game, watching, that three separate inner-type things come together and mesh. One is a feeling of deep personal privilege at being alive to get to see this; another is the thought that William Caines is probably somewhere here in the Centre Court crowd, too, watching, maybe with his mum. The third thing is a sudden memory of the earnest way the press bus driver promised just this experience. Because there is one. It's hard to describe—it's like a thought that's also a feeling. One wouldn't want to make too much of it, or to pretend that it's any sort of equitable balance; that would be grotesque. But the truth is that whatever deity, entity, energy, or random genetic flux produces sick children also produced Roger Federer, and just look at him down there. Look at that.

David Baggett

WHY ROGER FEDERER IS THE BEST

Or Is It McEnroe?

He who would be greatest, let him serve.
—Mark 9:35[1]

In *The Simpsons Movie,* Bart at one point sadly pronounces, "This is the worst day of my life," to which Homer, manifesting the full resplendence of his wisdom, soberly offers a needed correction: "The worst day of your life *so far.*"

The question of the all-time best (men's) tennis player requires such qualification.[2] Let's suppose for a moment that the answer is indeed Roger Federer. That would mean that Federer is the all-time best so far, which suggests that, before Federer, the title could have been held by another, maybe Borg or Sampras, perhaps Laver or Emerson before them. And it means that in the future a new contender might emerge, one even better than Federer.

The answer to the question of the all-time best is not something I will suppose or imagine but rather think about and argue for, even though the question is difficult.[3] What makes the question a hard one is also what makes it fun and philosophically interesting. For getting at the heart of the question, and attempting to generate an answer, requires, among other things, conceptual clarity, effective argument, and recognition of a range of potential approaches, all of which enable a deeper appreciation of the difficulty of the question, and all of which are in the particular province of the philosopher.

Why would philosophers care about such a question, though? Shouldn't they be concerned about loftier matters and more recondite questions? Well, philosophers sometimes are tennis fans too, and, in fact, some of them were lovers of tennis before falling in love with philosophy. Besides, the question of the all-time best is not just enjoyable to ponder and inherently fascinating, it broaches issues in both metaphysics and epistemology, important branches of philosophy—metaphysics asks "What is the case?" and epistemology asks "How is it we come to know what's the case?" Perhaps most important of all, though, asking and trying to answer the question of the all-time best is, like tennis, both a good exercise (a mental one, in this case) and fun.

As Federer surpassed the record of Slam victories, the question of where he stands in the line of all-time greats gained steam. So, one who studies great Greeks like Aristotle, Socrates, Plato, and Sampras is ideal to ponder the question of the all-time best tennis player. What are the criteria to qualify for the honor of the all-time best? Are there competing sets of criteria? Is one such set privileged or the "right" one? Can we know which set this is? Does "Federer is the all-time greatest tennis player" express a proposition? Is the sentence true? Is there a fact of the matter? Even if it's true, can we know it to be true? Are we confronted with intractable commensurability problems when comparing players from different eras, using different equipment, facing different opponents? These are among the distinctively philosophical questions that arise as we ponder the question before us.

I write this chapter as a tennis fan for fellow lovers of the game and its history. I also happen to be a philosopher, and my take on the question will be philosophical, without apology. As much fun as the question is to ponder, more important than my answer to the question will be the philosophical issues that arise along the way. The question thereby gives us a chance to discuss matters at the intersection of tennis and philosophy, so for fans of both, this should make for a good time.

The Competition

In the history of tennis, several great players have vied for the honor of the all-time best. From Roy Emerson to Pancho Gonzales, from Rod Laver to Björn Borg, from Pete Sampras to Roger Federer, each of these names has been in serious contention. It's impossible here to do justice to all the greats of the game. Unless Ellsworth Vines, Fred Perry, Lew Hoad, and Ken Rosewall are included, their fans will understandably cry foul. Although I love the sport and relish its history, my forte is not in authoritatively excluding such great players from the list; but for the sake of brevity and a manageable discussion, allow me, while paying due respect to those just mentioned, to defer to the most commonly cited players in the running.

Setting Federer aside for the moment, let's suppose we consider a pool of twelve potential candidates who belong to this elite company. In alphabetical order, here they are: Andre Agassi, Björn Borg, Don Budge, Jimmy Connors, Roy Emerson, Roger Federer, Jack Kramer, Rod Laver, Ivan Lendl, John McEnroe, Pete Sampras, and Bill Tilden. Readers will note that this list has only a slightly more contemporary feel, since it includes players from both before and after the start of the Open era in almost even numbers. It's admittedly more difficult when reaching farther back into history; doing so exacerbates the epistemic difficulties and commensurability challenges of comparison and contrast. So let's suppose I confine my attention to this group and then see how Federer stacks up against them according to the salient criteria by which to assess the players that grow out of our summaries. First I'll briefly review the credentials of each contender, going through the list chronologically.

I will focus on the quality of the tennis rather narrowly construed. Yet it remains true that an interesting essay could be written accentuating the many laudable personal qualities that all of these champions held in common and one would do well to emulate. An uncommon ability to focus, a penchant to overcome adversities ranging from hostile crowds to inclement weather to perpetual travel to jet lag to recurring or chronic injuries, a capacity to believe in themselves even when others don't, a knack for silencing self-doubts and rising to the occasion, a mental toughness and competitive resilience, an inner drive toward excellence, an unwillingness to rest on laurels or be content merely to beat the local opponent, an aspiration to be the best, a passion for improvement; to make the list, these giants of the game needed each of these characteristics and more.

Big Bill: Bill Tilden (1893–1953)

Pre–Open-era great Bill Tilden was an American tennis player who was the world #1 player for seven years.[4] Six feet, two inches tall, flamboyant, a smart tactician, a showman, and a good sport, Tilden was long considered the greatest tennis player ever. His record of Slam victories, in particular, was astounding. Between 1916 and 1930, he earned a mixed doubles title at the French, three singles titles and a doubles title at Wimbledon, and seven singles, five doubles, and four mixed doubles titles at the U.S. Championships. In the 1920s he also captured thirteen successive singles matches in the Davis Cup challenge round against the best players from Australia, France, and Japan, while leading his team to an unprecedented seven consecutive Davis Cup victories. He sustained an incredibly high level of play into his fifties on a variety of surfaces.

His serve was characterized as a cannonball, his passing shots were, like Borg's, impeccable, and his mastery of spins renowned. He wrote two books about tennis, including *Match Play and the Spin of the Ball*, which is still in print and considered something of a classic. Allison Danzig, the main tennis writer for the *New York Times* from 1923 through 1968 and editor of *The Fireside Book of Tennis*, called Tilden the greatest tennis player he had ever seen. And Jack Kramer included Tilden in a list of the six greatest players of all time.[5] In 1950, an Associated Press poll named Tilden the greatest tennis player of the half-century by a wider margin than that given to any athlete in any other sport. Bud Collins writes of Tilden, who had a .936 winning percentage as an amateur, that he was "perhaps the greatest tennis player of them all."[6]

The GOAT: John Donald Budge (1915–2000)

It was bound to happen; "Don" Budge's nickname among fellow players was "GOAT": Greatest of All Time. Perhaps he was, and still is. We can certainly make a case for it. *Inside Tennis* devoted parts of four issues to an article entitled "Tournament of the Century."[7] It was an imaginary tournament to determine the greatest of all time. Thirty-seven experts offered their ten-best lists. The third top point earner was Don Budge, who also garnered four first-place votes, beating McEnroe, Gonzales, and Hoad. E. Digby Baltzell wrote in 1994 that Budge and Laver "have usually been rated at the top of any all-time World Champions list, Budge having a slight edge," and Will Grimsley wrote in 1971 that Budge "is considered by many to be foremost among the all-time greats."[8] Paul Metzler ranks him as second only to Jack Kramer, who himself said the best player was either Budge (for his consistently good play) or Ellsworth Vines (at the height of his game).

Affable and good natured, Budge is reputed to have had the best backhand in the game. Budge was world #1 for five years, first as an amateur and then as a professional. His most famous achievement as a tennis player is that he was the first to win in a single year the Grand Slam. At Wimbledon he registered a double triple, winning singles, doubles, and mixed in 1937–1938, and tripled in the United States in 1938. After helping the United States retain its Davis Cup trophy over Australia in 1938, he became a professional in 1939, and on tour edged Vines 21–18, Perry 18–11, and forty-seven-year-old Tilden 51–7. But he would soon join the Air Force to serve in World War II and incur a torn muscle in his shoulder that never completely healed, which permanently hindered his playing abilities, although he still won more titles after the war. "I consider [Budge]," Tilden wrote in the 1947 edition of his *Tennis: The Greats* (1920–1960), "the finest player 365 days a year who ever lived."

Jake: Jack Kramer (1921–)

Although Kramer considered Budge (or Vines, whom Kramer as a boy saw play, inspiring Kramer to focus on his tennis) the all-time best, others would say the honor belongs to him. World #1 for a number of years, he was among the first to perfect a consistent serve-and-volley game and was known, like Borg later would be, for his ability to play "percentage tennis." Winner of ten Slam titles (counting singles, doubles, and mixed), all at Wimbledon and the U.S. Open, and champion at Davis Cup in 1946 and 1947, Kramer simply owned Gonzales in the latter's first year on the professional tour, 96–27, but again, this was when Kramer was near his peak and Gonzales still finding his game. Kramer's 1979 autobiography is called *The Game: My Forty Years in Tennis*. In the *Inside Tennis* hypothetical tournament, Kramer came in fourth place and received five first-place votes, more than Gonzales, Hoad, McEnroe, and Budge.

Gorgo: Ricardo Alonso ("Big Pancho") Gonzales (1928–1995)

A tempestuous and fiery competitor, Gonzales was one of the best ever to play the game. A Mexican American, he was self-taught and gradually rose to become the world's best player. In a career spanning three decades, his accumulation of Slam tournaments was hampered by his inability, through most of his career, to compete, since he was a professional and, as a result, ineligible before the start of the Open era in 1968. He was the world #1 player for eight years in the 1950s and early 1960s. Known for his powerful serve-and-volley game and excellent defense, he was also able, at the age of forty-three, to beat the nineteen-year-old consummate grinder Jimmy Connors from the baseline. He was as much older than Laver as Sampras is older than Federer (ten years), yet at forty-one beat Laver in five sets, just after Laver's 1969 Grand Slam. His ability to win matches long into their fifth sets earned him the honor of being perhaps the toughest long-match player in the history of the sport.

In addition to battling Laver several times, he also played other giants like Ken Rosewall, Jack Kramer, Don Budge, and Lew Hoad, each of whom has been argued by some to be the greatest of all time, or at least until their own time. Thirteen years Gonzales's senior, though, Budge was past his prime when Gonzales came into his own, and Gonzales had yet to come into his own while Budge reigned, requiring us to take with a grain of salt their head-to-head matchups. Gonzales said of Hoad, "He was the only guy who, if I was playing my best tennis, could still beat me. I think his game was the best game ever. Better than mine." Gonzales held a 101–59 lifetime record against Rosewall—admittedly six years Gonzales's junior. A 1999 *Sports Illustrated* article about the magazine's "favorite athletes" of the twentieth century said of Gonzales, "If earth was on the line in a tennis match, the man you want serving to save humankind would be Ricardo Alonso Gonzales."[9] In an interesting piece of historical serendipity, Gonzales's sixth and last wife was Andre Agassi's sister!

Emmo: Roy Emerson (1936–)

Roy Emerson's name suddenly became prominent again in 2000, when Pete Sampras, by winning Wimbledon, broke Emerson's record of Slam victories. Emerson's record of twelve, which had broken Tilden's previous record of ten, had held for thirty-three years. Over the four Slam tournaments and counting singles, doubles, and mixed, Emerson amassed twenty-eight major titles, a record for a male player. Gregarious, hardworking, and amazingly fit, Emerson was also a member of a record eight

Davis Cup–winning teams between 1959 and 1967. Because his career spanned the transition into the Open era, he spent most of his time playing as an amateur, so his victories at the Slams weren't usually against the arguably better professionals like Laver and Rosewall. Nonetheless, Emerson, two years Laver's senior, did show he could beat Laver, such as in the 1961 Australian and U.S. Championship finals. Emerson's six Australian titles is a record for a male player.

The Red-Headed Rocket: Rod Laver (1938–)

After losing to Emerson in two Slam events in 1961, the incomparable Aussie Laver would beat Emerson in three Slam finals the next year, the first of Laver's famed Grand Slam years. Then Laver turned professional and became ineligible to compete in the Slams until 1968, after which he won the Grand Slam again in 1969. The world's highest ranked player for seven consecutive years, 1964–1970, Laver is the only player to have twice won all four Grand Slam singles titles in the same year, and his eleven Slam singles titles have always left fans wondering how many he would have ended up with had he been able to compete in those intermediate years. Perhaps more than anyone else, Laver has been rated as the greatest male player of all time by several experts and polls.

For good reason, Laver has been long thought by many the all-time best. A leftie, Laver mastered a serve-and-volley game with aggressive ground strokes to boot. He hit with heavy topspin on both sides, not unlike Borg would later, while also demonstrating a feathery touch on drop volleys, not unlike McEnroe later. Like Federer, he indulged in too much adventurous shot-making early on and had to discipline himself not to show off his full array of talents when it wasn't high enough percentage tennis.

Although Jack Kramer claims Gonzales at his best would have beaten Laver regularly, many insist on demurring from Kramer's analysis. What often serves as the strongest evidence against Kramer's claim is Laver's remarkable achievement of winning two Grand Slams. In fact, for many, the caliber of this achievement renders the debate about the all-time best a no-brainer; others cite the statistic that adding up Laver's victories as an amateur, touring professional, and Open-era player, he won a record 184 singles titles. Even after turning thirty, he won a record forty-five Open titles. In an article in *Tennis Week* in 2007, the tennis historian Raymond Lee statistically analyzed the all-time best players, and Laver topped the list. In an August 2006 article for MSNBC, Bud Collins called Laver "in my eyes, the greatest player ever."[10] The aforementioned *Inside Tennis* "tournament" featured Laver, ranked first with nine first-place votes, against McEnroe, ranked second (with three first-place votes) in the final, with Laver winning in five sets.

Jimbo: Jimmy Connors (1952–)

A feisty, determined, passionate fighter, Jimmy Connors never lost zeal for the game or gave his opponents a break. Over the course of twenty years, he earned a 1,337–285 record, playing more tournaments (401) and winning more matches than any other male pro. He was in the U.S. Top 10 a record twenty times and the world's Top 10 a record sixteen times. His career included winning nineteen doubles titles, including Wimbledon and the U.S. Open, along with a mixed U.S. Open as well. Until Sampras broke his record, Connors held the longest Open stint at #1: five straight years. He was #1 an astounding 268 weeks, a record at the time. His five U.S. Open titles included wins on three surfaces: grass, clay, and hard court. Two Wimbledon singles titles and an Australian meant a total of eight Slam singles titles. His legendary 1991 run to the semifinal of the U.S. Open—the site of his greatest successes—when he was thirty-nine years old, did nothing less than electrify the crowds and mesmerize the attention of tennis fans worldwide. Connors is clearly one of the all-time greats. Arthur Ashe wrote, "Looking back from the early 1990s, with Connors still playing well, I see that he was the greatest male tennis player, bar none, in the two and a half decades since the Open era began in 1968."[11]

Ice Man: Björn Borg (1956–)

By the age of just twenty-six, the great Swede Borg had become a legend. Unsuccessful at the U.S. Open largely thanks to Connors and McEnroe, and largely untried at the Australian, he reigned as nearly untouchable at Wimbledon and the French. His stellar record of six French Open singles titles is the all-time record for a male player. He's the only player in the

Open era to win both the French and Wimbledon titles in the same year more than once, and he did it three consecutive times! In 1976 he won Wimbledon without losing a set, and he repeated the feat in 1978 and 1980 at the French. His 1980 defeat of McEnroe, to win his fifth Wimbledon title, is arguably the greatest tennis match in the history of the game.

The list of records Borg was able to compile is remarkable. His 41 winning percentage in Slams is the highest for a male in the Open era. His 89.8 winning percentage in Slam singles is better than any male player ever. He shares with Sampras the distinction of having won at least one Slam singles title for eight consecutive years (a feat Federer is poised to match in 2010). He was the first to win two different Slam singles tournaments at least four consecutive years. Along with Sampras and Federer, he won two different Slam singles tournaments at least five times. Borg and Nadal each won four consecutive French Open singles titles. And the list goes on interminably.

Known for his fitness, cool demeanor, heavy topspins, and percentage tennis, Borg was for a while in a class by himself. His winning percentage was higher than that of Connors, Lendl, McEnroe, Sampras, and Agassi. His Davis Cup singles streak of thirty-three was intact at his retirement, still a record. Borg was poised to tie Emerson's record of twelve Slam singles when he walked away from the game at twenty-six, shocking the tennis world.

Johnny Mac: John McEnroe (1959–)

One of the most talented individuals ever to play, John McEnroe was a master of the game, both singles and doubles.[12] His brilliant touch, innovative shot-making, unpredictability, and impossible angles made his tennis look like art. His 82–3 record in 1984 still stands, and his epic battle with Borg has already been mentioned. His 155 tournament wins (77 in singles and 78 in doubles) is an Open-era record. He is third in singles titles and tied for second in doubles. His longtime doubles partner Peter Fleming is famous for his modest quip that the best doubles team in the world is McEnroe and anyone else. Mac reigned for 257 weeks as the world #1 doubles player. He played Borg to a 7–7 career tie, beat Connors 31–20, but trailed Lendl 15–21, losing eleven of the last twelve (after his magical 1984). He also owns the distinction of having won a tournament in his teens, twenties, thirties, and forties, quite an accomplishment. No summary of his career is complete without noting Mac's commitment to Davis Cup. He set numerous Cup records, including years played (twelve), ties (thirty), singles wins (forty-one), and total wins and doubles (fifty-nine). His undying patriotism and brilliant, often selfless performances in Davis Cup play earned him deep respect even among those understandably critical of some of his infamous on-court outbursts, one of which served as the title of his engaging 2002 memoir: *You Cannot Be Serious.*[13]

Ivan the Terrible: Ivan Lendl (1960–)

Ivan Lendl, despite his nickname, wasn't terrible; he was an amazing player. Pete Sampras includes him in the list of the five greatest of all time (among players who played at least a significant portion of their careers in the Open era), and a case can be made for it.[14] He captured eight Grand Slam singles titles during his career and competed in a total of nineteen Slam singles finals, a record for a male player until Federer broke it. He won all the Slam events except Wimbledon and was in the final of the U.S. Open for eight consecutive years. Lendl was a model of longevity, finishing four years at #1 and occupying the top spot for 270 weeks, breaking Connors's record. His was a game built on power and a relentless all-court game. His conditioning regimen was legend, and among his achievements were that he reached the semifinals in twenty-seven of the thirty-four Slams he played, was second in career ATP tournament singles titles (behind Connors), and had most consecutive singles finals. His domination of McEnroe in the latter half of their rivalry wasn't due entirely to Mac's decline; Lendl made some key adjustments that reduced his vulnerability to Mac's volleys. Beating McEnroe at the 1984 French during Mac's golden year, which rivals Laver's 1969, is testimony to Lendl's greatness. His record against Connors was also an impressive 22–13, though it needs to be remembered that Connors was twelve years Lendl's senior.

The Punisher: Andre Agassi (1970–)

Agassi is definitely among the greatest of all time. Mats Wilander puts him in the top four, and McEnroe puts him in the top five or so. A winner of eight Slam singles titles, an Olympic gold medal in singles, and a record seventeen ATP Masters Series titles, he's one of only six male players to have won all four Grand Slam singles titles and the only men's player in history to have won all four Grand Slam titles on four different surfaces. McEnroe and Jim Courier have said Agassi's the greatest returner in the history of the sport, and Brad Gilbert called him the best ball striker ever to play the game. His penchant for relentlessly running players around earned him the nickname "The Punisher." Sampras admits that nobody pushed him as hard as Agassi did, requiring Sampras to make some necessary adjustments to his game. Their rivalry stands as one of the greatest in the history of the sport, alongside Borg-Connors, Navratilova-Evert, Laver-Rosewall, and Federer-Nadal.

Pistol Pete: Pete Sampras (1971–)

Nobody can exclude Sampras from serious contention for the title of the all-time best. Cool under pressure, never one to choke, a sportsman extraordinaire, with an iron will of resolve, Sampras won a record fourteen Grand Slam singles titles. He won two Australians and five U.S. Opens and showed such splendor in the grass on his way to winning seven Wimbledon titles that Wordsworth himself would have marveled. The year-end #1 for six consecutive years, he broke the Open-era record for that distinction. *Tennis* magazine named him the greatest tennis player from 1965 to 2005, which would put him above Laver, Borg, McEnroe, Connors, and Agassi. Since so many tennis experts put Laver as the best up until his day, this doesn't leave much room for anyone else to vie for the top spot. The only male player to win at least three consecutive Wimbledon singles titles twice in his career, he appeared in at least one Grand Slam final for eleven consecutive years. He's the only male player to have played in at least seven singles finals at two different Slam tournaments during the Open era. And the records and achievements go on and on.

Sampras's game was without any real weakness. From his versatile one-handed backhand to the weapon of his forehand, from his rifling serve to his flawless volley technique, he was nearly invincible out there. He had a winning record against every former world or U.S. #1 player, from Agassi to Becker to Courier. Although his personality wasn't flashy, his consistent excellence was nearly unparalleled, and the strength of his character and determination undeniable. A serious case indeed can be made for Sampras as the all-time best in light of the way he so dominated his awesome opponents for such a sustained period of time. Paul Fein's article on the all-time best concludes that Sampras indeed deserves the honor.[15] He may well. Even if Federer is the all-time best now, Sampras may well have held the title for a while, though not nearly for as long as many of us would have predicted.

The Criteria

The question of the all-time best is not the same question as who among the great players would win on any given day or on any given surface. Even the best of the best are liable to lose on any given day. Perhaps McEnroe was the all-time best, but he still lost that 1980 final to Borg; perhaps Borg was the best, but he still lost later that summer to McEnroe. This demonstrates the fallacy in thinking that, say, one tournament could settle the question. The difference between the players we just discussed is small enough that, on any given day, any one of them at his prime could have pulled off a win. The sample has to be bigger than just a point, a game, a match, or even several matches. It would likely take a sizable number of matches played on a representative sample of surfaces to get a good reading of who's better.

Nor is the question who the best was at his prime, because somebody's prime could pass too quickly. Ken Kramer says, perhaps rightly, that Ellsworth Vines at his prime could have beaten anyone. Perhaps that's true, but it's not enough to show that Vines is the all-time best. For someone's best has to be played consistently enough to show it wasn't a fluke, and a player arguably needs to demonstrate enough longevity in his career to show that his greatness could last more than a few seasons. The longer a dominant career the better, the shorter the worse in terms of our estimation of where he stands among the all-time elites. The needlessly fancy way a philosopher might put it is to say that the assessment needs to be done over time, diachronically, and not merely as a snapshot in time or over a short period, synchronically.

For now, too, we're setting aside aesthetic and moral considerations. How artistic a player appears or fails to appear won't be going into our calculation, for it would seem in principle possible that the all-time best wasn't very artistic in the least. Perhaps he was just an extremely hard-working grinder from the baseline who happened to be better than everyone else, however incrementally, including those more aesthetically pleasing to watch. Or a player's boorish behavior on the court, like Connors's outbursts, likewise wouldn't disqualify him from the race. The issue before us is not primarily one of ethical behavior, sportsmanship, or artistry on the court. Those are indeed worthwhile features to consider, and this book has whole chapters devoted to them. They very well may be relevant in a more expansive treatment of the all-time best, but here we will try to delimit our analysis—at least at first. Even if a player's strokes are aesthetically deficient or his conduct on or off the court unbecoming, we will set those shortcomings aside in the present discussion.

Nor is the question who had the best backhand, who had the best serve, who had the best forehand, or the like. Those questions aren't easy, though they're easier than the present question, but they are different. As a philosopher and tennis fan, I admit to finding the atomistic approach of dividing the game up in this way—forehand, backhand, et cetera—profoundly unsatisfying. McEnroe's serve and volley make up an organic unit, both a reflection of the heart and mind of the player and together comprising one fluid event. There's an integrity to the organic whole that one shouldn't violate. It's the players themselves we wish to compare, not parts of their game, as if one could artificially carve them out so neatly like a dissection.[16] Likewise I'm not simplifying the question by asking who's the all-time best clay-court player, or all-time best hard-court player, or even the all-time best singles player, but the all-time best tennis player, which ineliminably includes doubles.

In addition, I'm not exploring the question of who potentially was the all-time best, but who in fact was the all-time best. It's a hard question, and one may well face insuperable challenges to answering it confidently, but I'm at least striving to answer the latter question. Perhaps a case could be made that, had Budge not been injured or Hoad not grown bored and left the game when he did, one of those would have won the battle here. Maybe so, but I'm asking not who potentially was the all-time best, but rather who actually was.[17]

Finally, I'm not asking who's the all-time best based on any single criterion, like the all-time winner of Grand Slam titles or highest winning percentage. Any such criterion is susceptible to a defeater that demonstrates its inadequacy as the single determinant of the answer. Take the all-time winner of Slam singles titles. In Borg's day, it was much more customary to skip some of the Slams, which is why Borg played in only one Australian. And of course Laver, after winning the Grand Slam in 1962, became a professional and wasn't qualified to play in the Slams until the Open era began in 1968. Or a player who focuses on Davis Cup play, or plays doubles as well as singles, also jeopardizes his acquisition of Slam singles titles. Or in principle the player with the highest winning percentage may not have, during his career, had to face strong enough opponents. Similar deficiencies attend each criterion of all-time excellence when taken in isolation, so what we need to do, and I now will attempt, is identify a plausible range of criteria by which we can make a better cumulative assessment.

The criteria must capture the essence of our question, which is most directly a matter of excellence. The all-time best player is the most excellent player, which is related to winning matches, but not in a simplistic fashion. It also has to do with such qualities as the ability of a player to dominate his opponents, to show mental toughness, to showcase a complete game without weaknesses opponents exploit, the capacity to dictate play and play his own game, but also make needed adjustments depending on the nature of the competition. The excellence needs to manifest for more than a short period of time, must lead to a great many more victories than defeats, and is likely to lead to a number of records, though not a record in every category. It's just a logical mistake to think that the all-time best must be the best in every category, the player with the best serve, the best touch, et cetera. But the all-time best is the overall most excellent player who, as a whole, was better than all the rest.

Among the criteria, then, I could adduce for such purposes would be the following. The number of career titles and tournaments won is important, because it demonstrates the ability to dominate opponents, win matches, show tournament toughness, and demonstrate longevity. A player's winning percentage is similarly important, though if a player takes a while for all the pieces of his game to come together, his winning percentage might suffer in those early years without disqualifying him from the competition. The number of weeks at world #1 or end of years ranked #1 are another indicator of dominance and longevity. Winning percentage, tournaments won, and domination of the sport, of course, also need to be balanced against the quality of competition. It's customary to look at the number of Grand Slam singles victories in particular, and this is certainly one among other relevant considerations, so long as the needed caveats already mentioned are borne in mind. Assessments about completeness of game and mental toughness are also to be factored in.

Even with a list of such criteria, however, the question remains of how best to weight them comparatively. It's not obvious how best to assign priority to the various criteria, and since the race is potentially so close among the cream of the crop, small differences in priorities or value assessments can make the difference between, say, a Laver or a Borg. Nothing like a mathematical algorithm suggests itself as a foolproof way to effect the calculation. This is interesting in itself, but how best to interpret the significance of the fact isn't easy. Some might suggest that the implication is that there is no one right way to do it, that the best explanation of our inability to generate such an algorithm, even with a list of salient criteria in hand, is that no such algorithm exists. That's a metaphysical thesis, which implies that perhaps there's no such thing as the all-time best tennis player after all, perhaps owing to intractable commensurability challenges. But a different account would be epistemic: there may well be one right way to weight the criteria, and one right answer to the question, but we're just hard-pressed epistemically to know what that answer is. In principle, though, something like an omniscient knower would know, even if all we can do is our best, which might not be good enough. I'll look at a few reasons why the latter account may be preferable to the former in a moment, which would leave the question of the all-time best as a living one to which there may well be an answer, despite the difficulty of finding it. In general, philosophers are wont to remind us, echoing Aristotle and Kant, that we shouldn't expect more precision than is reasonable to expect. In the present discussion, this can be taken as a reminder that our inability to know with precision exactly how best to weight the criteria shouldn't surprise us, nor should it entirely discourage us. The challenge of the question is also its fun.

So now I'll face the question head on, with these tentative criteria in hand and at least a respectable sense of what I'm looking for. After seeing how Roger Federer fares in light of such criteria, I'll offer a bit of analysis of the question of the all-time best and will see what the range of alternative answers to this question looks like and why, in more detail, the question is both so interesting and so challenging.

The Lion: Roger Federer (1981–)

Stauffer's biography of Roger Federer is subtitled "Quest for Perfection." When Federer was just a teenager, frustrated over his tennis mistakes, he said, "One should just be able to play a perfect ga.ne." Like so many aspiring greats, his opponent wasn't the guy across the net. His goal was not just to win but to approximate perfection the best he could. The question of the all-time best isn't the same as who's the best possible tennis player. Like Guanilo's island, a tennis player likely doesn't admit of intrinsic maxima—there's no good answer to the question of how fast such a player serves or hits with a topspin—but nonetheless there's a connection between the all-time best and the best possible.[18] For what drives all the greatest competitors is the desire to get as close as they can to perfection. It's a goal that of course remains forever out of reach, but by reaching for it anyway, they go farther than they otherwise could. This is certainly true in Federer's case, whose early temper tantrums were, he later admitted, due to his expecting perfection too soon. Taming his inner beasts, he became better able to maximize his potential and improve his game to a level that may be unprecedented. John McEnroe has said of Federer that he's the most perfect player who has ever lived.[19]

A Swiss, Federer first gained a great deal of attention at Wimbledon in 2001, where he defeated Pete Sampras in five sets, ending Sampras's thirty-one-match winning streak there. He was still coming into his own, and the pieces of his game were still coming together, but within a few years he was the world #1, winning his first Slam singles title in 2003. From February 2004 to August 2008 he was the world #1 player, a record 237 consecutive weeks. As of the end of 2009, he has won fifteen Grand Slam singles titles, a record. A litany of his records is remarkable, from being the first player to have five consecutive wins at both Wimbledon and the U.S. Open to winning the Australian, Wimbledon, and U.S. Open titles in the same year three times (so far).

How does Federer compare to the other greats in our list? Recall the ten salient criteria: quality of competition, winning percentage, degree of dictating play and dominating opponents, completeness of game, success on various surfaces, singles and doubles performances, longevity, number of Slams and other tournament victories, weeks and years at #1, and mental toughness. Federer's ultimate place in the list of the all-time greats undoubtedly will be related to Rafael Nadal. A truly great player, Nadal has proven himself far more than a clay-court specialist.[20] Theirs is one of the greatest rivalries in the history of tennis; they are the only men in the Open era to play each other in seven Grand Slam finals. Their 2008 Wimbledon final is considered by some the greatest match of all time.[21] Whereas Laver had Rosewall, and Borg, McEnroe, Connors, and Lendl had each other, and Sampras had Agassi, Federer has Nadal; and tennis fans, including fans of Federer, should be grateful.[22] What most hurts Emerson's historical standing is that the bulk of his career was played as an amateur, rather than with Laver and other professionals. Great competition gives players a chance to prove their greatness, and, because of the dynamic, essentially relational nature of tennis, it elevates the games of the participants. Sampras admits that Agassi required him to add some new weapons to his arsenal and elevate his game. The question of the all-time best is who would, in the preponderance of those crucial moments of representative competition, rise to the occasion and find a way to win. Nadal offers Federer that chance, and all of us should hope, for Federer's sake, that guys like Djokovitch and Murray and del Potro continue elevating their games to push him to his limits.

Federer's winning percentage is lower than might be expected, but the reason largely has to do with the fact that his game took time to come together. Once he neared the peak of his performance, however, he's been nearly unstoppable, so this shouldn't hurt him too much. After his slow start, Federer's ability to dictate play and dominate opponents is impressive. A few telling statistics in this regard: in 2004 he didn't lose a match to anyone ranked in the top ten, won every final he reached, and was 74–6 for the year, with eleven titles. In 2005 he nearly matched McEnroe's 1984, with an 81–4 record. And when he won his third Wimbledon, he'd only lost four sets, whereas Borg had given up nine and Sampras eleven in their own first three.

Nobody would question the completeness of Federer's game. To the contrary, commentators often laud his versatility, all-court playing style, dexterity in just about every spin shot there is. David Foster Wallace likened the speed and fluidity of Federer's forehand motion to "a great liquid whip," and his footwork, balance, and speed are exceptional.[23] McEnroe says, "I dreamed of playing like Federer. Watching him play is the greatest treat. If he continues like this over the next three or four years, he'll become the greatest champion I have ever seen in my life." McEnroe said that in 2003, then in 2004, McEnroe affirmed that Federer was "probably the greatest player that ever lived."[24]

What about his success on various surfaces? He's built an incredible record, but of course, like some great champions before him, the French Open remained elusive until he finally won it in 2009. Clay is not the same problem for him as it was for, say, Becker, who never won a clay tournament. No, like Sampras, Federer had won tournaments on clay, but never at Roland Garros, until recently. This is why it had been suggested by some that the French would be the deal breaker for Federer, but for the same reason no one criterion should be counted as decisively settling our question in favor of one player, no one criterion should probably be a clincher against. Nevertheless, the case for him was certainly strengthened when he won the French.

Federer seems well on his way to an impressive enough singles record to vie for the top all-time spot, and he has demonstrated some success in doubles, too, though he's been focusing on his singles. He's won a handful of doubles titles and an Olympic gold in doubles, though of course his record in doubles can't compare to one like McEnroe's (seventy-eight) or even Laver's twenty-seven, though clearly trouncing Sampras's two. How much longevity he will have remains to be seen, especially if after breaking some more crucial records his passion to compete and will to win begin to fade a bit, which will happen eventually. Sampras predicted a few years ago that Federer will end up with seventeen or eighteen Slams, so we'll see.

What about Laver's two Grand Slams? Recall how some think this single criterion makes Laver the clear choice of the all-time greatest, and perhaps it does. But two points should be stressed. First, in Laver's day, three of the four Slam events were played on grass, and Laver himself—a model of modesty—has said this of Federer: "The best way to beat him would be to hit him over the head with a racquet. Roger could win the Grand Slam if he keeps playing the way he is and, if he does that, it will equate to the two Grand Slams that I won because standards are much higher these days."[25]

Add to all of this Federer's record number of consecutive weeks at #1 and his notorious mental toughness and ability to perform in high-pressure situations, often saving break, set, or even match points during a match, and a case can indeed be made for him as the all-time best. Ivan Lendl has said Federer will probably end up being the all-time best, and Andre Agassi, after resisting comparisons for a long time, and paying due deference to the greatness of Sampras, finally admitted, "I think [Federer's] the best I've played against."[26]

A Few Remaining Philosophical Issues

Most of the philosophical issues so far have been weaved into the discussion, but here I'll identify a few remaining ones and give them explicit attention in order to bring our discussion to a close. These issues are a comparison of the "better than" relation and the "likely to beat" relation, issues of commensurability, and issues of vagueness. Top-ranked American player in the 1970s, Cliff Richey was once asked to compare the all-time greats. Among those at the top in his estimation were the usual suspects: Laver, Tilden, Borg, Gonzales. "Pancho or Rod against Björn—all at their peaks? A helluva match no matter who wins."[27] He was no doubt right.

Of course, though, recognizing that much is easy. The all-time greats at their sustainable peaks would very likely be comparable players, even if their styles were widely different. This was readily apparent in some of the epic battles between Borg and McEnroe, who played to a 7–7 career tie. What is crystal clear is that no single match could settle the matter. If Richey's hypothetical match were played, it would surely be a great match, but it would also provide little help to know who was better, for a single victory isn't a big and representative enough sample on which to base such a conclusion. In a competition among the all-time best players, what would be needed is quite a number of matches, played on a variety of surfaces, while such players are at their sustainable best.[28] The tours and exhibitions between the top players in the first half of the 1900s provided the sort of real test to compare two players, but even then, players were often pitted against one another at different stages of their careers.

And this shows something important about head-to-head matchups: they tell something that's interesting but potentially limited. Unless the matchups are enough in quantity and representative enough in quality, they don't necessarily determine who's better. Few people think Borg and McEnroe were exactly the same in quality, despite their 7–7 record, with some choosing Borg and others McEnroe. Sampras had a career edge over Agassi, which is potentially significant, especially given their similar ages. At the same time, though, some players clearly not as good as Sampras had winning records against him over their careers (Stich, Safin, Krajicek, and Bruguera). This suggests that the "better than" relation isn't reducible to the "likely to beat" relation, even given optimal conditions.[29]

This isn't hard to see. Suppose someone is a local club player and the best in the neighborhood, but he can't beat his own dad, who taught him the game. For some reason, he can't overcome his dad's psychological edge, but he routinely beats and is clearly better than others his dad loses to. This would show that, though he's better than his Dad, since he's not likely to beat him when they play, "being better" isn't quite the same as "likely to beat" on a particular occasion. The "better than" relation is transitive, while the "likely to beat" relation is not.

What bolsters the conclusion that Sampras has an edge over Agassi isn't just their head-to-head matchups, but the rest of their careers. And as good as Agassi's was, including his career Slam, Sampras's was better. So even representative head-to-head matchups alone, real or hypothetical, aren't a decisive criterion to determine who's the best.

Next, in light of the increasingly difficult challenge involved in comparing players from before and after the Open era, there is probably good reason to confine discussions to one or the other set of players (recognizing that some, like Laver, were transitional).[30] This pays no disrespect to the old-time greats but allows for a more manageable discussion. If I were to thus delimit the discussion, I would suggest, given their records, that the top five players from the Open era, chronologically, are Laver, Borg, McEnroe, Sampras, and Federer.

If I were to argue that "Federer is the all-time greatest," what's the status of that sentence? It doesn't appear to be semantically defective, since "Federer is better than Blake" makes great sense, and the all-time status as best would just require that that same relation obtain between Federer and everyone else as well. Assuming the sentence isn't defective, then, what is its status? The challenge is that it's vague, meaning that it's very difficult to determine whether Federer's the right guy.

Think of an analogy: Imagine a tennis ball. Suppose it now with one less atom. It's still a ball. Likewise with one less atom than that, and one less than that. It remains a tennis ball. But suppose this keeps up for a very long time until there's only one atom left. At some point it ceases being a tennis ball, but when? With the removal of what atom does it stop being a ball? It's impossible for us to say, even if there's an answer.[31] What constitutes a tennis ball is a challenging question due to this "vagueness" problem, which happens to be ubiquitous in our language use. And it certainly applies to the qualification for the all-time best tennis player. Drawing the line between that very best player and the second best is notoriously difficult.

What philosophers teach about vagueness allows for three different ways to understand "Federer is the all-time best." One possibility is that the sentence expresses a single proposition whose truth is a matter of degree. Truth for such fuzzy logic is not an either/or. So perhaps, given the closeness of the race, "Federer is the all-time greatest" is true to, for example, a .78 degree, and that's all that could be said. The biggest challenge confronting fuzzy logic is that truth doesn't seem to work like this. Classical logic would demand that every proposition is either true or, if it's not, then it's false. Saying truth obtains to some matter of degree raises more questions than it answers—such as how on earth we can with confidence specify such particular degrees—while flying in the face of classical logic.

A second possibility comes from the supervaluationists, who might say that "there is an all-time best tennis player" is true, but it's not true of Federer or Borg or McEnroe or Laver. Why? Well, take "Federer is the all-time best." A case can be made for such a view. But so can one be made for Borg, and for McEnroe, and for Laver and Sampras. For in each case we can give a solid set of reasons and fashion a plausible set of criteria by which each of those gets the honor. Earlier I showed the inherent challenge of figuring out how best to weigh and weight the various criteria; the supervaluationists can be understood to suggest that there is no one right or privileged set of criteria, but a variety of them. The only way "Federer is the all-time best" could be true is if it were supertrue—true on every specification or set of criteria, but it's not. Since truth is supertruth, according to the supervaluationist, it's not true that Federer is the all-time best; nor is it true that Borg, Laver, McEnroe, or Sampras is. And yet, paradoxically, it is true that there is an all-time best! This at least seems to be an implication of supervaluationism.

The biggest philosophical challenge confronting supervaluationism is that it, too, would do too much violence to the principles of classical logic. I've just shown an instance of an objection to such a view. How could it be true that there's an all-time best tennis player (since there is one under every plausible construal of criteria) and yet that it's nobody in particular (since no one player is the best under every such construal)? Timothy Williamson also argues in his book on vagueness that super-truth can't be truth and thus that supervaluationism fails.[32] Supervaluationism is also supposed to be a theory of vagueness, but according to the theory it is never vague whether, say, "Federer is the all-time best" is su-pertrue, since it's supertrue that there are no borderline cases (given the set of criteria by which Federer is the best), and so there's no vagueness.

Because of the difficulties saddling fuzzy logic and supervaluationism, Williamson argues for "epistemicism," according to which, for example, "Federer is the all-time best" would be a sentence that expresses a proposition that is either true or false. On this view, which seems to have fewer philosophical problems than its alternatives, there's something about our language use that would pick out one and only one player as the all-time best. One set of criteria, properly weighted, really would be privileged. Where does the vagueness come from, then? The closeness of the competing sets of criteria. We aren't in an epistemically privileged enough place to recognize with enough clarity what set of criteria those are. We are thus relegated to a kind of ignorance about the answer to the question of the all-time best. But this ignorance is not evidence that there's no right answer, or a variety of equally right answers; no, there really is an answer to the question and a fact of the matter. God, presumably, knows the answer. But we don't. The best we can do is make our case. We can't get deliverance from our ignorance, because the players we're comparing are all so good and close to one another in quality that we could easily be wrong, and if we know something, presumably we can't be so easily wrong. Given this margin-of-error principle, we're left with ignorance.

The advantage of this approach is that it provides an account of vagueness without sacrificing classical logic and, for tennis fans, gives us reason to think there really is an answer to our question, even if it's an answer that potentially always eludes our confident grasp. The best we can do is make our case, as I have attempted to make the case for Federer, at least as the all-time greatest singles player. McEnroe might well be the all-time greatest tennis player, though, if we are entitled to accord much significance to his talents and achievements as a doubles player. Even if he was only the fourth or fifth all-time best singles player, if he was also the all-time best or second-best doubles player then he may well have been the best all-around tennis player ever. This might suggest, by the way, that Federer at his best (or Laver, Borg, or Sampras) might be likely to edge McEnroe in singles more times than not, especially depending on the surface, but McEnroe might still be the all-time best.[33]

Final Thoughts

In science, Einstein, by his own admission, was able to accomplish what he did because of thinkers like Newton.[34] I could ask who was the greater scientist, and it would be an interesting question, but perhaps most fruitfully asked not in terms of a zero-sum-game competition but a collaboration. Especially in light of the relational and dynamic nature of tennis, with opponents pitted against one another and pushing each other to new heights, Federer's attitude toward tennis is a good one for us to have in our speculations about the all-time best.[35] Federer sees his opponent not merely as a competitor but as someone sharing a journey with him, making excellence on the court possible. Federer grew up watching Sampras, and that experience helped shape him into the player he became; and likewise Sampras watched Borg, and Borg watched Laver. We have less a static competition here and more a dynamic collaboration in a shared quest for excellence. Tennis, at its best, is never merely a game. Like nearly any human endeavor conceived of nobly and practiced diligently, it's an opportunity for excellence and beauty to find expression, intrinsic goods both.

Earlier I set aside aesthetic and moral dimensions to our question, but if I was to bring them back into the discussion here at the end, it's clear that the case for Federer certainly wouldn't suffer. How he's conducted himself on and off the court with dignity, as an ambassador for tennis and model sportsman (four times named the Laureus World Sportsman of the Year), only strengthens the case for him as the all-time best construed more expansively. And beyond his technical skill and abundant natural talent is a kind of genius and artistry that has invoked in some, like Wallace, nothing less than a kind of transcendent religious experience.[36]

Federer remains a work in progress and a player in motion; his legacy will depend on what remaining achievements lie in his future. I can't know he's the all-time best, but perhaps I can be justified to believe it.[37]

Federer's serve.

Or maybe Mac's.

Notes

Thanks to Ginger Asel, Mark Foreman, Troy Matthews, and Jerry Walls for helpful comments on an earlier draft of this chapter.

1. It's been pointed out that my interpretive gloss on this verse might not withstand exegetical scrutiny.

2. This chapter will explore the question of the all-time best male tennis player, but of course an equally interesting and difficult question is of the all-time best woman player. That I'm not dealing with that question here is not meant to suggest that that exploration is any less worthwhile. Paul Fein, for one, takes up the question in his *Tennis Confidential II: More of Today's Greatest Players, Matches, and Controversies* (Washington, DC: Potomac, 2008), chap. 2, "Who is the Greatest Women's Tennis Player Ever?" (He also devotes a chapter to the greatest of all the male players.) I love Fein's dedication in that book: "To the unsung heroes in tennis: Tennis moms and dads, racket stringers, court maintenance workers, tournament volunteers, high school coaches, community organizers, TV camera operators, association and club committee members, and all those who work so others can play. Without them, where would we be?"

3. Evidence for the fascination people have had with the question of the all-time best can be found in the number of treatments devoted to the subject. In addition to Fein, see for example, Raymond Lee: "The Greatest Tennis Player of All Time: A Statistical Analysis," *Tennis Week*, September 14, 2007, http://www.tennisweek.com/news/story print.sps?inewsid=503656; and the 1986 *Inside Tennis* series devoted to "The Tournament of the Century."

4. Throughout these career summaries, I access key data from the online encyclopedia Wikipedia.

5. Jack Kramer, *The Game: My Forty Years in Tennis* (New York: Putnam, 1979).

6. Bud Collins, *The Bud Collins History of Tennis: An Authoritative Encyclopedia and Record Book* (New York: New Chapter, 2008), 633. This is an invaluable resource for all things tennis.

7. "The Tournament of the Century," *Inside Tennis*, 1986. References are to this series.

8. See Will Grimsley, *Tennis: Its History, People, and Events* (Upper Saddle River, NJ: Prentice Hall, 1971).

9. Richard Hoffer, "Our Favorite Athletes," *Sports Illustrated,* July 1999, 78.

10. Lee, "Greatest Player of All Time"; Bud Collins, "Top Stars of Tennis," *NBC Sports,* August 2006, http://nbcsports.msnbc.com/id/14489546/?pg=4#spt0823 Greatestplyr.

11. Arthur Ashe, with Arnold Rampersad, *Days of Grace: A Memoir* (New York: Ballantine, 1993), 82.

12. I refrain from the well-known but slightly snide "Superbrat" nickname, largely to keep alive my dream of one day hitting a few tennis balls with McEnroe.

13. John McEnroe, with James Kaplan, *You Cannot Be Serious* (New York: Putnam, 2002).

14. See Pete Sampras, with Peter Bodo, *A Champion's Mind: Lessons from a Life in Tennis* (New York: Random House, 2008), 204–5, for his praise of Lendl, which is undoubtedly well deserved.

15. Paul Fein, "Who Is the Greatest Men's Tennis Player Ever?" *Tennis Confidential II,* 14.

16. Here's an analogy: Love for another person is consistent with appreciating her beauty, but if the beauty is all that's loved, and replaceable by another equally or more beautiful, there's not genuine love for the person. Similarly, appreciating a tennis player involves recognizing and valuing more than just the parts of his or her game, but the way a player instantiates all the various parts of his or her game as a cohesive whole.

17. I can't help but think of Sartre's existentialism here as a philosophy of action; Sartre (1905–1980) denied transcendent entities and disparaged the emphasis we often place on possibilities and potentials that do not occur. As he says, there is no love except in being in love, there is no genius except as expressed in works of genius. Excuses and explanations of the sort, "Could've/should've," simply don't cut it. The student who says he could get A's but is lazy and doesn't like to study is saying nothing of value, in Sartre's view—likewise with the claim that someone who never picked up a racket could have been the best tennis player. Nonetheless, I suspect Sartre overstates his case, for a counterfactual like "If Laver had had a chance to compete for more Slams in the 1960s, he likely would have won several of them" is both perfectly coherent and very plausibly held to be (nontrivially) true.

18. Guanilo was a contemporary of medieval philosopher St. Anselm, who came up with an ontological argument for God's existence, the essence of which is that God, since he's perfect, must possess all the great-making properties to the maximal degree. Since it's better to exist than not to exist, God must have the property of existence, so God exists. Guanilo responded by suggesting that such an argument would show too much, for by parity of reasoning it could serve as the basis for arguing that, say, a perfect island exists. But the typical rejoinder to Guanilo is that whereas we know what a maximally perfect being would be like (omnipotent, omniscient, om-

nibenevolent, et cetera), we don't know what the perfect island would be like; for example, what's the temperature on the perfect island? What is its size? How many grains of sand are on its beaches? There's no nonarbitrary way to answer such questions; therefore, islands don't admit to intrinsic maxima the way a perfect being like God does.

19. Cited in Rene Stauffer, *The Roger Federer Story: Quest for Perfection* (New York: New Chapter, 2006), 198.

20. Here I must demur from Paul Fein's (excellent) analysis on the all-time best, since he's suggested that, since Nadal is a clay-court specialist, Federer has lacked solid competition. Although it's true that today's field isn't as rich as one inhabited simultaneously with Borg, McEnroe, Connors, and Lendl, the rivalry between Nadal and Federer is shaping up to be one of the all-time greatest, and Nadal's shown himself considerably more than a clay-court specialist at Wimbledon the last couple years. There's every reason to expect continuing excellence from him. At the age of twenty-two, he's already been in seven Grand Slam finals, winning five of them, including Wimbledon, plus an Olympic gold in singles. In fairness to Fein, though, he wrote his article in 2005, when the evidence did suggest Nadal might be primarily a clay-court specialist. Fein knew that his analysis could be falsified by Federer's and Nadal's continuing play.

21. The vexed question concerning the greatest tennis match raises parallel considerations to the ones this chapter explores. Demonstrating the power of the question to generate debate and capture popular imagination are two recently published books: L. Jon Wertheim's *Strokes of Genius: Federer, Nadal, and the Greatest Match Ever Played* (New York: Houghton Mifflin Harcourt, 2009) and Marshall Jon Fisher's *A Terrible Splendor: Three Extraordinary Men, a World Poised for War, and the Greatest Tennis Match Ever Played* (New York: Crown, 2009). Wertheim's book chronicles the 2008 Wimbledon final between Federer and Nadal, whereas Fisher's is a riveting and rich historical narrative of the deciding 1937 Davis Cup match between American Don Budge and Germany's Baron Gottfried von Cramm, a match significant both as athletic spectacle and for its social significance. My own nostalgic bet would still go with the 1980 Wimbledon final between Borg and McEnroe.

22. Two excellent reasons for this are as follows: It takes a player like Nadal to show us what Federer is made of; without Federer getting tested to the limits, his reputation suffers. In addition, watching two titans like this clash gives tennis fans something to cherish, for the tennis that results is priceless to watch. This is why the truest tennis fans, even if they're partisan by being, say, fans of Federer, won't be happy to see Nadal play less than his best even if it means a victory for their favored player. (Seeing an opponent double fault shouldn't be as gratifying as your hitting an ace.) Their love of the game trumps their love for a particular player. Not to overdo this analogy, but philosophers, similarly, are contrasted with sophists. Whereas sophists engage in disputes just to win arguments or at least project the appearance of

winning them, philosophers are interested in the truth. The most genuine tennis fans are more interested in excellence, beauty, and sportsmanship than merely a victory—either for themselves or even for their favorite player.

23. David Foster Wallace, "Federer as Religious Experience: How One Player's Grace, Speed, Power, Precision, Kinesthetic Virtuosity, and Seriously Wicked Topspin Are Transfiguring Men's Tennis," *New York Times PLAY Magazine*, August 20, 2006, 46–51, 80, 82, 83.

24. Cited in Stauffer, *Roger Federer Story,* 198, 242.

25. Ibid., 242.

26. Ibid., 202.

27. Cited in Björn Borg, with Eugene L. Scott, *My Life and Game* (New York: Simon and Schuster, 1980), 54.

28. The notion of "sustainable best" is designed to ensure that the play is representative, not just the occasional stellar performance unable to be sustained. How long such performance must be sustained is of course hard to say, but more than a couple years would probably be required. Beyond sustainable performance, representative matchups require that something like equipment and technology, something beyond the players' control, be held equal, but not necessarily physical conditioning or eating habits, which are under the control of the players.

29. A further interesting twist: Consider Justine Henin's controversial win over Serena Williams at the French in the 2003 semifinal. At a crucial point where Williams had the chance to nearly put the match away, she faulted on a serve when Henin raised her hand. The umpire didn't see it, Henin didn't volunteer she'd done it, the anti-American crowd loved it, and Serena became vulnerable, eventually losing a closely contested and otherwise magnificent match. One of Henin's comments afterward is germane to our present discussion: "[Serena] played very well today and she probably deserved to win. She was the better player today, really." Perhaps Henin didn't mean that, but if what she said is possible, it shows that, given the vagaries and dynamics of tennis, the better player on a given day may not win. See Mark Ryan's *Justine Henin: From Tragedy to Triumph* (London: J. R. Books, 2008), 95–96.

30. For one of the best discussions of issues related to commensurability problems, see Thomas Kuhn's classic *The Structure of Scientific Revolutions* (Chicago: University of Chicago Press, 1962).

31. The removal of atoms isn't like the straw that broke the camel's back in reverse. The straw that broke the camel's back involves a causal process; the weight becomes too much for the camel to sustain, causing his back to break. Removing the relevant bit of matter doesn't cause the ball to cease being a ball; rather, its removal constitutes the ball no longer existing. There's a metaphysical distinction here between "causes" and "constitutes."

32. Timothy Williamson, *Vagueness* (New York: Routledge, 1996), 142–64.

33. It's not unreasonable to suggest that Federer has yet to earn the title before winning the French and without more doubles success. Doubles tennis highlights the reality that tennis is a team game as well as an individual one, which elaborates on the

point that in tennis our competitors make us better in ways we don't see in golf, for example, since we're not responding to them in the same way. (See more on this in note 35). Doubles also requires us to be aware of and respond to three other persons, which is a more complex and demanding activity in certain respects than responding only to one. Singles and doubles test different skills; this is why it's rare that the best singles player is also the best doubles player.

34. And it was Newton of course who famously wrote, in a letter to Robert Hooke on February 5, 1676, "If I have seen a little further [than Descartes and Hooke himself] it is by standing on the shoulders of Giants."

35. In the sense of its relational and dynamic nature, tennis is more like boxing than golf. In golf a player can play the course and compete with his personal previous best, more effectively putting his other competition out of his mind, but in tennis there's more direct engagement with the opponent, though not bodily contact as in boxing. James Blake reflects on a few more differences between golf and tennis in Stauffer's *Roger Federer Story*, 170–71, especially as they bear on the question of the all-time best. Boxing, due to the goal of inflicting bodily harm, is suspect as a sport, in my estimation; but setting that issue aside, the last *Rocky* movie featured an interesting scene. A computer program, fed information about Rocky and the now current world champion, models a simulated fight between them at their primes. On this basis it predicted that Rocky would win. I'd suggest that no such static algorithm would work (in either tennis or boxing) when the competitors are among the all-time best and so close in quality—because of not just our epistemic limitations, which are bad enough, but also the dynamic nature of the envisioned interaction, which has the potential to bring out new aspects of the competitors never quite seen before.

36. Stauffer characterizes Federer's game as the perfect blend of art and science, while making it look easy, almost effortless, and like he's never in a rush (*Roger Federer Story*, 191). Björn Borg once contrasted tennis players and painters; see his *My Life and Game*, 52. McEnroe, whose artistry on the court is also legend, now owns an art gallery in New York City and reflects on what tennis players and artists have in common in Fein's *Tennis Confidential II*, 90.

37. We can handle this point in various ways. We can affirm that we can be justified to believe that, say, Sampras is the best without our knowing it, either since it's not true or it is and we have a counterexample to knowledge as justified true belief and/or justification isn't a requirement for knowledge; or we can deny that we can be justified even though we can make a plausible case for Sampras, so we wouldn't have knowledge because of that lack of sufficient justification; or we can affirm both justification and the possibility of our genuine knowledge here, despite the vagueness and the closeness of the call between Sampras and the other candidates. I resist the last option because of the nature of vagueness and what strikes me as the ignorance it's likely to entail.

Mark R. Huston

WHY ARE ALL TENNIS FILMS BAD?

The American Film Institute (AFI) recently presented its list of America's ten greatest films in ten classic genres.[1] The movies that made it into the top ten of each genre were based on the votes of a jury that contained over fifteen hundred members pulled from the film world (from critics to directors). The members voted from a list of fifty nominated movies for each of the ten listed genres. Not only is there no tennis movie on the list of the fifty nominated films, there is only one film that even has tennis in it at all.[2] In fact, my guess, based on anecdotal evidence, is that if some-one were to ask you if you know of any tennis movies, probably the only one you could come up with is the 2004 Kirsten Dunst movie *Wimble-don*—and that is due much less to the quality of the work than to its obvious tennis title. There are very few tennis films, and most of those that do exist are pretty awful, which brings us to the driving question of this chapter: Why are all tennis films bad? Another way of approaching this question is to ask whether or not there could ever be a truly great film centered on tennis, say a *Raging Bull* of tennis? Unfortunately, I think the answer is: "No, there never will be a truly great film, the caliber, for ex-ample of a *Raging Bull,* related to tennis."

To explore these questions and defend my conclusion, some ground-work and analysis is in order. In terms of categorizing this chapter, it should be understood as falling into the category that crosses between philosophy of sport and philosophy of film/film theory.[3] I will first start with a brief, general discussion of genre and then move to an analysis of the sports film as a genre. That needs some defense because the sports film is usually assumed to be a subgenre, but regardless of whether it is a genre or subgenre, the goal is to figure out some of the core features. I will then look specifically at how to understand a film as a "tennis" film versus a film that merely has tennis or a tennis player as a component, then give a closer reading of three (and a quarter) tennis films: *Nobody's Perfect, Wimbledon,* and *Tennis, Anyone . . . ?*[4] *Tennis, Anyone . . . ?* is actually a decent movie (though not great), and so it provides a nice counterpoint to the other movies. The close readings will serve (get it?) the function of highlighting the, possibly insurmountable, difficulties in making a truly great tennis movie à la *Raging Bull.*

Genres in General

Whether genre is represented in literature or film, its study traces back to Aristotle. In the *Poetics,* Aristotle sets out to separate and define various species of poetry including "epic and tragic poetry, comedy and dithyrambic" which are all considered varieties of mimesis or representation. He locates their respective differences in the media, the objects, and the mode of representation.[5] It is under the influence of Aristotle that any discussion of genre, particularly by philosophers, takes place.[6]

By way of example, Noël Carroll has done extensive work defining the genre of horror in art (which includes books, plays, films, et cetera). According to Carroll, a horror fiction is "a narrative or image in which at least one monster appears, such that the monster in question is designed to elicit an emotional response from us that is a complex compound of fear and disgust in virtue of the potential danger or threat the monster evinces and in virtue of its impurity."[7] While I will not bore you by explaining all of the gory details of Carroll's definition, such as his very specific definition of "monster," it is worth noting that he is explicitly working within an Aristotelian framework.[8] His definition is *essentialist,* in the sense that he is giving necessary and sufficient conditions for a work to be considered a work of horror. In addition, an important part of his definition defines art horror in terms of the emotions that are supposed to be evoked by the work in much the same way that Aristotle defined tragedy, partly in terms of the evocation of pity and fear in the audience. This style of defining a genre provides one clear model for defining any genre whatsoever.

An alternative approach to Aristotelian essentialism is a Wittgensteinian family resemblance approach, in which one looks for similarities to already accepted core examples when categorizing something new or uses core features of those examples to attain conceptual understanding.[9] Wittgenstein calls this a "family resemblance" approach to stress that, while there are no essential or defining features of any category, there are complicated networks "of similarities overlapping and criss-crossing: sometimes overall similarities, sometimes similarities of detail."[10] In terms of establishing a genre on this model, one would pick out various core features from a variety of works that are accepted as paradigms of the genre. For example, one might look at *Dracula, Frankenstein,* and other similar works to find the core overlapping features that earn a work acceptance into the horror genre. A main point of emphasis, however, is that this approach is much more open-ended than the Aristotelian one.[11]

It is important to note that no matter which approach is taken toward understanding and/or establishing a genre, there must be a constant recognition of the tug-of-war between looking at actual films (the empirical side) and theorizing or defining a genre (the abstract/conceptual side). The tug-of-war occurs in the art world in general, with theory sometimes driving art production versus the actual production of artists influencing the work of theorists.[12] In keeping with this tradition, I will look closely at works that are clearly sports films (and I will focus only on *film,* not literature in general) in order to eke out a few core overlapping features that are needed to understand what makes a sports film; hence, I will be taking a Wittgensteinian approach.

What Is Wrong with *Bull Durham?*

There are several reasons for the development of genres, or generic film categories. Originally genres developed as a means for movie distributors to understand what they were buying, and later they became a means for audience identification.[13] Genre as a means of film criticism came about as a response to auteur criticism that was prominent in the 1960s, when many developments in defining various genres occurred.[14] The western is the first, and possibly the most obviously identifiable, genre, with the gangster genre following fairly soon thereafter. Establishing a genre is tricky because the category must be neither too wide nor too narrow. If it is too wide, then so much will be allowed in the category that it will not be informative enough to be very useful for either the critic or the audience. That is one reason the AFI's listing of animation as a genre is wrong; animation is a very general film category within which various genres may take place (there can be animated westerns, dramas, and so on). However, even though Thomas Wartenberg provides an interesting defense, the "unlikely couple" is probably too narrow to be considered a genre and is better understood as a figure that pops up in different genres.[15] Yet, while there are a very few clear-cut cases of accepted genres, such as the western, mostly there is widespread disagreement among theorists attempting various defenses that some grouping or other should be recognized as a genre or major subgenre. It is into this fray I step with sports films.

The day after the AFI list aired on television, I was driving in the morning and listening to sports talk radio.[16] The hosts were arguing about some of the sports movies on the list, a list that includes the following, from tenth to first: *Jerry Maguire, National Velvet, Breaking Away, Caddyshack, The Hustler, Bull Durham, Hoosiers, The Pride of the Yankees, Rocky,* and *Raging Bull.* Independent of the fact that virtually everyone I have spoken with about this list agrees that *Jerry Maguire* is not a sports movie but primarily a romantic comedy, the radio hosts were concerned about *Bull Durham.*[17] I found this particularly interesting, because I had never heard anyone really challenge the sports status of that movie; indeed, it was even chosen in 2003, by no less an authority than *Sports Illustrated,* as the #1 greatest sports movie of all time.[18] Now, while it may be possible to challenge the sports status of the film, on similar grounds to *Jerry Maguire,* as primarily a romantic comedy, that was not the challenge presented by the radio hosts. The primary challenge—and this is what piqued my interest—was that *Bull Durham* does not contain a culminating sporting moment, in their view, a necessary condition for a film to be considered a sports film.

By examining the AFI list, it is clear that a culminating sporting event or moment is certainly a typical element. Most of the movies on the list, *Hoosiers, Breaking Away, Rocky,* and even *Caddyshack* do indeed contain just such a moment, but is that moment essential? If it is, then not only is *Bull Durham* off the list, but so is *Raging Bull,* which is the #1 movie on the AFI's list. I believe the mistake is to assume that a typical feature is a necessary (or essential) condition without which the film in question fails to be a sports film. Following a Wittgensteinian model, I maintain that a culminating sporting event or moment is a core, but not a necessary or essential, feature of a sports film. *Wimbledon,* for example, does have this feature, while *Raging Bull* does not.

Digging a little more deeply, there are other important aspects of the culminating moment. The most crucial of these is that the final sporting event is usually a triumphant moment where the lead character/team overcomes long odds to win it. *Hoosiers, A League of Their Own, Major League,* and *The Longest Yard* provide clear examples of this for team sports. For individual sports, *Breaking Away, Caddyshack,* and *Rocky II* are all good examples. Importantly for the analysis, neither *Bull Durham* nor *Raging Bull* contains a culminating sporting event or moment in the traditional sense. Even the original *Rocky,* #2 on both lists, plays with the final event. While it is true that *Rocky* contains one of the most famous culminating sports moments, the final fight against Apollo Creed, Rocky does not win the fight, hence the triumph of the moment is not the typical triumph of winning. So of the three possibly greatest sports films of all time, two do not contain, and one manipulates, one of the core features of sports films.

Now some of you may think that I have jumped the gun a bit by discussing sports films without first giving at least a suggested definition or list of features. However, as there is a constant tug-of-war between theorizing and empirically examining elements of accepted paradigmatic films, I have started with films first. But it is now worth stepping back to try and gain a bird's-eye view of possible features of the category.

A Wittgensteinian Account

The obvious place to start is with the notion of sports outside of film. Whether or not an event or activity is categorized as a sport depends on cultural, social, and institutional factors completely independent from the film world. So on first blush, and without begging the question, an apparent necessary condition of a sports film is that it represent an actual sport. Here is a case where an Aristotelian approach would seem to make most sense; surely an essential feature of any film deemed to be a sports film is that it contains an actual representation of a sport: a tennis film represents tennis, a basketball movie represents basketball, and so on.[19]

Let's now contrast this feature with the suggested AFI definition, which is an attempt to provide necessary and sufficient conditions of the sports genre as *"a genre of films with protagonists who play athletics or other games of competition."*[20]

There are two ways this definition is defective, both of which result in including too many films in the sports film category. The first is in the portion of the definition that insists the protagonists play, apart from athletics, "other games of competition." While I have mentioned that many find *Jerry Maguire* to be a contentious inclusion on AFI's list, the film I actually find to be the most clearly erroneous an inclusion is *The Hustler*. While no doubt an exceptional film, I am hard-pressed to understand counting pool as a sport. The "games of competition" clause makes this possible, but the problem should be obvious: the AFI is conflating the concept of "sport" with that of "game."

Without attempting the difficult and dubious task of clearly defining "sport" and "game," some clarity is still possible and should presently suffice. Bluntly put, all sports are games but not all games are sports. Hide and Seek, Monopoly, Twister, Checkers, and Tiddlywinks are all games, but they are not sports. Minimally, a sport must contain some combination of competition and athletic activity to even begin to get into the category, and Monopoly and Chess just do not make the cut. There may, of course, be borderline cases; for example, I have had arguments with people over whether golf or auto racing should really be considered sports, but no one is arguing over whether or not Candyland should be considered a sport.[21]

Additionally, without a lot more defense and clarification, other clearly unacceptable films would get into the category if "games of competition" are sufficient. For example, the Steve Martin comedy *Dirty Rotten Scoundrels* is a movie in which two con artists (the other played by Michael Caine) actively compete for a woman, yet it would be perverse to categorize this as a sports film. Again, the main problem is the conflation of "games" and "sports." The feature under question might make sense if the attempt was to understand a game genre of film, but this is neither the task nor the proper clarifying terminology.

The "other games of competition" clause is clearly neither necessary nor sufficient for a sports film (it's the *"other* games" that is the real problem), and so it is now time to turn to the other clause of the definition: "protagonists who play athletics." This clause is less problematic, and may even be necessary, but that depends on the proper analysis of "athletics." Prior to that discussion, a couple other points are in order. If that clause is taken to be sufficient, then again it is too broad. In fact, there are nice, clear examples using tennis and film that illustrate this problem.

In the movie *Annie Hall,* both of the protagonists *play* tennis, yet there is very little actual tennis in the movie, and tennis is not a major theme, so *Annie Hall* is not a sports film (though it is a great romantic comedy). Maybe one could respond by amending the clause to say not merely "playing athletics," but by featuring a recognized sport as the profession of the protagonist. So, much like one could argue that westerns need cowboys, sports movies need professional athletes. That emendation, though, would still result in including too much in the category. Two specific examples illustrate the problem: *Match Point* and *Strangers on a Train.*[22]

Both of these films include protagonists who are professional tennis players, yet again neither should be considered a sports film. They are both better understood as thrillers or suspense films, but why? It might be argued that, with *Match Point* in particular, especially given the title, the driving metaphor of the film is that of the back-and-forth between the leads, much like players in a tennis match, and so the movie is really a tennis-thriller. The same could even be said of *Strangers on a Train,* with the back-and-forth and crisscrossing between the two lead characters. So, here are two examples where the protagonists are professional tennis players and, arguably, tennis provides a metaphorical foundation for each film. The question this drives to: Is metaphor enough?

The answer is "no." While the metaphorical elements provide some interest, and possibly even some clarity, when one reads the films, there needs to be much more related to the sport in question for a film to be a sports film. So, even though there are scenes of tennis in each of these, there is not enough emphasis literally (not metaphorically) on tennis to make either of them tennis films. This point generalizes to all sports films. Two lessons can be drawn from these examples. The first is that merely having a protagonist who plays athletics, professionally or not, is not sufficient to make a film a sports film: *Marathon Man* is not a sports film just because the lead runs marathons and the title contains the word "marathon." The second is that there needs to be a literal, and not merely metaphorical, emphasis on the sport under question for a film to be a sports film.

To sum up, by examining the AFI and *Sports Illustrated* lists of great sports films and also by criticizing the suggested AFI definition, I have been attempting to ferret out at least some of the core, but not necessarily essential, features for a film to be considered a sports film. The core features so far include (1) that the film has to be a representation of an actual sport as understood by a culture, (2) that the representation needs to be literal, not merely metaphorical, (3) that there is a culminating sporting event or moment, and (4) that the protagonist plays athletics or sports. Other elements that may be core features are settings and imagery—which for the sake of brevity may be safely folded into (1) and (2). For example, the movie *Wimbledon* takes place at Wimbledon, *Bull Durham* largely takes place on a baseball field. Another point (5) is that there needs to be a fairly substantial amount of the sport actually being played in the film. *Strangers on a Train* only has one brief (but quite chillingly effective) scene of tennis, while *Tennis, Anyone . . . ?* has several. Now, there is no set percentage that is needed, but if the sport is barely played in the film, then it is probably not a sports film. However, proper genre categorization depends on the overlapping of the five elements, not on just one or two being present, and on how those features are emphasized.

These core features, then, are the generic elements that allow categorization of a film as part of the sports genre of films. Plotlines that take a protagonist that plays a sport, by showing the playing of the sport, to a culminating sporting moment/event is the typical story arc. Additionally, various themes such as perseverance, redemption, and overcoming of odds (the underdog phenomenon) are common. One of the difficulties in categorizing sports films is that they often cross other genres, such as romance (e.g., *Rocky*, *Bull Durham*), fantasy (*Field of Dreams*), and biopic and drama (*Raging Bull*). Each film has to be examined individually to understand whether the level of emphasis is on a particular sport enough to categorize it as a sports film. For example, since *Raging Bull* is a biopic of a boxer, it is almost impossible to separate these elements, but since some of the other features are present to a high degree—in particular, there is a substantial amount of boxing itself—the film is a sports film (even without a culminating sporting event). However, even though these features provide a Wittgensteinian family resemblance account (in fact, because of that), *none* are necessary. I have already discussed some of the reasons, so I will only briefly look at the two I think many would consider clearly necessary and provide counterexamples: (1) and (4). I will first look at (4): the protagonist plays athletics.

I have already provided reasons the protagonist playing sports or athletics is not sufficient to make a film a sports film, but it still might be thought a necessary element. While it is typical, and hence a core feature, there are filmic counterexamples already in this movie lexicon. The respective protagonists in *Hoosiers* and *Miracle* do *not* play the sport in question (at least not in the film). The lead characters are the *coaches* of sports teams, yet given the other elements of the films, they are both clearly sports films.

It is, however, feature (1) that I suspect many would consider the best candidate for a necessary condition. In fact, I used to think it was, before fully reflecting on certain problematic examples. Recall that this feature is that the film represents an actual sport as understood by a culture. So tennis and basketball get in, but so do cricket and soccer. At #29 on the *Sports Illustrated* list is a movie that, if it is a sports movie, shows that this feature is unnecessary: *Rollerball*, a 1975 film set in a future where a brutal sport, "rollerball," is the main form of entertainment. I have to admit that I loved this film as a kid (hey, I was a kid after all), but is it a sports film? This is not the same problem of conflating "game" with "sport," which is what ruled out *The Hustler*. Rollerball clearly represents what other real sports have in terms of competition and athletics, and so if it existed it would clearly be categorized as a sport. Obviously one might argue that since the film is set in the future, then it is a science fiction film; however it has already been granted that sports films often blend with other genres, so the issue is emphasis. Given that the protagonist is a professional rollerballer, there are several scenes of the sport being played, and there is a culminating sporting event, there is a strong case to be made that this is a sports film. If so, then even condition (1) is not necessary. This is clearly the most contentious point, but I think it is plausible, and so I propose to move forward.[23]

Tennis Films

In this section I will look closely at three films in which tennis plays a significant role. I will use the established criteria to figure out whether the films in question should be categorized as sports (tennis) films and contrast these with some of the films already discussed. There are actually not a lot of tennis films to choose from, and one of the most infamous, *Players,* is very difficult to find. I actually saw it when I was quite young (about ten), because I loved tennis so much; the film famously includes many pros playing themselves (in 1979), such as Vilas, McEnroe, Nastase, and several more. The reviews I have read, and McEnroe's own comments on one of the extras on the DVD of *Wimbledon,* confirm what I knew even as a kid—the movie is awful. However, it's worth watching, if for no other reason than to see the cameos.

Nobody's Perfect

Nobody's Perfect is a cross-dressing "comedy" about a character named Stephen, played by Chad Lowe, who, upon entering a small college in southern California, falls madly in love on first sight with Shelly.[24] Stephen is so in love that he is unable to concentrate, gets kicked off the tennis team (coached by Vitas Gerulaitis), and with his wily schemer friend concocts a plan to dress as a woman, Stephanie, in order to get close to Shelly.[25] The movie is even worse than it sounds, and there is little reason to go into much more detail except to figure out whether or not it fits into the sports genre as a tennis film.

Even though appalling as a movie, it provides an interesting test case because it really is on the borderline. Of course, one of the virtues of a Wittgensteinian account is that it allows for borderline cases, whereas an Aristotelian essentialism does not. *Nobody's Perfect* is clearly supposed to be a comedy, possibly even a romantic comedy (the execution is so bad it is hard to tell), but it is unclear if it is also supposed to be a sports film. The protagonist does play tennis as both Stephen and Stephanie—he even joins the college women's tennis team as Stephanie to stay close to Shelly. There are several shots of tennis being badly played, unlike in *Strangers on a Train* and *Match Point,* and there is a culminating sporting moment when "Stephanie" dramatically returns to the women's tennis team to help them win the final tournament.

Given these elements, an argument could certainly be made that this is a tennis film; however, due to its emphasis, it is much better thought of as a romantic comedy with a significant amount of tennis. Although there are a few tennis scenes, other than the culminating moment, tennis is not discussed and merely functions to move along the nontennis romantic/comedic elements. In other words, there is very little thematic or story emphasis on tennis. Contrast this with *Bull Durham,* where even the romantic elements often revolve around baseball discussions and/or in a baseball setting—it is partly because of the thematic emphasis that *Bull Durham* is a baseball movie.

Take another example: *Caddyshack.* It might be thought that *Caddyshack* is merely a (very good) comedy that happens to have some golf elements. But in contrast to *Nobody's Perfect,* there are even more scenes of golf being played, there is a triumphant culminating moment, and, clearly unlike in *Nobody's Perfect,* the primary setting is a *golf course.* Because of this emphasis, I believe it makes good sense to categorize *Caddyshack* as a golf movie that is also a comedy, in contrast with *Nobody's Perfect.*

Wimbledon

One might think that the title, *Wimbledon,* makes clear that this is a sports film, but given that *Match Play* and *Marathon Man* both use their titles primarily metaphorically and not literally, it is only on close examination of the movie in question that its status is to be understood. *Wimbledon* has all the elements of a traditional romantic comedy: the meet-cute, the movement from mere attraction to love, the roadblocks (her father, their careers), and a final wrap-up with the couple together. Given these elements, it might be thought the analysis would be the same as *Nobody's Perfect,* the difference being, of course, the emphasis and setting. We will argue, though, that *Wimbledon* really is a tennis movie (and also a romantic comedy).

Lizzie and Peter are tennis pros, she very successful and he about to retire. They meet when he accidentally enters her hotel room, and the romance quickly unfolds from there. As for the tennis, there is clearly an attempt to capture at least some of the feel of professional tennis. The movie is largely set on the actual grounds of Wimbledon; there is the obligatory cameo from McEnroe and Chris Evert as announcers; there are many scenes of tennis, and a very unbelievable final, culminating tennis moment when the wildcard Peter actually wins Wimbledon![26] In addition, special effects are used to illustrate the power of tennis and the difficulties that arise—crowd noise, anxiety, et cetera—when playing at the highest level. Given all of these elements and the thematic emphasis, this is definitely a tennis movie. The emphasis on the tennis at least equals, perhaps exceeds, the emphasis on the romance. Unfortunately, while this is not an awful movie, it is incredibly mediocre.

Tennis . . . Anyone?

Tennis . . . Anyone? is an even more recent, independently made movie. Following two wannabe actors, one of whom becomes somewhat famous and the other who instead makes a living teaching tennis, this movie blends the genres (or subgenres) of the sports movie, buddy movie, and Hollywood movie. While the protagonists are both playing actors, they become ensconced in a world of celebrity doubles tennis tournaments, in which they keep playing, and losing to, a particular doubles team, setting up the triumphant final tennis moment. There are several relatively lengthy scenes of tennis play and some interesting discussions of tennis that, combined with the other elements, establish this as a tennis movie.[27] In light of these brief synopses, I will now turn toward the general problems that arise in portraying tennis in film.

The *Raging Bull* of Tennis?

Aesthetically evaluating art is notoriously difficult, especially since a large portion of the population thinks it is impossible because, as the platitude says, "beauty is in the eye of the beholder." Yet, people do present arguments and reasons for their aesthetic judgments, unlike with mere matters of taste (such as: "I like cherry ice cream better than vanilla"), and so I proceed on the assumption that some works can reasonably be judged as better than others, with the obvious caveat that all judgments are open to critique and debate.

Raging Bull was judged by a group of critics as the best film of the 1980s.[28] Not the best sports film or biopic, but the best film. So it should be no surprise that it is recognized as one of the top sports films of all time. Reasons for *Raging Bull*'s aesthetic greatness are several, but at least some of the reasons include the incredible acting (DeNiro famously gained roughly fifty pounds and also trained extensively to learn boxing), the cinematography and general look (the stark black and white giving the story a timeless quality), and the basic brutality and realism of the boxing scenes. Supposing I allow that *Raging Bull* is an excellent film, the question presented earlier, and really the driving question of the title, is: Could there be a *Raging Bull* of tennis? Even though I love tennis and sincerely wish there could be such a movie, I believe because of certain critical problems with sports films in general and, further, specific features related exclusively to tennis, there will not be a tennis movie that achieves the critical level of *Raging Bull*.

To be fair, it is not clear that many other sports films have reached that level either. This brings one to the general problem that it is very difficult to make a truly great film that also falls in the sports genre. Certainly if one looks, for example, at the *Sight & Sound* list there has never been a sports film in the top ten of all time (note: *Bicycle Thieves* is not a sports film).[29] However, unlike in some literature criticism, this cannot be seen as a bias against genre work in general, since the list has contained westerns (*The Searchers*), mystery/suspense films (*Vertigo*), and musicals (*Singin' in the Rain*) among others. I would even venture to guess that *Raging Bull* is the only sports film that has been close. This naturally leads to the possibility that there is a limitation with sports films in particular.

Most films, historically, that have been evaluated as great tend to be of serious subjects and so tend to be dramas, tragedies, or epics or have serious crossover with these areas. Most sports films, though, are uplifting and triumphant, with the culminating sporting moment as one of their core features. Comedies, which are also rarely at the very top of any lists, are similar to sports films on this point, in that they uplift the viewer. And, whether ultimately justified or not, works that are serious and (at least emotionally) realistic tend to be evaluated as more aesthetically valuable.

A long history of theorists and critics have criticized popular art, including popular, or mass, films.[30] Part of the criticism is that films are thought somewhat frivolous, a distraction from the important things in life, hence the notion of "mere" entertainment. The same criticism is often leveled at games and sports—as recently as 2001 a philosopher called them "pointless and childish tasks."[31] If this is at all true, then sports films become a kind of double frivolity or, mirroring Plato, a frivolous representation of a frivolous activity. While I think this is definitely too strong, at least psychologically there may be something to this analysis.

Sports films, again like comedies, rarely deal with serious life issues, and even when they do, those issues are usually too easily resolved along with the culminating sporting moment. This is exactly what happens, and it is just one of the problems with the end of *Wimbledon*. When Peter wins *Wimbledon*, he basically wins the girl; everything is nice, tidy, and easy. Now, I happen to believe that sports themselves, and tennis in particular, provide an opportunity to reflect on a specific kind of technical beauty, much like in the case of dance, and so are not as frivolous as some have suggested. But the beauty involved with tennis is particularly difficult to convey on film. So, the problem of conveying this on screen, combined with the fact that sports films in general rarely deal in a serious way with serious issues, leads to a general psychological attitude of a popular, and critical for that matter, dismissal of most sports films.

Boxing movies stand out in this respect and highlight the difficulty of seriously dealing with life issues. Boxing is almost by definition serious, since the very nature of boxing qua boxing often results in the injury and possibly even death of one of the competitors; contrast that with "winning the big game" or the final match—the gravitas is often not there, and definitely not as part of the sport itself. These various points help establish why, in general, sports films are rarely considered truly great films; however, there are also some other issues related specifically to tennis.

When sports films are very good, this is largely due to the believability of the sport being played. For example, the boxing scenes in *Raging Bull* are incredibly believable. In fact several actual boxers, upon viewing the movie, thought DeNiro could have been a boxer. I take it also that this is why Kevin Costner keeps popping up in baseball movies: he can believably portray a baseball player. Even the golf scenes in *Caddyshack* are fairly realistic, if one realizes that the players in the movie are supposed to be not professionals but merely normal club players. Tennis film has a particular difficulty with believability because of two factors: the lack of background knowledge of the audience and the difficulty of representing tennis on a movie screen.

Really appreciating any sport requires some degree of background knowledge. Yet this is a double-edged sword. On the one hand, if the viewer does not know enough about a sport, then it is difficult to fully appreciate a representation of the sport.[32] On the other, if the viewer knows a lot about a sport, then it is easy to be distracted and frustrated by its portrayal. *Wimbledon* illustrates both problems. As a tennis fan, I enjoyed the representation of the behind-the-scenes elements at Wimbledon (the place)—in fact, it is those elements that made the film even tolerable. On the flip side, the actual tennis-playing scenes verge on the excruciating, especially given that the players are supposed to be world class. The cuts and special effects used to convey the tennis only served to highlight the deficiencies in both representing tennis and the tennis abilities of the actors.[33] Possibly if I knew less about tennis, the tennis scenes would not bother me as much, but then the Wimbledon scenes would also be less interesting, and the only thing left to focus on would be a nearly unbearable, formulaic love story.

David Foster Wallace helps highlight the problem of representing tennis at all. He beautifully discusses the contrast between watching tennis live and watching on television, going so far as to claim "one thing [tennis] is not is televisable."[34] He points out that if you have only seen professional tennis on television, then "you simply have no idea how hard these pros are hitting the ball, how fast the ball is moving, how little time the players have to get it, and how quickly they're able to move and rotate and strike and recover."[35] The upshot is that trying to convey the beauty and power of professional tennis on film verges on the impossible because of the representational limitations of movies combined with the fact that few, if any, actors have the tennis ability to come close to representing top-level tennis. This is the problem with movies like *Nobody's Perfect* and especially *Wimbledon*.

Tennis . . . Anyone? comes the closest so far and is certainly the best tennis film available, because it is clear that the lead characters really do play tennis, as demonstrated in tennis-playing scenes that limit the cutting away from the entire point.[36] In addition, similar to *Caddyshack*, there is no attempt to make the players seem much better than they are—decent to good normal players. While I do not think *Tennis . . . Anyone?*

reaches the level of *Caddyshack*, I do think there could be a *Caddyshack* of tennis. However, there will not be a *Raging Bull* of tennis. There will not, because of the various problems we have discussed, be a tennis film that realistically represents tennis and that is serious enough to be considered a great film in general. Either the film will fail to contain enough tennis to be a tennis film—for example, *Strangers on a Train*—or will fail to represent tennis well, or, if it does both, then it will fall into the trap of trying to dramatically engage a serious subject matter via a medium and genre in which it is notoriously difficult to do so; and so, in all likelihood, it will fail to achieve the aesthetic heights of, say, *Raging Bull*. My great desire is that a director who understands tennis makes the *Caddyshack* of tennis, since no one can make a *Raging Bull* of tennis.

Notes

I would like to thank Alec Thomson and Eric Mortensen for helpful discussions, Helen Ditouras for her knowledge and discussions of film and genre, and Daryl Fisher for his vast knowledge of tennis.

1. The American Film Institute, "Top Ten Sports," *AFI's 10 Top 10*, 2008, http://www.afi.com/10top10/sports.html.

2. Most of the information about AFI's list comes from the critic Tim Dirk's website. Tim Dirk, *Greatest Films*, http://www.filmsite.org. The one film on the list that has any tennis at all of the fifty nominated films is *Pat and Mike*, DVD, directed by George Cukor (1952; Los Angeles, Warner Home Video, 2000).

3. The philosopher Noël Carroll provides an exceptional model; he and David Bordwell use the term "post-theory" to describe this new approach to film studies. See David Bordwell and Noël Carroll, eds., *Post-Theory: Reconstructing Film Studies* (Madison: University of Wisconsin Press, 1996).

4. The "quarter" refers to the movie *Jocks*, which was so horrible that I truly could not watch anymore. In fact, claiming that I watched even a quarter of the movie is probably a stretch.

5. Aristotle, *Poetics*, trans. M. E. Hubbard, in *A New Aristotle Reader*, ed. J. L. Ackrill (Princeton, NJ: Princeton University Press, 1987), 540.

6. For a good discussion of Aristotle's influence on genre, see Rick Altman, *Film/Genre* (London: British Film Institute, 1999).

7. Noël Carroll, "Horror and Humor," *Journal of Aesthetics and Art Criticism* 57, no. 2 (Spring 1999): 151. For his most extensive treatment of horror as a genre see Noël Carroll, *The Philosophy of Horror; or, Paradoxes of The Heart* (New York: Routledge, 1990).

8. Carroll, *Philosophy of Horror*, 7–8.

9. For those philosophers who are interested, using this approach with defining

genres is merely a special case of the general debate over whether or not we should approach defining any categories in an Aristotelian or Wittgensteinian way. So, traditionally, philosophers lean more toward Aristotle while psychologists tend to work more from a Wittgensteinian model when attempting to understand the nature of concepts.

10. Ludwig Wittgenstein, *Philosophical Investigations*, 3rd ed., trans. G. E. M. Anscombe (New York: Macmillan, 1958), sections 66–69. Wittgenstein uses the concept of "game" to illustrate family resemblance.

11. I have presented two very general approaches, but there are many more within genre studies; however, most of them end up falling roughly under one of these two. For a nice, brief summary of four approaches toward genre theory, see Deborah Knight and George McKnight, "Whose Genre Is It, Anyway? Thomas Wartenberg on the Unlikely Couple Film," *Journal of Social Philosophy* 33, no. 2 (Summer 2002): 331–32.

12. For example, Clive Bell's theory of significant form is famously a response to developments in modern art and the work of Cezanne in particular.

13. Michael Allen, *Contemporary U.S. Cinema* (Harlow, England: Pearson Education, 2003), 177–200.

14. Christine Gledhill, "Genre," in *The Cinema Book,* ed. Pam Cook (New York: British Film Institute, 1985), 58–112.

15. For the criticism and the point that the unlikely couple is best thought of as a figure, see Knight and McKnight, "Whose Genre Is It, Anyway?" For Wartenberg's argument that he has established a new genre, see Thomas Wartenberg, "Can Romance Function as Social Criticism? A Defense of *Unlikely Couples*," *Journal of Social Philosophy* 33, no. 2 (Summer 2002): 310–21.

16. I don't do this often, because half the time the hosts either don't talk about sports or they only talk about football, baseball, or basketball (almost never tennis), and so the discussions grow quite tedious.

17. *Bull Durham,* DVD, directed by Ron Shelton (1988; Arlington, TX, Mount Company).

18. See the list at Tim Dirk, "Sports Films: The Greatest Sports films of All-Time," *AMC Filmsite,* August 4, 2003, www.filmsite.org/sportsfilms.html.

19. I do not mean anything fancy by "represents," only that the film presents images of people playing whatever sport is under consideration (tennis, basketball, etc.).

20. American Film Institute, *AFI's Top Ten,* emphasis added.

21. The existence of borderline cases is evidence of some vagueness to the word "sport," but this is hardly surprising, since vagueness is a ubiquitous feature of language. David Baggett's chapter in this volume, "Why Roger Federer Is the Best: Or Is It McEnroe?" touches on this topic of vagueness further.

22. *Match Point,* DVD, directed by Woody Allen (London, BBC Films, 2006). *Strangers on a Train,* DVD, directed by Alfred Hitchcock (1951; Danbury, CT, Warner Bros., 1995).

23. Even if one were to argue that the futuristic elements overwhelmed the sporting elements (which they do not) and so the movie is best understood as only part of the science fiction genre, surely it is plausible that there could be a movie of a purely fictional sport. Suppose, for example, a fan of the Harry Potter books received the rights to make a movie that focused almost exclusively on Quidditch, the sport played by Harry Potter in the books. Surely, if the right elements were emphasized, then the film would be a sports film, even though the sport in question does not actually exist.

24. *Nobody's Perfect*, DVD, directed by Robert Kaylor (Los Angeles, Panorama, 1989).

25. Gerulaitis, as many tennis fans know, has the best tennis quote of all time. On finally beating Connors at the 1979 Masters after losing to him sixteen straight times, he reportedly said: "Nobody beats Vitas Gerulaitis seventeen times in a row!"

26. I suspect, but have no evidence, that Chris Lewis is part of the inspiration for Peter's character. For those of you who don't remember, Lewis was an unseeded player who came virtually from nowhere, and went back just as quickly, to make the 1983 Wimbledon finals (where, unlike in the movie, he was handily dispatched by McEnroe).

27. There is even a humorous discussion of how good of a movie *Caddyshack* is, providing a nice meta-film moment.

28. One such list, from the well-known film magazine *Sight & Sound*, is at "The Sight & Sound Top Ten Poll 2002," *Sight & Sound*, http://www.bfi.org.uk/sightand sound/topten/.

29. The *Sight & Sound* poll of several critics worldwide is considered the master list of great films. The list, which started in 1952, is voted upon every ten years, 2002 being the most recent.

30. For a good overview and interesting definition of mass art, see Noël Carroll, *A Philosophy of Mass Art* (Oxford, England: Clarendon, 1998).

31. Frans De Wachter, "Sport as Mirror on Modernity," *Journal of Social Philosophy* 32, no. 1 (Spring 2001): 90.

32. Boxing stands out in this respect as well. While one does need to know quite a bit to understand the intricacies of boxing, one does not need to know much to understand what it is like to be hit repeatedly very hard. Because virtually everyone has this basic understanding, it is much easier for boxing films to deal with serious issues in a way that does not need a lot of set-up (and a lot of set-up is the aesthetic downfall of many a sports movie).

33. It was no surprise at all to find out, upon watching one of the extras on the DVD, that neither of the leads had ever played tennis prior to training for the movie.

34. David Foster Wallace, "Federer as Religious Experience: How One Player's Grace, Speed, Power, Precision, Kinesthetic Virtuosity, and Seriously Wicked Topspin Are Transfiguring Men's Tennis," *New York Times PLAY Magazine*, August 20, 2006, 49.

35. Ibid., 50.

36. Many, if not most, films showing tennis will often show a player hitting, say, a forehand which, if one knows anything about tennis, one can tell that the shot will go into the net, but there will be an immediate cut to the other player flailing at the shot and missing. This is the worst possible way to represent tennis on screen, yet some version of this happens repeatedly. *Tennis . . . Anyone?* admirably avoids this for the most part.

Kevin Kinghorn

EXCUSES, EXCUSES

Inside the Mind of a Complainer

As rational creatures, humans have the unique ability to reflect on their personal successes, and they can identify with gratitude the reasons for them. Unfortunately, humans have the corresponding ability to complain and offer excuses when things don't go their way. But why do people do it? More specifically, why would a tennis player—who already faces the mental demands of concentrating on shot after shot in a competitive match—take the time and energy to complain about a line call? Or why would a frustrated amateur feel the need to make excuses as to why he's not in the professional ranks? What lies behind the human drive to complain and make excuses?

To use the psychology of a tennis player to gain insight into human psychology in general, I'll first need an accurate picture of the mind of a tennis player. Obviously, it would help if I could draw from the thoughts of someone who works closely with actual tennis players. And if I'm going to get input from a tennis professional, I might as well opt for the top coach in the world. That would be Brad Gilbert, who has coached two players (Andre Agassi and Andy Roddick) to a #1 ranking and whose advice is sought by players and tennis federations around the globe. Brad was himself a top player in his own right, winning twenty ATP tournaments and achieving a #4 world ranking at one time. If there's anyone who understands the mentality of a tennis player, it's Brad Gilbert.

I had the chance to talk with Brad about this issue of complaining and excuse-making. His insights helped me understand some of the reasons players might complain about things liked missed line calls. And I was left with no doubt about the self-destructive nature of excuse-making. As I go along, I'll draw from some of the comments he offered.

As a final point of introduction, it's worth mentioning that philosophers have sometimes offered advice on avoiding the pitfalls of complaining. The school of thought called Stoicism (founded in Ancient Greece by a philosopher named Zeno [344–362 B.C.E.]) urged that people should avoid any emotional state of mind which might give rise to complaining. Indeed, stoics were concerned that people never be controlled by any of their emotions. The key is to suppress one's expectations and desires, so that one is indifferent to those negative aspects of the world over which one has no control. The fiery temperament of a competitive tennis player, however, wouldn't be compatible with this kind of philosophy (although the case of Ivan Lendl is perhaps debatable). At any rate, my concern is not so much with what strategy a player might adopt to limit complaining as it is with the question of what causes a player to complain in the first place.

The Fact of the Matter Is: That Call Merits Complaint!

The first and most obvious reason a player might complain about line calls is that the calls really are going against that player. If someone plays in enough competitive events, then the statistical odds are pretty good that some of these matches will be unbalanced in terms of the calls that go for or against him or her. Brad recalls, "I played in eight hundred matches. Sure, there are days when everything seems to go against you. And there are days when things seem to go for you as well. There were times when my opponent kept arguing over everything, and you begin to think, 'Maybe I am getting a lot of these calls.'"

So, sometimes complaints on the tennis court are straightforward observations of objective facts. Line judges and umpires don't always make correct calls, and sometimes a string of incorrect calls go against a player. At such times, it is understandable that a player might draw this fact to the umpire's attention. A player might do this because he is angry and wants to make a retributive comment on the umpire's competency, or he might do it more shrewdly as an attempt to influence the umpire's future rulings on close calls. But as far as the player's initial belief about the repeated, unfavorable calls which led to the complaint, this belief is simply an observation of objective facts.

Sometimes it can *seem* that one is observing objective facts, when really her own intellectual limitations are influencing what she believes. An honest attempt to assess a situation is no guarantee that one will not be prone to errors in the way she draw inferences. When people observe an equally weighted coin land on "tails" three times in a row when flipped, there is a common tendency to expect that the next flip of the coin is probably due to land on "heads." But of course there is no "law of averages," whereby the result of the next flip of the coin is in any way influenced by previous results. Similarly, volunteers in psychology experiments may be asked whether the births of six children in a family are less likely to have the gender sequence of MMMFFF than the sequence FMMFMF. Many people answer that the first gender sequence is a less likely scenario than the second. Because the first sequence seems less representative of the random process by which gender is determined, these people see the first sequence as less likely. But of course each is equally likely. These kinds of mistakes in drawing inferences and reaching conclusions are limitations on our ability to think rationally. They are actually, therefore, forms of irrationality.

Lest we think ourselves above such rational shortcomings, we would do well to consider the many ways all of us at times succumb to powerful imagery. Have we ever been surprised to learn that an actor was, in real life, quite unlike the character he or she played so well in a TV series? But in having our belief about an actor dispelled, we must concede that our belief was originally formed despite knowing that actors are paid to play specified roles, not simply to portray their real-life personalities. Have we ever heard a stirring rendition of the national anthem at a time of national crisis or mourning and become more resolved in our belief that we live in a great country? But of course the emotional impact of a song is no good reason to think that a country is or is not great.

Frequently, it is the vividness of evidence that leads a person to give that evidence a certain weight she would otherwise not give it. As the psychologists Richard Nisbett and Lee Ross have confirmed through experimental testing, "the news that a bank in one's neighborhood has been robbed just an hour ago is more vivid than the news that a bank on the other side of town was robbed last week. The former bank robbery, accordingly, is likely to have a greater impact on one's views of the seriousness of the crime problem in one's city or the need for stiffer prison sentences for bank robbers."[1] Any number of everyday examples abound where the vividness of evidence causes one to form beliefs she otherwise would not form. A married couple may continually have to compromise about what sporting events to watch on television, with the woman always wanting to watch tennis and the man always wanting to watch football. Perhaps the objective fact is that each person has had an equal number of instances watching his or her preferred sport. Due to the vividly remembered frustration associated with those previous times when one had to defer to the other person's preference, though, each may earnestly believe that he or she is the one who has done the majority of the compromising in the past. Such differences of opinion are surely common on a whole range of everyday issues, and these differences reveal that people are probably not as objective in evaluating evidence as they think they are!

There are certainly instances where the vividness of a bad tennis call might understandably stick in a player's mind. Who can forget John McEnroe's famous outburst at umpire Ted James during the 1981 Wimbledon tournament: "You can't be serious, man. You cannot be serious! That ball was on the line. Chalk flew up! It was clearly in. How can you possibly call that out? How many are you gonna miss?!" A call like that sticks in the mind. And, as with the example of the married couple watching sporting events, most any call going *against* a player will be felt more deeply, and remembered more easily, than one that goes *for* the player. So it would be understandable that a tennis player might commonly perceive the bulk of an umpire's missed calls as going against him, when in fact his perceptions are explained by his emotional responses and not by the simple facts themselves. Indeed, I would have thought that some players might genuinely come to believe that a particular line judge or umpire is "out to get them." But Brad Gilbert is dismissive of such an idea: "You can't be a champion and have one ounce of that way of thinking. None of the top players think like that. No one thinks the umpire is out to get them, or the world is out to get them. You can't think like that and be a champion."

So how does one explain a player complaining against particular umpires, as John McEnroe did in his animated pledge to an umpire at the 1986 Paris Open: "You'll never work another one of my matches!"? Is it a matter simply of a player not having confidence in the umpire's overall competency? Brad looks at it like this: "Yeah, umpires are going to miss calls, and players know that. But no one is going to think in terms of some conspiracy theory. . . . You're going to get some bad calls. There's obviously such a thing as human error. I think technology is helping to eliminate some of that."

This last reference to technology includes Hawk-Eye, a computer re-creation of a ball's flight path, which is now used in major tournaments as a way of appealing line decisions. If the possibility of human error remains a concern for tennis players, then players will consider the introduction of Hawk-Eye to be a good thing, right?

Roger Federer has openly lobbied *against* Hawk-Eye, stating publicly, "I think it's nonsense anyway in the first place."[2] But what reason would Federer have for opposing Hawk-Eye, given that its sole design is to increase the overall accuracy of line calls? To answer this question, I'll explore a different kind of reason that lies behind the complaints of some tennis players.

Complaining and Eliminating the Distractions

What makes Federer's attitude toward Hawk-Eye so odd is that, as the current best player in the world, he seemingly has more reason than anyone to avoid the possibility of a match being influenced by human error or anything else besides the sheer performance of the players. But Federer seems truly to despise Hawk-Eye, telling an umpire during a Wimbledon 2007 match that Hawk-Eye is "killing me" and asking (out of exasperation more than hope) if it could be turned off.

Of course, one explanation of Federer's attitude would be that he simply thinks Hawk-Eye is not in fact providing accurate results. His complaint at Wimbledon followed a controversial line call in his finals match against Raphael Nadal, in which Federer was absolutely convinced that a shot from Nadal, which landed a few feet from Federer, was past the baseline. He remarked after the match, "I told the umpire I was happy Nadal was going to challenge because I knew the ball was out. Then to see that it was in on a 30-all point, which was such a huge point, I was shocked. . . . The umpire told me, too, he saw the ball out. He couldn't believe it was in."[3] Other players also have at times questioned the accuracy of Hawk-Eye. Nadal himself, in commenting on another of his own matches during the same 2007 Wimbledon tournament, admitted, "I think the Hawk-Eye has mistakes sometimes." And indeed, because Hawk-Eye only reconstructs—rather than photocopies—the ball's likely landing spot by taking trajectory data and computing statistical likelihood, there is no 100 percent, conclusive proof that a Hawk-Eye call will be accurate. So perhaps one might think, following from the discussion in the previous section, that Federer's objection to Hawk-Eye is primarily a reaction to objective facts involving machine error.

This explanation, however, is far from complete. To begin with, it is far from clear that Hawk-Eye gives inaccurate results, even in cases where the human eye seems to suggest otherwise. Dr. Paul Hawkins, creator and managing director of Hawk-Eye technology, assures us that his line-calling system has undergone more than a thousand tests and says, "We've gotten every single one of the tests correct." He acknowledges that within Hawk-Eye's computations there is a margin of error of less than four millimeters. And so while admitting that Hawk-Eye "isn't infallible," he quickly adds, "but it's pretty damned close."[4] In response to Federer's description of the specific line call in his match with Nadal, Hawkins contends that the ball was indeed "definitely in." He explains that when a tennis ball touches down, "The ball will be in contact with the ground for about 10 cm. In the very first impact, it will compress so that the bottom half is flat. Then it will start to roll and skid and uncompress."[5] The result is that, because the naked eye does not detect the skidding of the ball, we will not typically be able to discern exactly when the ball first made contact with the ground. Even a television freeze-frame may show a ball after it has skidded for several inches, making a ball that actually touched the baseline on impact seem long to television viewers who are watching a replay.

Although Federer may not have reflected on the intricacies of Hawk-Eye technology, he would surely have to concede that, at the very least, Hawk-Eye provides an accurate result more times than not. So, his adamant resistance to Hawk-Eye cannot be explained simply by an appeal to some perceived machine inaccuracies. What seems a more likely explanation is that Hawk-Eye has become a distraction to him. That is, it is just one too many a thing to have to worry about while on the court. Federer seems to want simply to concentrate on playing the match. Andy Roddick defends Hawk-Eye, saying that it helps keep umpires "in check a little bit more." And Lindsay Davenport agrees that "it takes a lot of pressure off the umpires to try and make too crazy of a call and interject."[6] But Federer complains that Hawk-Eye, in taking pressure off the umpires, puts it on the players. Here is Federer's take: "Now [the umpires] can hide even more behind these calls, that's for sure. It makes it really hard for us. Of course, we would like to be able to rely a little bit on umpires as well. They tend to now just let us do the work, you know, the tough stuff. They let us get embarrassed basically."[7] Federer is alluding to the fact that appeals to Hawk-Eye are made by players during a match, with each player allocated a limited number of appeals. He finds it irritating that, as a player, he is forced to do a job he sees as the responsibility of umpires. The whole system seems to distract him from what he's always done in competitive matches: focus on playing the next shot and find a rhythm of play that is comfortable. Plus, let's face it: Federer is simply not very good at knowing when to challenge a call by appealing to Hawk-Eye. During the 2006 U.S. Open, when he was first given the opportunity to use Hawk-Eye, he made seventeen challenges during the course of the tournament—and he was wrong ten times. So, in addition to his added responsibilities of deciding when to appeal to Hawk-Eye, a player may be faced with questioning his own eyesight! In the end, Federer's ardent complaints about Hawk-Eye seem best explained as a reaction to what has become for him a big, ongoing distraction.

The link between complaining and feeling distracted may account for quite a lot of the outbursts we witness from tennis players. When I asked Brad Gilbert about his own squabbles with umpires, he said: "If I felt something was not right, I'd want to be heard. But then I'd go on. If I felt like I wasn't being listened to, then I'd get upset. I wanted to be heard."

It is indeed a basic human need that others at least hear and understand what we're saying. We often speak of the need to "get something off our chests." And once we do that, we usually can move past the issue and focus on the next task. Without expressing ourselves and being understood by others, we may continue to dwell on the issue in a continually self-destructive manner. So perhaps many of the outbursts we witness from tennis pros are simply attempts to get annoying line calls "out of their systems" so they can refocus their attention on the task at hand.

Complaining as Self-Motivation?

It is one thing for a player to have a brief outburst that serves as a way of eliminating a potential distraction as he refocuses his attention on the match. It is quite another thing to have an ongoing argument with an umpire during which one becomes more and more upset. Such sustained complaining would seem naturally to provide *more* distraction to the player, instead of helping to eliminate it. Yet, I have heard more than one tennis commentator suggest that players like John McEnroe may have sometimes *looked* for a controversial call as a way of "firing themselves up" during the course of a match. Is it ever the case that arguments are intentionally sought by players as a way of motivating themselves to concentrate and play harder?

Brad Gilbert thinks this is an unlikely suggestion. He doubts that even McEnroe ever went looking for an argument with an umpire. Certainly, he responds, "I never went looking for it." But what of this idea that a player, by drawing from the emotional energy of a confrontation with an umpire, could actually become inspired to play better? "For 99.9 percent of the people, that doesn't work. There are a select few who can do that, who are true genius. They can get pissed off, and when their opponent starts to react to it, they can then raise their game to another level. It's genius. But that's one in a million. For the rest of the people, once they start complaining, their games go right in the shitter. . . . For me, when I got pissed off, I'd play worse." So although it seems likely that players might have an outburst as a positive way of letting off steam so that a perceived bad call won't continue to distract them, it's unlikely anyone would actually want to believe that the calls in a match are going against him.

Admittedly, in team sports like football or basketball, a team coach may tell his players that other people are hoping the team fails and that the league referees, influenced by public or league pressure, probably aren't going to do them any favors. This occurrence is evidenced by the frequent statement from players after winning a championship: "They said we wouldn't do it, but we proved them wrong!" (It's never been clear to me who "they" are; but that's another matter.) Such a scenario seems best explained in terms of a coach trying to instill an "us against the world" mentality, so that the players set aside egos and work together for a common purpose. In other words, the coach tries to foster team unity by designating common enemies. Perhaps this approach is effective in some cases as a way of team-building. Nevertheless, in the context of an individual tennis player, this kind of mentality seems utterly incapable of providing the sustained motivation one needs to reach the top. Consider again Brad's assurance that, when it comes to the idea that others may be "out to get us": "You can't be a champion and have one ounce of that way of thinking." Becoming a champion in tennis requires years and years of physically grueling and mentally taxing work. As Brad says, "What people don't understand is how incredibly difficult it is to be a top-five player. It takes an incredible amount of work, and an incredible mental effort to do it."

An "us against the world" mentality may help a basketball coach focus a team's attention for the playoffs, but over the long haul it simply is not compatible with the kind of drive and focus needed to become a tennis champion. To those who make a habit of blaming others and making excuses, Brad's response is simply, "I don't want anything to do with people like that."

Whether the context is the short-term effects of getting caught up in an argument with an umpire during a match, or the long-term effects of associating losses on the court with unfair treatment from others, complaining is a self-destructive practice for the serious tennis player. No player who has achieved anything noteworthy will *want* something to complain about as a way of self-motivation toward success.

Experiencing Relief Instead of Disappointment?

An interesting psychological possibility arises when we consider a scenario in which a person benefits in some way from a line call that goes against him because he actually doesn't want to win the match. On the surface, this scenario seems far-fetched. But a recent admission from Andrea Jaeger seems to raise some questions about the mixed motivations people are capable of having. Jaeger was a teenage tennis star in the early 1980s, becoming a finalist at the French Open (at the age of sixteen) and at Wimbledon, and earning a #2 world ranking. She has since become a nun and has devoted her adult life to helping children living with cancer. Andrea admitted recently that she never wanted the spotlight of a top-ranked tennis star and that she sometimes intentionally didn't play up to her abilities. For instance, she recalls, "the second pro tournament I ever played in, I was 14 and beat a few seeded players, one of whom, Wendy Turnbull, took out a bottle of wine in the locker-room and asked me for a corkscrew. I thought, 'Oh, she's having a drink because I beat her? I've upset her? I don't want to have to deal with this all the time.' That haunted me my entire career. Every time I played her from then on, I tried to give her the match because I felt so bad."[8]

Of course, this is not to say that Andrea regularly shied away from winning. She was, after all, known for her frequent flare-ups when line calls didn't go her way. And, interestingly, her attitude toward Wendy Turnbull helped at times to strengthen her resolve to win: "At Wimbledon in 1983, Billie Jean King beat Wendy Turnbull and whoever beat Wendy, I always had to beat them because it bothered me so much. When we were going on Centre Court for our semi-final, a lady offered her a towel and Billie Jean said, 'No, I won't need one. I'm not going to sweat in this match.' I thought, 'Not only did you beat Wendy, now you've said this so I have to try hard.' So I went out and beat her 6–1, 6–1."[9]

It is remarkable that Andrea could have had the success she did if there was even the very occasional time when she intentionally didn't play to her own highest standard. But what for our discussion is most crucial is the question of why in the world she would be ambivalent about winning. Watching a defeated opponent open a bottle of wine is hardly cause to rethink one's career goals. Andrea's recent admissions, though, extend to a range of issues having to do with her extreme discomfort at the ruthlessly competitive approach of her father and coach, Roland.[10] She has lamented, "We didn't really have a father-daughter relationship; we had a [daughter]-coach relationship."[11] And she recounts stories such as the time her father hurried her into the family car after she lost at the U.S. Open—not even allowing her to shower—and drove the thousand miles home, berating her along the way.[12] Andrea was always more interested in helping children than in achieving fame and fortune on the tennis court. Certainly, she resisted her father's apparent view that these goals should be pursued with single-minded focus and at all costs. When former rival Chris Evert heard of her decision to become a nun, she remarked, "Andrea has found her niche, her calling in life. I don't feel she was cut out for cutthroat competitive tennis. She never looked very happy."[13] Perhaps, then, some tennis players really *don't* want, on some level, to win matches, so they actually are relieved when a close line call goes against them.

In noting that this desire may occur "on some level," I mean to draw attention to the fact that we can have desires of which we're not fully, consciously aware. For instance, a son may not see that his rebellion is in part an attempt to get his parents to listen to him. A daughter may not see that her eating disorder is in part an attempt to gain some control over her life. Frequently, our motivations are mixed. A recent college graduate may enter medical school believing that she is motivated by desires to have financial stability, develop her abilities in a meaningful way, help others in need. All these motivations may be present. She may also believe that her parents, who are both physicians, will approve of her if she follows in their footsteps. Although she may not recognize that this last motivation is indeed partly responsible for her decision, it may nonetheless be a contributing factor.

Given the complex nature of human motivations, one can easily imagine a case in which someone is motivated to do one thing, while also desiring (at some psychological level) to do the very opposite. This seems to be the case for Andrea Jaeger. The competitive spirit of a professional player was clearly present when she played (evidenced by her outbursts at umpires when things didn't go her way). At the same time, by her own admission, she felt a deep uneasiness with the competitive atmosphere of the professional circuit and at times became aware of her own desire not to see an opponent lose. Perhaps there are budding tennis players today who, as did Andrea, have a desire on some level to rebel against a domineering parent-coach or against some other aspect of the demands of competitive tennis. There may be a part of them that therefore experiences relief when one of their shots is called out and they go on to lose a match. Certainly the case of Andrea Jaeger provides insight into people's truly mixed motivations.

Why Excuse-Making Is So Prevalent

Almost any budding tennis player with such mixed motivations will probably be a player you'll never hear about. It is a marvel that with her ambivalent attitudes Andrea Jaeger could have been a top pro for a while.

It *is* incredibly difficult to become a top player in tennis. Brad Gilbert notes how tennis is very different from team sports: "I don't tell people not to go into tennis, but it's not like other sports like baseball or basketball where there are lots of other people who are at the top. To be a Grand Slam champion takes incredible talent and toughness. It is so, so difficult."

In sports like baseball, basketball, and football, there may be dozens of players who are widely viewed as elite, championship-level players. But there can only be one winner of a Grand Slam tennis event, the pinnacle of tennis success. In terms of sheer numbers, there is far more room to be an all-star caliber player in a professional team sport. Brad emphasizes, "And think about all the college players who were good enough to be all-stars on their teams and they're at the end of the bench in the pros!" Indeed so, and success at the college level in a major team sport may gain a player the kind of notoriety that opens marketing and business opportunities, even if the player never establishes himself at the professional level. Clearly, the same cannot be said for collegiate tennis players.

Given the extremely small number of tennis players at any one time who would widely be recognized as among the elite of the professional ranks, the odds are exceptionally long for anyone hoping to gain fame and fortune by means of playing tennis. Yet, the ranks of junior tennis leagues continue to swell. This leads to the question that so many players and their families will inevitably face: What happens when things don't work out as we had hoped?

To be sure, the prospect of unmet expectations can be difficult for the family of a tennis player to accept if that family has invested a great deal of time and money in the player's development. Brad sees that "parents invest in their kids, and their kids work hard, and they think they're owed something because of all that. They have this expectation that their kids are going to be champions. They all expect great things for their kids. And parents should want great things for their kids. But guess what, there are three hundred thousand other kids who are working hard. What about them?" So much of the time there simply is going to be no real prospect of a young tennis player developing into one of the elite, tournament-winning players on the professional tennis circuit. Realistically, he adds, "Look, you need a certain gene pool if you're going to be a champion. If your parents are short, or if your parents are thick, and you want to be a tall, seven-foot basketball player, it's just not going to happen."

Yes, there may be any number of budding tennis players who are really good athletes and who possess above-average mental toughness. But nearly all these hopefuls may yet fail to possess the rare combination of physical skills and mental abilities that sets apart the very top players in the sport. When young players do not progress as they or their families expected, the most obvious explanation is what we have already noted: it simply is incredibly rare for any person to make it to the elite level of a tennis champion. But of course it may be difficult to accept that one's hopes and plans—along with one's investments of time and money—have no real chance of bearing fruit. Faced with the uncomfortable thought that one has invested heavily in an ultimately hopeless cause, alternative explanations may be sought. Brad sees that "parents invest all kinds of money in their kid's future, and they want results. If things don't go well, they'll find some excuse." It is understandable that parents who have already invested heavily in their child's tennis development would resist admitting that they have overestimated their child's athletic potential.

Psychologists have documented how people can sometimes go to extraordinary lengths to avoid uncomfortable conclusions. Tennis parents, like anyone else, can turn their attention away from the thought that they might be wrong in their analysis, choosing instead to reflect only on the evidence that supports their position. So, parents might quickly change the subject when a tennis coach mentions that their child's serve and foot speed are not improving much, instead asking the coach to repeat the positive message that the child's drop shot technique is really coming along. Parents can explain away evidence that undermines their favored conclusion by describing it as an anomaly. So they might describe a child's losses in terms of temporary and uncharacteristic lapses, holding up her few outstanding matches as the norm. In the end, parents may say any number of things to themselves and others as a way of both keeping alive their dreams for their child and justifying their decision to invest in their child's tennis career.

While it may not be too surprising that people can lie to themselves rather than tell themselves the truth, what is particularly interesting is that people often end up believing the lies they tell themselves. The act of lying to others or to oneself involves our pretending that things are a certain way, even while we know (or at least secretly fear) deep down that they are not. And psychologists have shown that this phenomenon of pretending can actually have powerful effects in terms of people truly coming to believe what they once only pretended. In everyday language, we sometimes talk of people "convincing themselves" of something.

To see why the act of pretending can be so effective, we will need to recognize that a good deal of what we believe about ourselves comes from how we observe others behaving toward us. A toddler who is not treated by others as though she is valuable and loved will grow up with a negative self-image. Psychologists have shown through experiments that the complex nature of social interaction can blur the distinction in our own minds between how people are relating to the "real us" and to the persons we are pretending to be.[14] As a result, we may come to believe the things we were once only pretending to believe. If parents act as though their child is surely destined for tennis greatness, and if enough people relate to them over time as parents of a child destined for greatness, then they can become genuinely convinced that they are in fact parents of such a child.

In addition to the effects of making a pretense for others and then observing their behavior as they relate to oneself, a person's observations of his own behavior—as he pretends that something is the case—can have surprisingly strong effects on what he comes to believe about himself. At first glance, it may seem odd to think that parents could simply act as though they were the best evaluators of their child's potential as a tennis player—and by observing their own behavior come to truly believe this about themselves. Consider, though, a fascinating story told by Sigmund Freud that shows how people's beliefs about themselves really can be based on their observations of their own behavior. Freud describes an experiment in which a hypnotized subject was ordered to open an umbrella five minutes after he awakened. The subject carried out the instruction and was then asked why he was acting in this way. Freud reports that "instead of saying that he has no idea," the subject felt "compelled to invent some obviously unsatisfactory reason."[15] Specifically, he claimed he wanted to make sure the umbrella was in good working order (which is a motivation we might naturally attribute to any person we observed opening an umbrella indoors). Freud's example seems to show that people's understandings of their own motives can indeed stem from observing their own public behavior. If parents of a tennis player act as though they are the best evaluators of their child's potential, then they can come to believe this. Subsequently, if the opinions of coaches, talent evaluators, and so forth conflict with the parents' conclusions, then the parents will naturally view them as flawed in some way.

Brad Gilbert does not think that players themselves are typically the ones who go to elaborate lengths to find excuses when hopes and expectations for their development aren't met. Rather, his view is that the tennis prodigies' caretakers will be the ones who cultivate the mentality of excuse-making: "I think it usually comes from outside influences—parents, or even doctors [i.e., sports psychologists]—who find something to complain about and some excuse to make."[16]

If parents can convince themselves that their child has more promise than his match results thus far indicate, and if they convey this idea repeatedly to their child, then it is understandable that the child will follow suit in seeking to blame someone or something else when match results aren't as hoped.

Do these excuses sometimes fly in the face of any reasonable assessment of objective facts? Brad says, "You wouldn't believe the people that phone me up or visit my website and whine and bitch about everything. It's always some reason why they or their kid isn't progressing or isn't where they should be." Starting down the path of making excuses, Brad says, is a sure-fire indication that a player will never become a champion. Again, his attitude toward excuse-makers is simple: "I don't want anything to do with people like that."

Philosophers and psychologists may find it interesting to explore the various motivations and strategies people have for avoiding tough truths about their own limitations. But it's understandable that a tennis coach like Brad Gilbert, who wants to work with champions, would have no interest in such things. After all, the coach has to deal with the actual person day after day. And the simple fact is that any real-life psychological issues the player has—whatever their causes—hamper a coach's efforts to help mold a player into a champion.

Brad comments, "Like you said, I'm a realist. I'm dealing with the person. It sounds like they're [philosophers and psychologists] dealing with the reasons behind the person." And this is fair enough. Philosophers may seek to analyze and systematize the possible reasons a player may make excuses—an exploration that reveals interesting possibilities about the human penchant for selective evidence and self-delusion. But a coach ultimately confirms the fact that excuse-making is an obvious sign that a player lacks the mentality to become a champion.

Notes

1. Richard Nisbett and Lee Ross, *Human Inference: Strategies and Shortcomings of Social Judgment* (Englewood Cliffs, NJ: Prentice Hall, 1980), 49–50.

2. Leo Schlink, "Federer Attacks Hawk-Eye," *Melbourne Herald Sun,* January 18, 2007, http://www.heraldsun.com.au/sport/tennis/federer-attacks-hawk-eye/story -e6frfgao-1111112849297.

3. "Federer's HawkEye Frustration," *Melbourne Herald Sun,* July 9, 2007, http://www.heraldsun.com.au/sport/tennis/federers-hawkeye-frustration/story-e6frf gao-1111113917297.

4. "Two British Scientists Call into Question Hawk-Eye's Accuracy," *Associated Press,* June 19, 2008, http://sports.espn.go.com/sports/tennis/wimbledon08/news/ story?id=3452293.

5. Will Pavia, "Hawk-Eye Creator Defends His System after Federer's Volley," *London Times Online,* July 10, 2007, http://www.timesonline.co.uk/tol/sport/tennis/ article2051307.ece.

6. "Two British Scientists Call into Question Hawk-Eye's Accuracy."

7. Schlink, "Federer Attacks Hawk-Eye."

8. Peter Robertson, "Why I Became a Nun, by Former Tennis Star Andrea Jaeger," *London Mail Online,* April 19, 2008, http://www.dailymail.co.uk/femail/ article-560743/Why-I-nun-tennis-star-Andrea-Jaeger.html.

9. Ibid. The next match for Andrea, the 1983 Wimbledon final against Martina Navratilova, is the one for which she has drawn the most attention in claiming that she purposefully tried not to win. For her reasons, see Peter Robertson, "Jaeger's Confession—I Let Martina Win the Title," *London Mail Online,* June 4, 2008, http://www.dailymail.co.uk/sport/tennis/article-1031959/EXCLUSIVE-Jaegers -confession--I-let-Martina-win-title.html.

10. Andrea Jaeger, *First Service: Following God's Calling and Finding Life's Purpose* (Deerfield Beach, FL: Health Communications, 2004).

11. Douglas Robson, "Jaeger Now in Service to Next Calling," *USA Today,* March 9, 2007, http://www.usatoday.com/sports/tennis/2007-03-08-jaeger-cover_ N.htm. Happily, Andrea and her father later reconciled.

12. Robertson, "Why I Became a Nun."

13. Robson, "Jaeger Now in Service to Next Calling."

14. See Daniel Gilbert and Joel Cooper, "Social Psychological Strategies of Self-Deception," in *Self-Deception and Self-Understanding,* ed. Mike Martin (Lawrence: University Press of Kansas, 1985).

15. Sigmund Freud, "The Interpretation of Dreams," in *The Standard Edition of the Complete Works of Sigmund Freud,* vol. 4 of 24, ed. and trans. James Strachey (London: Hogarth, 1953), 148.

16. As to Brad's view of sports psychologists in general, let's just say he's not a fan.

Kevin Kinghorn

AUTHORITARIAN TENNIS PARENTS

Are Their Children Really Any Worse Off?

The latest story to make headlines about a tennis child prodigy is almost unbelievable. To be sure, there have been a long line of players labeled as the "next great champion" before they entered puberty. The accuracy of these predictions has, of course, been mixed. Tracy Austin did become a lasting champion. Andrea Jaeger (and countless others you've never heard of) did not. Child prodigies, by definition, are identified at an early age. But the case of Jan Silva has even Tracy Austin shaking her head in disbelief.

Jan was born in November 2001. He showed such aptitude as a . . . well . . . toddler that he attracted media attention by the age of three. When he was the ripe old age of four, his parents quit their jobs and moved the whole family (Jan has two siblings) from Sacramento to France so that Jan could attend the prestigious Mouratoglou Tennis Academy. The Academy provides Jan with a cadre of coaches and physio advisors, and his scholarship covers the family's living expenses—reportedly to the tune of $140,000 a year. The Academy's founder, Patrick Mouratoglou, estimates that, all told, he'll probably invest $2 to 3 million in Jan's career. If you think your own involvement in competitive sports as a youth gave you an understanding of pressure, you may want to think again.

To be fair, the Silva family seems like a well-adjusted group. I don't think you'll see Jan as a teenager having to issue restraining orders against aggressively domineering parents. (Think Mary Pierce and Jelena Dokić.) Still, there is a sense in which we might wonder if Jan's future—even if it turns out fine—has been unduly "mapped out" for him. Even though Jan enjoys playing tennis (as do presumably most other tennis prodigies), does someone in his circumstances really have much of a psychologically viable choice whether to continue down the path he is on?

I might ask readers who have any uneasiness about Jan's situation: What exactly is wrong with mapping out a child's future? Perhaps it just seems intuitively obvious that a person's well-being would be harmed in the long run if he were not allowed to make autonomous decisions about his own future. But is that really the case? When so-called tennis parents channel their children's energies into an exacting regimen from a very early age, are they actually undermining a child's well-being in any way?

To answer such a question definitively, I will examine the general issue of what makes anyone's life "go well" for him or her. Philosophers have a long history of debating this very question. True to form, they have frequently disagreed as to how we should measure the quality of a person's life. Three main perspectives on well-being have developed over time, and there are insights to be gained from each of them. I will explore what is correct and incorrect about these classic theories of human well-being: perfectionist, mental-state, and desire-satisfaction theories.

And when the truth about what makes for a "good life" is clear, it will also be evident—somewhat surprisingly—that tennis parents might not actually deserve the tarnished reputation they're often given.

Perfectionist Theories (If Only He Were More Like Rod Laver!)

The first philosopher to provide a comprehensive theory of what it means to lead a "good life" was Aristotle (384–322 B.C.E.). Aristotle started with the assumption that any creature will flourish when it performs those functions for which it is uniquely equipped. For example, a beaver will thrive when it is cutting down trees with its teeth and building dams, not if forced to graze in open fields like a gazelle. So, what activities are humans uniquely designed to pursue? Aristotle remarks that humans are unique within the animal kingdom in their ability to reason. More specifically, they are able to use reason to navigate between behavioral extremes and achieve the kind of balance of life that Aristotle considers virtuous. For example, humans can recognize the opposite extremes of cowardice and foolhardiness; and they can chart a middle course of prudence. When a person therefore uses reason to achieve a constant and proper balance between opposing extremes, he or she achieves a "good life."

Aristotle's theory is perfectionist in character in the sense that it presents a specified ideal for humans. Aristotle himself wanted to emphasize the point that very few people can attain a life of ideal human flourishing. Most subsequent perfectionist theories have sought to focus also on the extent to which a person's life might go well for him or her, even if that life is not ideal. On such theories, the goodness or value of a person's life becomes a measure of the extent to which his or her life exemplifies the specified ideal. This approach is analogous to measuring tennis players on the basis of how they stack up against "the perfect player," Rod Laver, for example, who could play every shot in the book and dominate opponents on every surface. A given tennis player, then, can be judged if one measures the extent to which he or she approximates the total skill level of Rod Laver.

I think the perfectionist approach to human well-being is correct in its basic insight. However, the key question is: *Which* ideal really does constitute the height of human flourishing?[1] Aristotle's answer to this is decidedly flawed. His starting point is that a creature's uniqueness allows us to identify how that creature will maximally flourish. But this assumption seems just plain false. Whether some other creature does or does not have the faculty of reason is surely irrelevant to whether our own flourishing is best achieved by developing our faculty of reason. Further, some unique human attributes seem clearly to undermine our well-being. If humans have, for instance, a unique capacity to engage in self-destructive behavior as a way of making others feel guilty for not returning their romantic feelings, surely one will not want to conclude that humans will genuinely flourish only if they develop this capacity. In the end, then, Aristotle's uniqueness criterion does not provide a proper way of determining what makes humans flourish.

As I look for a better criterion, I do not want to identify anything too specific. Given the wide range of human personalities, it would be far-fetched to think that humans flourish only when they are as free with their emotions as John McEnroe or as self-controlled as Pete Sampras. People have different gifts and talents, and a pattern of activities that leads to happiness for one person may not bring it to another.

There is, though, a general feature about humans that I think holds the key to every person's well-being. Humans are very much relational creatures, needing love from infancy and craving human touch and fellowship. Indeed, a person who is continually left in complete isolation from others will literally go insane. Consider also how trips to the therapist's office seem inevitably to stem from some relationship—with family, friends, or one's wider community—that is unhealthy. Indeed, it is difficult to imagine a case where a person would be less than joyful if absolutely all the relationships in her life were flourishing wonderfully. So, it seems at first glance that there really may be something to the idea that healthy relationships hold the key to having a good life.

The critic has two ways of arguing against this idea. He could argue either that healthy relationships aren't always necessary for a person to flourish or that healthy relationships aren't sufficient to guarantee that a person will flourish. Are relationships necessary if we are to flourish? The critic might argue that people can flourish in a number of ways that have nothing to do with relationships. I watch a romantic movie on television and feel warmly pleased. I sample an award-winning chef's custard tart and feel happily indulged. I observe Bud Collins wearing a bizarre pair of trousers and feel greatly amused. The critic might point to these examples as proof that there are indeed other things people enjoy besides healthy relationships with others.

In response to this argument, though, I would suggest that humans in fact don't enjoy these things outside of the context of ongoing, healthy relationships. A wonderfully acted movie will fail to inspire if one is feeling alienated from those she loves. A wonderfully prepared meal will not be enjoyed if eaten amid strife. Even a Bud Collins outfit will fail to amuse the person in the throes of depression. However, when one is enjoying other people's company, even an inane B-movie can be an occasion of great fun and laughter. And for honeymooners enjoying their first dinner together as a married couple, even basic fare will seem like a feast of delights. So, rather than viewing movies and meals and comic moments as sources of human happiness, perhaps one should view them as occasions that allow people to reap the benefits stemming from their healthy relationships with others. In the end, healthy relationships do seem to be necessary for humans to flourish.

Even if healthy relationships with others are necessary, the critic might still claim that they are not sufficient to ensure a good life. After all, people participating in healthy relationships can still experience the pain associated with tennis elbow or blisters on the feet. Indeed, professional tennis players have had to retire from matches on account of the discomfort from such things. And doesn't this show, so the critic might insist, that other conditions are needed—such as physical health—for doing well?

In response to the critic, two points can be made. First, people in physical pain typically are at least capable of having moments when the physical trauma to their bodies does not prevent them from being happy. For example, a hospital patient recuperating from painful surgery may, upon seeing the door to her room swing open (possibly heralding the visit of another friend), experience the pleasant feelings we associate with anticipating good news. People talk sometimes in terms of "forgetting" that they are in pain. And if this is possible for a moment, then, in principle, it seems possible for longer periods—assuming deeper relationships with others, which foster much greater comfort, or assuming a greater mental ability to focus full attention on relationships irrespective of surroundings and circumstances. In short, in truly ideal human relationships it might well be the case that outside factors like physical trauma are rendered inconsequential as determinants of a person's well-being.

Even if this line of response to the critic fails to be fully convincing, I can offer a second one. Admittedly, there are cases where harm to the physical body does rob one of the benefits that would otherwise come from relating to others. But this fact does nothing to refute my earlier claim about the source of well-being. Physical health is not itself a source of well-being; one can be free from physical injury and even have access to a well-acted movie or a gourmet meal, and still be absolutely miserable. The source of well-being is, once again, healthy relationships with others—even if further conditions must be met for one to enjoy the benefits of these healthy relationships.

Why do healthy relationships with others provide positive experiences? There is a certain feeling that comes with positive encounters with others. Perhaps the term "connecting" best captures this feeling. People often describe their special relationships with spouses or best friends in terms of a "special connection." Equally, I can feel a connection to a stranger who hears my life story and seems to understand me. There is an enormous healing quality to the connections made with others, which seems further evidence that humans' well-being really does ultimately hinge on the status of their relationships. I suggest that a life of continual, positive experiences of connecting with others is the ideal of a good life. The extent to which one approximates this ideal is the extent to which her life goes well.

I will finish this section by returning to the example of the tennis prodigy who is pushed to succeed from a young age by demanding tennis parents. Although the young person will not be given the freedom to begin plotting his own career path, such autonomy of choice isn't a part of the perfectionist theory of well-being outlined here. In fact, it seems clear that some people's lives do not go well when they are given lots of self-directing choices. For example, too many choices can create great anxiety for some people or can lead to compulsive second-guessing. Even professional tennis players can be wracked with indecision and self-doubt, as evidenced by the lost look in a player's eyes as she searches the crowd for a coach or relative, seeming to hope for some sign of direction. So, it would be far-fetched to think that continual autonomous choice leads to the height of human flourishing for all people.

Admittedly, some people do possess strong desires to make choices for themselves. I will consider this point later when I explore desire-satisfaction theories of well-being. But for now, I'll note that, whatever insights perfectionist theories give into the common source of flourishing for all people, these insights do not help make the case that autonomous choices are somehow vital for a person's well-being. If authoritarian tennis parents really do undermine their children's well-being, I will have to look elsewhere for reasons that support this conclusion.

Mental-State Theories (Am I a Wimbledon Champion if I Think I Am?)

The theory of human well-being I outlined in the previous section is a kind of mental-state theory. Mental-state theories see flourishing as entirely a matter of one's mental experiences. Since the feeling of connecting with others is clearly a type of mental phenomenon, it warrants the description of a mental-state theory.

The best-known proponent of mental-state theories was the Victorian philosopher John Stuart Mill (1806–1873), who defended a version of hedonism. In everyday language, the term "hedonism" has become associated with debauchery and sensual overindulgence. But in philosophy circles, it simply refers to the idea that pleasure—as opposed to pain—is the only ultimate good. Playing tennis, taking walks in the park, and reading a well-written book help one to flourish only inasmuch as they produce in us a balance of pleasure over pain.

Some hedonists do not make any distinctions among the types of pleasure one might enjoy. They see pleasure as a single kind of mental state, regardless of the differences that exist among the various activities that produce it. Mill's own brand of hedonism distinguished "higher" from "lower" pleasures, the former being for Mill more lasting and therefore more key for long-term happiness. The theory of well-being I have outlined so far identifies the mental experience of connecting with others as the key to human flourishing. And if one wants to think of the feeling of connecting as a kind of pleasure, then this theory would qualify as a particular version of hedonism.

Mental-state theories of well-being are fairly unpopular with philosophers these days. Much of the ongoing criticism centers on a famous thought experiment put forward by Robert Nozick (1938–2002): "Suppose there were an experience machine that would give you any experience you desired. Super-duper neuropsychologists could stimulate your brain so that you would think and feel you were writing a great novel, or making a friend, or reading an interesting book. All the time you would be floating in a tank, with electrodes attached to your brain. Should you plug into this machine for life, preprogramming your life's experiences?"[2] Nozick goes on to point out, correctly, that people desire to do things—not simply to believe they are doing things. So, a tennis prodigy practicing on the courts desires someday to be a Wimbledon champion—not simply to believe someday that he is a Wimbledon champion. If we were to hook someone up to Nozick's experience machine and program the machine to give him the mental experiences of winning Wimbledon, he would think his life was going really well. For that matter, he could be given the mental experiences of having lots of great friends and marrying the girl of his dreams. But Nozick argues that life in an experience machine is surely not a good life.

A number of philosophers view Nozick's line of argument as decisively undermining mental-state theories of well-being. But this conclusion is misplaced. It relies on the assumption that the mental-state proponent cannot accept Nozick's point that we desire a range of things outside our own mental states. The Oxford moral philosopher James Griffin (1933–) is among those modern-day thinkers who share this assumption. Notice the way he criticizes three well-known mental-state proponents for affirming that things have value, or utility, only if they involve one's mental experiences: "Bentham, Mill, and Sidgwick all saw utility as having to enter our experience. But we desire things other than states of mind: I might sometimes prefer, say, bitter truth to comforting delusion."[3] In response to philosophers like Nozick and Griffin, I do not wish to deny that people desire things other than their own favorable mental sensations. A tennis professional may desire to hear the "tough truths" about her weaknesses rather than the comforting affirmations continually coming from her entourage. What I do wish to deny is that this point has any direct bearing on whether one's well-being is solely a matter of having favorable mental experiences. There simply is nothing in the claim that "my well-being is enhanced only through my own mental experiences" that commits me to the further idea that the objects of my desires are merely my own experiences. Put another way, a mental-state theorist need not claim that it is the thought of having enjoyable mental states that motivates people whenever they act. A mental-state theorist simply claims that, as a matter of fact, one's welfare is enhanced solely by his own mental states. It is a failure to recognize this point that seems to have led so many philosophers to insist (wrongly) that Nozick's experience machine provides decisive reason to reject mental-state theories of well-being.

Henry Sidgwick (1838–1900), one of the mental-state proponents Griffin criticizes, noted how people can often best enhance their own well-being by focusing their attention on things other than their own well-being. He commented, "The pleasures of thought and study can only be enjoyed in the highest degree by those who have an ardour of curiosity which carries the mind temporarily away from self and its sensations. In all kinds of Art, again, the exercise of the creative faculty is attended by intense and exquisite pleasures: but it would seem that in order to get them, one must forget them: the genuine artist at work seems to have a predominant and temporarily absorbing desire for the realisation of his ideal of beauty."[4] Sidgwick is saying that pleasant mental experiences often occur only when one loses himself in some pursuit. When one is playing a point in tennis, he should be telling himself, "Get to the next shot. Get to the next shot." When one focuses intently on the game itself—people sometimes call it "getting in the zone"—he'll receive a lot of enjoyment. However, if he were to focus simply on his own experiences of enjoyment, saying to himself "Enjoy the moment more! Enjoy the moment more!!" while playing, the game isn't going to be nearly as fun. Sidgwick called this the "paradox of hedonism." Mental-state theorists of well-being acknowledge that one often can, and should, concentrate on achieving things outside one's own mental experiences. But this acknowledgment does not detract from their theory that well-being is indeed a matter of what mental experiences people end up having.

I will finish this section by returning to the question of whether authoritarian tennis parents restrict their children's freedom in a way that undermines their children's well-being. Autonomous choices focus on actions one can perform, but they are not themselves mental states. Admittedly, when one makes an autonomous choice, there is a certain feeling that comes with it; I might describe this as a "sense of being in control." But this kind of feeling surely does not hold the key to our flourishing. The feeling of connecting remains a far better explanation of why people's lives do or do not go well for them.

Now, what would have a profound impact on one's well-being is a scenario where a lack of choice prevented a child prodigy from connecting with others. Admittedly, this scenario might occur when tennis parents are too authoritarian in dictating a child's practice routine, weekly schedule, and so forth. If children develop resentment or long-term codependence or for any other reason fail to develop the capacity to connect positively to the people around them, they will fall far short of the human ideal of well-being (which involves continually connecting with others). Accordingly, their lives will not go well. So, it seems appropriate to caution tennis parents against creating an environment in which their children have difficulty forming healthy connections with others. But of course this is a caution we would want to give to any parent. There is nothing inherent in mapping out a child's schedule—or indeed in planning the long-term career direction of a child—that itself precludes a child from connecting with the people around him as he grows up. In Jan Silva's case, I don't think there is any reason to doubt his dad when he says,

"Yes, Jani's life is organized, but he's having fun with it."[5] Many people have, after all, developed positive relationships (and positive lives) while growing up with authoritarian parents. So, whatever misgivings one might have about the personality or motivations of an authoritarian tennis parent, the actions of such a parent do not automatically compromise his or her child's well-being. Or at least I haven't come across good evidence for this so far in this investigation.

Desire-Satisfaction Theories (Just Give the Child Prodigy What He Wants!)

At this point someone might insist that surely every child desires, at some level, freedom from parental control. Hence, every child of an overbearing tennis parent will have at least some feelings of frustration or resentment at the lack of opportunity to make autonomous decisions. As much as Jan Silva enjoys playing tennis, there are still times he doesn't have a real desire to do tennis drills. His father, while remarking that Jan "is always smiling and laughing on court," also admits to occasionally resorting to ice-cream bribes to overcome Jan's resistance to finishing a practice session.[6] The idea of a potentially frustrated child provides a useful way to introduce our third and final general theory of human well-being. Desire-satisfaction theories view well-being as essentially a matter of having our desires fulfilled. If my life unfolds as I desire it to, then my life goes well for me; if it doesn't, then my life does not go well. It's as simple as that. If this theory gives the truth about well-being, then authoritarian tennis parents are undermining their children's flourishing every time they insist on one more practice session that their children really don't want to undertake. But does the desire-satisfaction theory really describe what a "good life" looks like?

I will compare the desire-satisfaction theory with the mental-state theory I defended in the previous section. I noted that, even though well-being rises and falls with mental states, people admittedly do desire things other than simply to experience pleasant mental states. I can agree here with James Griffin's comment, "If either I could accomplish something with my life but not know it, or believe that I had but not really have, I should prefer the first."[7] Probably many people will share his sentiments. That is, probably most will desire to accomplish certain things with their lives—not just believe they are accomplishing them. However, let me press the question of what actually enhances one's welfare. Surely, it is the belief that one is accomplishing certain things. Suppose I have as a goal the writing of a tennis instruction book that details ways inner-city youth can use tennis to obtain college scholarships and in general better their lives. If I am successful in doing this but am completely unaware that my book has been of any help to anyone, in what sense is my well-being enhanced? I may believe my efforts to have been completely in vain; and as I think of all the people I (mistakenly) believe are still in need of help, I will experience the same sadness and melancholy that, we suppose, motivated me to write the book in the first place! I cannot see how my well-being is enhanced by the fact that I have accomplished what I desired.

To enforce the point, I might suppose that my goal is not accomplished. For example, perhaps my publisher never actually publishes my manuscript. Nevertheless, if I *believe* that my book is helping others (and I can suppose my perverse publisher shows me fake letters from people thanking me for my "help"), then I will experience delight, fulfillment, and so forth. Surely when considering *my* well-being—that is, what is good *for me*—the sole thing directly relevant is whether I have an experience of believing that I have helped others. The actual accomplishment of my goal only leads to an increase in my welfare on the condition that I form true beliefs about this accomplishment.

One might be tempted to think at this point that desire-satisfaction theories are at least correct on the point that it is the perceived achievement of her existing desires that makes a person's life go well for her. However, even this would be too great a concession to make to desire-satisfaction theories. If a person's desires come to fulfillment, there is no guarantee whatsoever that she will end up contented, happy, or in any way enjoying her life. A quick glance at the biographies of sports stars, rock stars, and actors shows pretty clearly that achieving one's childhood dreams provides no immunity from discontentment and depression. Hence, the well-known adage: "Be careful what you wish for," which stems from the fact that there will inevitably be some gap between what one thinks will make her life go well and what really does.

In an attempt to overcome this gap between true flourishing and beliefs about where true flourishing lies, some desire-satisfaction advocates have sought to amend their theory. In the amended theory, it is not the fulfillment of just any desire a person has that will make the person truly flourish. Instead, it is the fulfillment of the desires of the well-informed person that will lead to that person's flourishing. Simply put, one's life goes well when one's desires are fulfilled, provided she is wise enough to know what really will bring her contentment and happiness.

The problem with this amendment is that it renders the desire-satisfaction theory utterly vacuous. To see why, I will consider the thought processes of the well-informed person. What criteria will such a person use in determining whether some particular desire, if fulfilled, really will make his life go well for him? Presumably, the person foresees that he will be happy, contented, and so forth. But happiness and contentment are clearly mental states. So, the well-informed person ends up assuming that mental states are what make a person's life go better or worse. This is the thesis of mental-state theories; and it is precisely this thesis that desire-satisfaction theorists were originally seeking to refute! So in the end, desire-satisfaction theories seem fatally flawed. If the theory proposes that well-being is a matter of having one's desires fulfilled, then the theory is clearly wrong, given the frequent gap that exists between what actually will make people happy and what they desire or think will make them happy. If the theory is amended so as to close this gap, then I move away from the original desire-satisfaction thesis, which posits that fulfilled desires make people flourish; I instead end up measuring well-being in the same way mental-state theorists do.

Despite the acute shortcomings of desire-satisfaction theories, they do serve as a useful reminder that a child prodigy's desires play a part in his ability to relate positively to others and thereby flourish. Although the level of fulfilled desires won't single-handedly determine whether a child's life goes well for him or not, continually unfulfilled desires do tend to produce frustration, resentment, and other attitudes that hinder positive, fulfilling relationships. One can of course acknowledge that an authoritarian tennis parent—like any parent—may at times have a better idea than the child as to "what is really good for him." Children often lack the ability to see that short-term sacrifices can lead to overall, long-term benefits. But there are limits to this. A parent cannot continually drag a child kicking and screaming to the practice court in the name of "what is really good for him." At some point, the child's frustrated desires will begin to undermine his positive, long-term relationships with the people around

him. Desire-satisfaction theories, for all their shortcomings, at least remind us of this fact.

A Theory of Children's Rights (Life, Liberty, and the Pursuit of Non-Tennis Activities?)

So far, I have not found any reason for thinking that authoritarian tennis
parents actually compromise their children's well-being. Certainly, there
are cautions for parents. Children's well-being potentially can be undermined if they are pushed to the point of resentment or for whatever reason fail to form the kind of meaningful connections with others on which
their well-being ultimately hinges. But from the mere fact that a child's
daily schedule and long-term career path are mapped out by parents, it
doesn't automatically follow that the child's well-being is undermined.

Aside from the issue of well-being, however, could it be that children
have a right to determine for themselves the trajectory of their future careers? Certainly, everyone will agree that children have some established
rights, such as the right to be loved, to be protected, to be nurtured, and
so forth. The philosopher Joel Feinberg has argued that children also
have a "right to an open future." From the fact that adults have the right
to choose a career, it follows that children have the right for this future
interest to be protected. They have "rights-in-trust," which parents must
guarantee (just as a trustee must guarantee the contents of an escrow account held for a child until adulthood). Feinberg emphasizes that "an
education that renders a child fit for only one way of life forecloses irre-
vocably his other options." The best course of action is therefore to send
a child "out into the adult world with as many opportunities as possible,
thus maximizing his chances for self-fulfillment."[8]

If Feinberg is correct in his line of reasoning, then authoritarian tennis parents are straightforwardly wrong in mapping out their children's
futures. An inalienable right to an open future would trump any previous
discussions about the effects on children's well-being. But when one considers the implications of Feinberg's conclusion, she finds good reason to
reject it. Would one really want to send a child out into the world "with
as many opportunities as possible"? A tennis lesson for a child would be
good, since it would introduce the child to the possibilities of a career in
tennis. But a second tennis lesson would come at the expense of one of

the endless number of other activities to which parents might expose their children. To reach the goal of "as many opportunities as possible," parents would do better to offer their children one tennis lesson, one squash lesson, one racquetball lesson, one ping-pong lesson, and so on. And of course when one turns to nonracket sports, ping-pong is only the beginning. A music career is also an option, so each child will need one clarinet lesson, one trumpet lesson, one harp lesson, and so forth. And of course there are careers in art, biology, forestry, woodworking, antique car repair. . . .

Feinberg's conclusion, as it stands, leads to the absurd implication that parents should offer to their children no more than introductory lessons in any subject. Perhaps I might amend his conclusion to say that parents should do a reasonable job balancing the concern for a child's "open future" with the need for the child to pursue specific options in more depth if she is to attain more than a superficial familiarity with them. (Feinberg hints at this kind of amendment when he discusses the reasonableness of thinking that children have "a right to an open future only in some, not all respects.")[9] But who decides what a "reasonable balance" is? Some pursuits, like tennis, take sustained dedication if a person is to reach anywhere near his or her potential in that discipline. What is a reasonable balance of activities when tennis is one of them? Any answer to this question seems hopelessly subjective. In the end children don't seem to have any objective "right" that entitles them to a specific, limited time each week on the practice courts so they can pursue a range of other potential interests. Feinberg's idea of a child's "right to an open future" is an interesting one, but it fails to establish any objective standard that tennis parents might be said to violate.

Opportunities Missed (Why Can't They Just Let the Child Have a Normal Childhood?!)

Whatever the merits of the philosophical arguments offered thus far in defense of tennis parents, one may still have nagging feelings that child prodigies like Jan Silva are simply missing out on the "normal" activities of childhood. "We're only children once," someone might say, "and once your childhood is gone, you can never get it back." That sentiment is perhaps understandable, though it's not immediately obvious exactly what objection is being raised. Perhaps the concern is that, even if the child is happy and enjoying some level of a good life, she is missing something that other children enjoy and that would make her life even better. On closer analysis, though, this objection turns out to be fairly unpersuasive.

Even if I suppose a particular tennis child prodigy would enjoy his relationships—and his life in general—a bit more if he were able to make a few more autonomous decisions for himself, what exactly follows from this? What I mean is that any number of things could potentially make a child's life go a bit better for him. What child is given the truly optimal ratio of playtime versus work time each day? What child is given the exact number of calories each day for optimal physical development? What child is given the optimal amount of fish oils to aid in concentration and brain development? The list here is endless as to the ways in which a child's life could be improved. No matter how well a child's life is going at any particular time, there is always scope for it to go better.

Surely it would be unfair to insist that a tennis parent—or any parent—provide a life of flourishing for his or her child that is maximal in a strict sense. Instead, parents should make a reasonably strong, concerted effort to ensure that their children are happy. No, parents should not prioritize their own personal interests to the extent that they rarely have time to read a story to their children or to share a meal with them. And, with instances of child neglect still a real problem in our society, perhaps the time is right for a national campaign to educate and motivate parents to nurture more actively their children's development. But the point is that parents are rightly allowed some leeway to balance the various demands on their time and attention that children, careers, charity work, and hobbies bring. The strict, maximal flourishing of a child is a noble goal; but it is not the only one a parent may rightly see as important. As long as parents are actively working to ensure that a child's life is in general going very well, the parents are not regarded as irresponsible if they do not seek to improve the child's well-being in every conceivable way and at the expense of anything else in life. So, from the fact that the child of tennis parents may have flourished a bit more if his life had been different, it does not automatically follow that the parents have acted outside the range of behaviors acceptable for all parents.

Some readers may still find themselves unable to shake nagging thoughts about the "lost childhood" of tennis prodigies. Perhaps it just seems intuitive that a child, even if he is enjoying his life, should not be missing out on what other children are enjoying—for example, a less-structured routine where there is freedom to choose between activities each day. But at this point one would do well to remember the flaw in Aristotle's theory of a flourishing life. I think back to his emphasis on the unique ability of humans to reason. In analyzing Aristotle, though, I saw that the question of how someone else flourishes does not directly determine how I truly flourish. Similarly, the question of how other children are flourishing is not directly relevant to the question of whether some particular child is or is not flourishing. If it is a fact that a tennis child prodigy is flourishing in a certain way, then this fact remains the same regardless of how other children are or are not flourishing. Of course, it would be another matter if, in some particular case, a child prodigy were thrust into the grown-up world so that he was hindered in his ability to form healthy relationships with peers as he grew into adulthood. Clearly, his life would not be going well for him. But from the mere fact that most children are forming relationships and flourishing in a certain way, it does not follow that a child prodigy is worse off if he forms relationships and flourishes in a different one.

So, I conclude that overbearing tennis parents aren't necessarily compromising their children's well-being in any objectionable way. Children's decisions to "plot their own course" are not part of any ideal state of human flourishing that one must approximate if his life is to go well. The mental feelings associated with making autonomous decisions are not—unlike the feelings of connecting with others—the source of human happiness. And even when children desire to make more decisions for themselves, there is no automatic correlation between fulfilled desires and ultimate happiness. Of course, there may be reason to object to the personalities and motivations of certain authoritarian tennis parents we have met. But that's a whole other issue! One cannot object to the mere fact that tennis parents control their children's schedules more than other parents do, for this does not automatically cause their children's lives to go any worse for them.

In case the reader is wondering, no, I'm not a tennis parent. My four-year-old daughter recently attended her first tennis camp. But my wife has made it clear that we will ask if she would like to continue taking lessons, not forcefully suggest she do so. Steffi Graf and Andre Agassi have a daughter the same age as mine. I wonder if she's been to a tennis camp. Talk about the pressure of expectations!

Notes

1. Even in tennis, Laver's greatness didn't exactly constitute perfection. David Baggett's chapter in this volume, "Why Roger Federer Is the Best: Or Is It McEnroe?" compares the all-time best tennis player with the in-principle best tennis player.

2. Robert Nozick, *Anarchy, State, and Utopia* (New York: Basic, 1974), 42.

3. James Griffin, *Well-Being: Its Meaning, Measurement, and Moral Importance* (Oxford: Clarendon, 1986), 13.

4. Henry Sidgwick, *The Methods of Ethics,* 7th ed. (Indianapolis: Hackett, 1981), 49.

5. Tom Perrotta, "Wunderkinds: The Future of the Tennis Prodigy," *Tennis .com: The Official Site of Tennis Magazine,* December 12, 2007, http://www .tennis.com/features/general/features.aspx?id=108988.

6. Mark Hodgkinson, "Jan Silva: The Roger Federer of the Future," *London Telegraph,* October 31, 2007, http://www.telegraph.co.uk/sport/tennis/2324582/ Jan-Silva-the-Roger-Federer-of-the-future.html; Scott Silva, interview by Meredith Viera, *NBC's Today Show,* August 3, 2007.

7. Griffin, *Well-Being,* 19.

8. Joel Feinberg, "The Child's Right to an Open Future," in *Freedom and Fulfillment: Philosophical Essays* (Princeton, NJ: Princeton University Press, 1992), 82, 84.

9. Ibid., 77.

David Detmer

"YOU CANNOT BE SERIOUS!"

The Ethics of Rage in Tennis

Few would disagree with the claim that it is impolite for a tennis player to interrupt a match by throwing a temper tantrum. But when a player—let's call him, to pick a name utterly at random, "Johnny Mac"—flies into a rage, verbally abuses the umpires or his opponent, and causes play to grind to a halt until he has finished his screaming and sulking fit, is this more than a mere transgression of etiquette?[1] Has he also done something immoral?

In attempting to answer this question, let's turn to two of the leading ethical theories from the history of western philosophy, focusing especially on what they can teach us regarding our general responsibilities toward others. While the theories in question, utilitarianism and deontology, differ from each other in multiple ways, for present purposes it will not be necessary to choose between them. Rather, since it will prove useful to approach our question from a variety of perspectives, the diversity of moral considerations emphasized by the competing theories should aid, rather than hinder, our inquiry.

Utilitarianism

Utilitarianism is a future-oriented moral philosophy. It holds that actions should be evaluated on the basis of their consequences. The morally right action in any situation is the one that would bring about the best results. But what counts as a good result? In Jeremy Bentham's original version of the theory, the answer is "happiness."[2] Thus, in Bentham's view, in any circumstance our goal should be to act in such a way as to maximize the happiness and to minimize the unhappiness of everyone who might be affected by our choice of action. We should try to bring about "the greatest happiness for the greatest number," as the popular slogan for this philosophy puts it.

In evaluating Johnny Mac–like behavior, then, utilitarianism would instruct us to consider its consequences. Such an inquiry immediately suggests two grounds for criticism. First, those placed at the receiving end of a tennis player's red-faced screaming tirade surely do not typically enjoy the experience. Most people find it embarrassing to be reprimanded in public. And tennis umpires and line judges are likely to regard the task of having to deal with the ravings of a raging tennis star as an irksome burden—an introduction of additional stress into the already quite demanding task of officiating a high-stakes tennis match.

Second, tennis tantrums interfere with the enjoyment of those spectators who wish to see a tennis match, as opposed, say, to a display of boorish conduct. The late Arthur Ashe, himself a tennis champion (and briefly, in his capacity as captain of the U.S. Davis Cup team, John McEnroe's coach), explains the harm of a McEnroe tantrum this way: "If you are a real tennis follower, it disrupts the continuity of your enjoyment. You are sitting there, really into watching a terrific struggle, and all of a sudden McEnroe explodes. It is like a five-minute commercial. Then when the match starts up again, you've got to get back into it."[3]

At the same time, some people seem to enjoy the spectacle of watching a tennis player throw a public fit. Such viewers may find the mere drama of competition, even when coupled with the exhibition of athletic excellence, insufficiently entertaining without the added ingredient of Johnny Mac–style histrionics.[4] Indeed, Richard Evans, author of an authorized biography of McEnroe, offers just such a claim in his defense: "People are increasingly bored with the commonplace and McEnroe, through his exceptional skills as well as his frequently outrageous behavior, [has] ensured that pro tennis continues to be compulsive viewing for millions around the world. Professional sport . . . is also show business— and those who believe otherwise are deluding themselves."[5]

Evans's point suggests that verbally abusive behavior on the part of tennis stars might be morally justifiable on utilitarian grounds. The argument would be that the happiness such conduct generates, by entertaining those many persons who enjoy watching it, outweighs the unhappiness it engenders in the fewer people who find it unpleasant to watch (and in the even fewer people—tennis officials, opposing players, and, on occasion, individual spectators—who are directly victimized by it). In short, it may be that the net balance of happiness over unhappiness produced in a tennis match that includes explosive displays of temper will tend to be greater than that produced in an otherwise identical match in which both players remain calm and conduct themselves politely.

One might plausibly claim, however, even without abandoning utilitarianism, that this argument fails because it focuses exclusively on the immediate consequences of the conduct in question and utterly neglects its long-term effects. In particular, it fails to take into account that some people, and especially children, often imitate the behavior of those they admire. In particular, some young tennis players might be expected to mimic the actions, including the throwing of spectacular temper tantrums, of famous tennis champions. So Johnny Mac–like behavior at Wimbledon or the U.S. Open might reasonably be expected to lead to an increase in such behavior at the local park and at youth tournaments.

And that would seem a bad consequence, since our initial utilitarian argument for tennis tantrums remains plausible only when it is applied to matches that attract a large audience, many members of which, it must be supposed, would be entertained by such antics. For in matches in which only a few tirade-loving spectators are deriving enjoyment from the cursing and screaming, it would seem likely that their enjoyment would be dwarfed by the displeasure the recipients of the verbal abuse would experience. So Johnny Mac–like conduct will not pass the utilitarian test at, for example, the local park, when two competitors are playing a match alone. (Think of how unpleasant it would be, in that situation, to have to put up with an opponent who constantly whined about line calls and occasionally screamed obscenities.) Similarly, it will not pass the test at a youth tournament or school match, where the crowds are small and are dominated by friends and relatives of the competitors. For then, not only would there not be a large audience of persons who would find such behavior amusing, but also, and more important, nearly everyone present would likely find it unpleasant. After all, the friends and relatives of the opponent of the player engaging in such behavior would almost certainly find it obnoxious and offensive, and the friends and relatives of the player who is behaving rudely would probably feel embarrassment on his or her behalf. So, taking into account this plausible long-term consequence of Johnny Mac–like conduct, it could very well fail to maximize the net happiness and compare poorly in this regard to polite behavior in competitive tennis.

The problem with this counterargument, in turn, is that it is speculative. Whereas we can be fairly confident of most of the immediate consequences of tennis tantrums, the indirect and remote effects of such conduct are much more difficult to determine. This point exposes a general limitation of utilitarianism as a moral theory. Since utilitarianism holds that actions are right or wrong solely in virtue of their consequences, it follows that when, as is often the case, we do not know what the consequences of various actions available to us in a given situation will be (and, in particular, we do not know which action would bring about the best consequences), we also do not know which action would be right. So utilitarianism appears open to the serious objection that it fails to guide our actions, that is, it fails to perform one of the essential tasks we demand of a moral theory—that it help us, when we are in doubt, to determine what we should do.

In fairness to utilitarianism, it should be noted that knowledge of the consequences of actions is not an all-or-nothing thing. Just as we rarely (if ever) can know with certainty what all of the effects of a given action will be, so are we rarely completely ignorant as to the identity of some of its most likely results. A utilitarian might then argue that this knowledge, though admittedly incomplete, is sufficient to offer us some guidance in figuring out what we are morally obliged to do. The fact that the theory fails to offer an infallibly accurate algorithmic decision procedure is not, so the argument might continue, so much a weakness of utilitarianism as a simple limitation of the human condition. As finite beings, perhaps we simply cannot be in a position to know everything relevant to determining the moral rightness or wrongness of our actions. The most we can ask of a moral theory is that it tell us, in general and in principle, what sorts of considerations are relevant—and utilitarianism, so the argument goes, definitely does that. In this way it genuinely does help to *guide* our judgment, even though it does not remove the need to *exercise* that judgment.

Still, by claiming that the rightness or wrongness of an action is to be determined solely by considerations of its consequences, utilitarianism, more so than some other moral theories, unwittingly opens the door both to uncertainty and to the possibility for abuse. For if we are forced to speculate about the indirect, long-term consequences of actions, it is easy enough to manipulate the speculation (even if unintentionally) so as to make it come out the way we want it to. So someone who is inclined to disapprove of Johnny Mac–like conduct can easily make a plausible case that the remote effects of such behavior are likely to be strongly negative. And a person of the opposite inclination can, with roughly equal plausibility, point both to the highly uncertain nature of those claims of long-term negative consequences and to the much greater confidence with which we can establish that thousands of spectators thoroughly enjoy the experience of watching such conduct.

Before concluding that utilitarianism is incapable of resolving our issue, however, let's consider one interesting modification of the theory, that offered by John Stuart Mill in his classic work, *Utilitarianism.*[6] While Mill's main concern in that work is to defend Bentham's theory, he does fault Bentham for failing to distinguish among different *kinds* of pleasure. Whereas Bentham had explicitly argued that when evaluating the consequences of actions we should consider only the *amount* of pleasure and/or pain they produce (so that, for example, if breaking dishes while intoxicated produces more net pleasure than does reading Shakespeare, then the former act is better, morally speaking), Mill maintains that it is also necessary to take into account differences in *quality* among those pleasures and pains.

His reasoning is this: experience is the proper foundation of value judgments. To know which of two things is better, we are wise to consult the judgment of those who (a) have experienced both and (b) are competent to appreciate both. If the testimony of these witnesses is relatively consistent and establishes something close to a consensus, this should be taken as reliable information concerning the relative value of the items being compared. Now, according to Mill, that is the situation we find ourselves in with respect to the distinction between what he calls "higher pleasures" (roughly, distinctively human pleasures, such as pleasures of the intellect or of one's aesthetic or moral faculties) and "lower pleasures" (chiefly physical pleasures but essentially any pleasures that do not appeal to the distinctively human faculties just mentioned). Mill's claim is that no one capable of appreciating both kinds of pleasure would be willing to give up the higher kind even in exchange for such a greater amount of the lower kind as to make one's overall happiness quantitatively greater. Thus, for example, no intelligent persons would be willing to be made stupid (and thereby to forego all the pleasures of the intellect), even if they got in the bargain so much more of the other kinds of pleasure as to allow them to achieve more net happiness following the transaction than they had enjoyed previously. Similarly, no knowledgeable person would willingly become ignorant, or morally sensitive person selfish and base, or aesthetically attuned person become indifferent to art and beauty, even in exchange for a life that would be, on balance, happier, from a purely quantitative standpoint, than it had been previously.

Let's now apply this point to the question of Johnny Mac–like conduct. While Mill does not address the pleasures of watching sports, one could perhaps argue that watching a great tennis match in the manner of a true aficionado—where the focus is on, and delight is taken in, the dazzling skill of the players, the grace of their movements, the brilliance of their strategies, and so forth—produces aesthetic pleasures analogous to those experienced when listening to excellent music, viewing fine paintings, or reading great literature. If so, it produces higher pleasures, in Mill's sense. Moreover, tennis fans, probably more so than fans of most other sports, tend to be players themselves. The firsthand knowledge of tennis that they have by virtue of playing the sport undoubtedly deepens their aesthetic appreciation of the excellence of the best players. Such fans also frequently experience the elevated pleasures of study and of learning, as they attempt to appropriate from the great stars they watch techniques, strategies, and shots that they might adopt for their own game.

But the enjoyment of public temper tantrums appears to be something in an entirely different category. In a tennis match involving a player the caliber of John McEnroe in his prime, the intrusion of his typical antics requires that those who would enjoy this spectacle as entertainment suddenly shift from admiring extraordinary skill to gawking in amusement at boorish behavior. I think Mill would argue that any pleasure one might derive from watching such behavior would fail to engage any higher human faculty (unless it would be the pleasure one might get by studying it from a psychiatric, sociological, or anthropological point of view) and thus should not be given much weight in comparison to the higher-order pleasure the true aficionado would get from appreciating the tennis itself or to the pain of frustration that such a viewer would get from having this pleasure rudely (in the most literal sense) interrupted. So Mill's version of utilitarianism seems to arrive at a clear conclusion. Because it affords less weight to the lower pleasures of enjoying the spectacle of watching an adult behave in public like a spoiled child and more weight to the pleasures that are interrupted and diminished by such conduct, Mill's revision tips the balance in the utilitarian calculation away from sanctioning Johnny Mac–like conduct as morally acceptable.

Deontology

And things only get worse for Johnny Mac when we turn from utilitarianism to our second ethical theory, deontology. The most important point to make about deontology here is that it rejects the consequentialism that is central to utilitarianism. For notice that one implication of consequentialism is that it regards no actions as wrong in principle, that is, wrong simply because of its nature. Rather, actions are held to be wrong only if they fail to bring about the best results in comparison to other acts that might have been performed in the circumstances. Such an approach usually generates uncontroversial results, since the kinds of actions typically condemned on principle (for example, lying, breaking promises, assaulting people, and so forth) are also open to the objection, at least in most circumstances, that they fail to bring about the best consequences. Utilitarianism does leave open the possibility that, say, cruel, or unjust, or unfair actions might have to be regarded as justified, if for some reason they seem likely, in a specific situation, to bring about better consequences than any alternative courses of action. Deontology, as defended most famously by Immanuel Kant, blocks this possibility by holding that we have definite duties to others that are not derived from consequentialist principles and also that some actions are wrong because of their intrinsic nature, and not because of their likely effects.[7]

To see the relevance of this to the present case, let's return to our utilitarian defense of tennis tantrums (setting aside criticisms of that defense based on considerations of long-term consequences or of Mill's distinction between higher and lower pleasures). The argument was that such tantrums might be justified as optimific, because the pleasure they produce for those who are entertained by them might outweigh the pain they produce for the much smaller number of people who are offended by them. However, from the standpoint of Kantian deontology, if the acts in question involve treating people unjustly, they are wrong in principle, a judgment that cannot be altered by the mere fact that they might also amuse some onlookers.

But is Johnny Mac–like conduct really wrong in principle? Does it involve treating people unjustly? Well, let's consider the act of publicly yelling at a person for making a mistake. Generally speaking, a necessary (though not a sufficient) condition for such an act to be justified is that the person being berated really is guilty of having made the mistake in question.[8] In other words, while a person who has made a mistake still might not deserve to be reprimanded for it, a false accusation of error, especially if issued loudly and publicly, is an injustice on its face. So tennis players who are inclined to yell at officials over erroneous calls should, if they are interested in conducting themselves ethically, be concerned about whether or not they can be sure they are right in judging that the officials have indeed made a mistake.

McEnroe, for his part, entertains no such doubts: "I know I can see the ball better than the officials. I can 'feel' when a ball is out or not. What's so frustrating is to know you're right and not be able to do anything about it."[9] But is McEnroe right about this? Can he really see the ball better than the officials can? It seems highly unlikely that he can, since the officials are in at least four ways better positioned than he to make accurate calls.

First, there is the simple issue of the spatial location of the viewer. McEnroe complains about calls all over the court, including calls on balls that land across the net from him and those he must observe from a difficult angle. The linespersons he abuses, by contrast, are placed so that they judge balls from a close proximity and can look directly down the line they are judging. Second, while McEnroe is frequently in motion when he watches a ball land, the officials are stationary. Third, while a line judge's sole job is to make line calls, McEnroe is multitasking. He has to make thousands of split-second decisions. He must think about strategy, anticipate his opponent's shots, decide how and where he will try to hit the ball, and, of course, execute his shots. Noticing the precise place where the ball lands ranks far down on the list of his concerns, in quite radical contrast to the case of the line judge.

Finally, McEnroe is, for obvious and unobjectionable reasons, a strongly biased observer. He is a competitor and very much wants to win. Accordingly, when he hits the ball, he wants it to be in, and when his opponent hits a ball that he can't reach, he wants it to be out. The officials, by contrast, are extremely unlikely to be as strongly biased. Many of them, simply because they have no particular reason to care one way or another who wins or loses, probably achieve, or at least approach, the ideal state of harboring no bias whatsoever. And even if some of them fail to overcome the natural human tendency toward favoritism, it is difficult to imagine that any of them, unless they are so corrupt as to be involved in wagering on the outcome, could possibly care as much about it as the competitors themselves do. This is significant because a strong rooting interest distorts one's perception of the fairness of the officiating of an athletic contest, as was demonstrated in a classic experiment conducted by psychologists A. Hastorf and H. Cantril over fifty years ago.[10] Shortly after rivals Dartmouth and Princeton had played a particularly violent football game, the investigators showed a film of the game to fifty students from each college, asking each student to identify as many violations by both sides as they could find. Naturally, students from each school saw far more infractions committed by the other team than by their own.

Moreover, tennis umpire Dr. Charles F. Beck reveals that early in McEnroe's career, he (Beck) and some other tennis officials, concerned over McEnroe's frequent complaints about their competence, conducted an informal experiment. They arranged to have off-duty umpires sit in the stands opposite the assigned linespeople, so that, in effect, they had two people on each line. The results were consistent from match to match. The extra pairs of eyes occasionally agreed with McEnroe—the assigned linespeople did miss a few calls. And, as might be expected, many of the calls could have gone either way—they were either "a millimeter in or a millimeter out." But the most interesting result was that McEnroe, not just once in a while, but with great frequency, argued some calls when he was dead wrong—calls in which both of the relevant linespersons (the official one on the court and the unofficial one seated nearby) had a clear, unobstructed view and found that the call was not a particularly close one. The ball was clearly in, even though McEnroe screamed that it was out (or vice versa). In analyzing this result, Beck concedes that McEnroe "has excellent vision" but adds that "it is not so special that he can over-come the scientific evidence that a linesman, in his fixed position, has the best view of the ball. These linespeople all have 20/20 vision or they wouldn't be certified in the United States."[11] Indeed, even Evans, who bends over backward to present McEnroe's behavior in the best possible light (his book is, after all, an *authorized* biography), states that "there is no doubt that [McEnroe] often complains needlessly about perfectly good calls."[12]

So there is every reason to believe that when McEnroe publicly be-rates an official for allegedly blowing a call, his charge of error is itself often culpably erroneous. If so, the embarrassment and stress suffered by the official is undeserved, and its infliction unjustified. And if the Kantian deontological perspective is sound, this wrong act cannot be made right by incidentally providing amusement to thousands of onlookers.

Kant provides an additional reason why McEnroe himself should be able to appreciate the moral wrongness of a factually wrong accusation: Kant argues that it is the essence of immorality to act on a maxim, or principle, that one could not consistently will to become a universal law. One way certain Kantian scholars understand the import of this approach is as something of a variant on the Golden Rule, according to which it is wrong to do what you would not be willing to let others, if similarly situ-ated, do as well—expressed positively, moral behavior would be the way we do wish for others to treat us. So if McEnroe were to claim that it is not morally wrong, but instead, perhaps, merely a minor and forgivable mistake, to issue factually inaccurate public criticisms of others, he would, by this Kantian test, have to commit himself to the same tolerant attitude toward others when they erroneously criticize him. But of course, that is not his attitude at all. He is rather, by all accounts, quite thin-skinned, and easily enraged by what he takes to be inaccurate criticism. For ex-ample, Evans reports that "nothing infuriated [McEnroe] more than the totally erroneous reports concerning a driving offense" that were report-ed throughout the world. (McEnroe had been in the car in question, but he had not been driving.)[13] If McEnroe doesn't like being publicly ac-cused of offenses he did not commit, then he shouldn't do it to others. The only way to escape this charge of hypocrisy would be to make the case that the accusations of error that he routinely hurls at officials are accurate. But we have already observed multiple grounds for doubting such a claim.

But now let's suppose, for the sake of discussion, that McEnroe is usually (factually) right when he claims that an official has blown a call. Would that make his conduct in publicly berating them for their errors justifiable? It is far from clear that it would. Ashe quotes McEnroe as frequently explaining his behavior by saying, "I'm trying as hard as I can, so I shouldn't have to deal with linespersons who make bad calls."[14] But this is not a cogent argument. First of all, it's a non sequitur. How is the conclusion—that McEnroe shouldn't have to deal with linespersons who make bad calls—supposed to follow from the premise that McEnroe is trying as hard as he can? Everyone agrees that good (accurate) calls from linespersons are better than bad (inaccurate) ones and that, ideally, all of the calls should be accurate. But one has no right to demand perfection of fallible human beings. The obligation of the linespersons is to *try as hard as they can* (to borrow McEnroe's language) to get the calls right— and notice that they have this obligation quite apart from the issue of whether or not McEnroe is trying as hard as he can. One could understand McEnroe's anger if he had evidence that the linespersons were failing to meet this obligation—if he caught them, for example, waving to friends in the stands while the ball is in play. But instead he blows up at them when, in his estimation, they have merely gotten the call wrong— and that, by itself (even if we waive the question of whether or not it might be McEnroe, rather than the linespersons, whose judgment is wrong), is evidence merely of fallibility, and not of a failure to meet their obligations. And it would be difficult to make the case that anyone deserves to be berated publicly for that. Second, McEnroe's complaint is groundless, since he doesn't have to "deal" with the linespersons at all. He could, instead, choose to focus on playing his match and accept in the spirit of good sportsmanship, and on the basis of a tolerant understanding of human fallibility, that occasionally there will be errant calls by linespersons—which, by turns, may help or hurt him.

Ashe also quotes him as saying, "I'm going to fight for what I think is right."[15] This confuses principles with judgments based on sense perception. Principles are often worth fighting for. One can give arguments, and cite evidence, as part of a rational process of defending them. But how can one argue over a simple matter of sense perception? Everyone agrees with the relevant principle—a ball that is in should be called in; a ball that is out should be called out. So there is no principle to argue about. "That ball was in!"—when screamed in the petulant tone of a spoiled six-year-old who has not gotten his way—is not exactly an "argument."

And questions about the justice of Johnny Mac–like treatment of officials are not confined to considerations concerning the officials themselves. For it can be argued that opposing players are also unfairly affected by such conduct in at least two ways. First, while umpires ideally should not allow the players' conduct to compromise their own impartiality, they are human and may very well be affected. If so, I think that players who berate officials are more likely to benefit than to suffer as a result of such behavior. To be sure, some officials might, quite understandably, resent being abused by a player, and then, even if unconsciously, hold a grudge and tend to punish the offending player by giving his or her opponent the benefit of a doubt on close calls.

But any such effect would likely be overweighed by three factors pushing in the opposite direction. First, as proud professionals, the officials would likely be highly conscious of the danger of developing such a bias against a player who had abused them. In their zeal to avoid acting on such a bias, and to avoid the *appearance* of doing so, they might inadvertently tend to bend over backward in giving the offending player the break on close calls.

Second, as human beings, tennis officials are vulnerable to self-doubt. So, when a player, and especially a great player like McEnroe, who presumably would have excellent vision, tells them not only that they have missed a call, but that it was an obvious error, indicating incompetence and meriting public vilification, it may very well shake their confidence and push them, however unwittingly, toward their critic's point of view.

Finally, and most important, it is highly unpleasant to find oneself, as an official, on the receiving end of a Johnny Mac–like tirade, both for the obvious reason that it is humiliating to be censured in public and because it also places one in the unwelcome position of having to make a transition from merely overseeing a tennis match to the much more demanding task of managing a raging star's tantrum. Adding to the stress is the fact that officials know (and know that the players know) that they cannot respond in kind. An umpire must deal with McEnroe's tantrum politely and respectfully and cannot simply bark at him, "Why don't you shut your stupid mouth and play tennis, you whining, spoiled crybaby!" I suspect that many officials are anxious to avoid such an unpleasant experience and thus are inclined, even if only unconsciously, to "see" close calls in such a way as to keep it at bay. If I am right in arguing that vilification of umpires gives the vilifier an undeserved and unfair advantage, this is another reason to regard such conduct as unjust. Such conduct puts Johnny Mac's opponent in the dilemma of having to choose between matching Johnny Mac's ugly behavior, and thereby cancelling out this effect, or else simply giving up an unearned competitive advantage to Johnny Mac.

In support of this analysis, consider the following example. In a match against Ivan Lendl in 1990, McEnroe, upset over what he claimed were some blown calls, summoned Gayle Bradshaw, the officiating supervisor for the tournament, and demanded that the linesperson be replaced. Bradshaw, hoping to prevent a McEnroe explosion, gave in. When the new line judge appeared on court, Lendl spoke up: "That's [a] big mistake. If I want someone changed you better change him real quick." Lendl's complaint clearly has merit. It would not be fair to give in to one player's demands without also doing so for the other player. But it would obviously not be workable to let both players discard linespersons at their whim throughout a match. So neither player should be given this power. This is an example of McEnroe benefitting unfairly from his whining and his star power. Because he is a star, the officials are loath to default him. So, because his atrocious behavior puts him in jeopardy of a default, officials are excessively (and unfairly) willing to accommodate him. The next day, Bradshaw admitted as much: "I made a mistake. Lendl was right."[16]

The second way Johnny Mac–like conduct unfairly affects opponents is that they must stop play and stand around and wait for the tantrum to end. Even McEnroe's defender, Evans, acknowledges the legitimacy of this concern: "Four or five minutes is a long time to hang around on court, trying to maintain both concentration and body warmth while your opponents argue over a point of law."[17] In fairness to McEnroe, much of the responsibility for this problem must be attributed to the officials, who have the discretionary power to stop debate by ordering the continuation of play and then assessing code violations (first a warning, then a penalty point, then a forfeiture of the match) if the offending player does not comply. But on the other hand, McEnroe, by his own admission, is not above exploiting his star power—the fact that paying customers and a television audience want to see him play—for his advantage. He explains in his autobiography,

> I noticed that the better I got, and the more money I made (for myself and for the events that were selling tickets and television rights), the more that linesmen, umpires, referees, and tournament organizers had to put up with from me. The more that professional tennis's money depended on me, the more that things seemed to be under my control when I got on that court. . . .
>   They had a show to put on, and my presence put behinds in the seats. . . . If I went home, they lost money. The tournament directors know it, the umpires (who got paid by the tournament) knew it, and the linesmen knew it. I knew it. The system let me get away with more and more.[18]

Since McEnroe's conduct is open, and involves no attempt at deception (thus, no attempt to subvert the discretionary power of officials to stop it), it would not be fair to categorize it as cheating. But since it also involves taking unfair advantage of his status as a star, it can rightfully be accused of "gamesmanship," that is, winning by unsporting behavior without actually breaking the rules.

Johnny Mac's Theory of Professionalism

McEnroe disagrees: "I always felt, 'Look, if you can't handle my having an outburst, then you shouldn't be in the profession.' . . . If by questioning a call for whatever period of time an umpire allowed, it threw off my opponent's game, I simply felt, 'That's too bad. That's not winning or losing points. That's what goes on between the points. If you decide you're going to sit there and get hot and bothered because I'm doing this, then you're allowing yourself to be psychologically affected. It's your job not to be.'"[19]

This argument calls for several comments. First, is it not arrogant and presumptuous of McEnroe to think he can decide who should or should not be in the profession? Many observers, including some champions, feel that his conduct was so poor that it rendered *him* unfit for the profession. But in McEnroe's unique worldview, the person who rudely interrupts play to scream insults at people is not the one whose attitude and conduct need changing, but rather those who are negatively affected by such a boorish display.

Second, one might also question the hard distinction McEnroe draws between what goes on when the points are played and what goes on between the points, as if the latter had no effect on the former. Muscles that would have stayed limber with continuous play can stiffen up during a protracted delay; such a delay can result in a player having to stay out in the sun longer than he otherwise would have; it can also result in a break in one's focus and concentration. Practice, rest, and diet are obviously important; but none of those happen while points are being played. Does that mean that they have no effect on the playing of the points, or that McEnroe would be within his rights in somehow interfering with his opponent's efforts at eating, resting, or practicing?

Third, while McEnroe is right that, ideally, a professional tennis player ought to be able to remain unaffected by his tantrums, it is also true that a professional tennis player ought to be able to avoid double faulting or hitting easy volleys into the net. But in reality, professional tennis players are human, and, while they make such mistakes much more rarely than do less accomplished players, they do make them occasionally. Indeed, one of the factors determining who wins or loses the match is precisely the ability to avoid such errors. As a tennis fan, I want to see the outcome determined by superior tennis play (that is, superiority in serving, ground strokes, volleying, shot-making, speed, power, stamina, and so forth), not by superior ability to maintain focus in the face of the spectacle of an adult throwing a temper tantrum.

Fourth, McEnroe holds his opponents more responsible for their conduct in response to his tantrums than he does himself for the tantrums themselves. If his opponent gets "hot and bothered" by McEnroe's tantrum, it is because he has "decided" to do so—which implies that the reaction is voluntary. But McEnroe repeatedly insists that his own outbursts are involuntary—beyond his control. Similarly, he castigates his opponent for "allowing" himself to be "psychologically affected" by his conduct, adding that it is his opponent's "job" not to be. But why is McEnroe not to be blamed for "allowing" himself to become infuriated at officials? Why is it not his "job" to behave more professionally and courteously? Why can't we say, "If you can't keep your cool and refrain from blowing up at the officials, you shouldn't be in the profession"? Where are those high standards to which he claims to hold himself?[20]

Finally, and perhaps most important from a Kantian standpoint, McEnroe frequently demonstrates that he does not uphold this position consistently, but rather only when doing so helps to justify *his* conduct. When he suspects others of engaging in gamesmanship, including the use of delaying tactics, in competition against him, he strongly objects. He complains about such things repeatedly in his autobiography, without apparently so much as noticing, let alone adequately addressing, the fact that such complaints appear to fly in the face of his rationalization of his own conduct. For example, he criticizes the tactics of the Argentinean doubles team that he and his partner, Peter Fleming, faced during the 1981 Davis Cup competition. At a certain point, the Argentinean team appealed to the umpire that the carpet on which the match was being played was coming apart and needed to be repaired before play could continue. McEnroe comments: "From our perspective, these guys were just trying to throw us off—break our rhythm. . . . They wanted to take a break, marshal their strength . . . and come out smoking. . . . They got their delay, and we were just steaming."[21]

Indeed, despite Evans's claim that McEnroe "is a living, breathing antidote to hypocrisy," he in fact consistently fails to hold himself to the same standards of conduct that he demands of others. For example, when a British journalist took McEnroe to task for his obnoxious conduct at Wimbledon, calling him "loud, rude, vain, childish, [and] sulky," not to mention "a spoilt child only his mother could love," McEnroe was, according to Evans, both "hurt" and "genuinely perplexed." He explained his perplexity this way: "I mean, I know I lost my cool and shouted at a couple of people when I shouldn't have, but I didn't expect everyone to react like they did. I thought they might understand or give me a second chance or forgive or whatever."[22] It does not seem to occur to McEnroe, who hurls ugly epithets nearly as casually as other people exchange hellos, that the officials whose rulings displease him might also like, and deserve, "understanding, a second chance, or forgiveness." So when he complains that he doesn't like to be called names, and he'd rather be given a second chance, it requires a measure of discipline to restrain oneself from replying: "You *cannot* be serious!"

Ethics or Etiquette

While it is widely conceded that Johnny Mac–like conduct is objectionable, some defend it, in a limited way, by arguing that it amounts to nothing more than a transgression of the rules of etiquette—a case of bad manners, as opposed to bad morals. And since rules of etiquette are often arbitrary and trivial, it is but a short step to argue that such conduct isn't really wrong at all. McEnroe himself implies as much: "I thought tennis had had enough of manners. To me, 'manners' meant . . . bowing and curtsying to rich people with hereditary titles who didn't pay any taxes. Manners meant tennis clubs that demanded you wear white clothes, and cost too much money to join, and excluded blacks and Jews and God knows who else."[23] So, don't you see, by screaming at linespeople when he disagreed with their calls, McEnroe was really striking a blow against racism and anti-Semitism!

But while Johnny Mac–like conduct does indeed violate rules of tennis etiquette, I have attempted to show that it also violates significant general moral principles, the scope and validity of which do not depend on the arbitrary traditions that have arisen over the course of the historical development of one particular sport. There is a world of difference between, on the one hand, a rule requiring the wearing of white clothes at a tennis club, and, on the other hand, an ethical rule, such as that one should avoid causing others unnecessary pain, should refrain from publicly issuing false accusations against others, and should treat one's opponent fairly in an athletic competition. The violation of the former rule hurts no one and violates no one's rights. But Johnny Mac–like conduct hurts and is unjust and unfair. So it is immoral, and not merely a transgression of etiquette.

Notes

1. I should make clear that the point of this chapter is to evaluate certain kinds of conduct on a tennis court from the standpoint of ethical theory rather than to slam John McEnroe as a person. My criticism of him is intended to apply only to his abusive conduct during tennis competition. I am not offering an overall evaluation of his moral character. Moreover, the point of criticizing his behavior is not to enable myself or my readers to feel superior to him but rather to make it clear that it is morally wrong to emulate such conduct.

2. Jeremy Bentham, *The Principles of Morals and Legislation* (1789; repr., New York: Hafner, 1948).

3. Arthur Ashe and Arnold Rampersad, *Days of Grace: A Memoir* (New York: Knopf, 1993), 84.

4. At the 1992 Beckenham (England) tournament, 83 percent in a poll of spectators said they preferred to watch someone like John McEnroe blowing his top rather than to see a top-class tennis match, Paul Fein reports. See his *Tennis Confidential: Today's Greatest Players, Matches, and Controversies* (Washington, DC: Brassey's, 2002), 95.

5. Richard Evans, *McEnroe: Taming the Talent* (New York: Stephen Greene, 1990), 201.

6. John Stuart Mill, *Utilitarianism* (1861; repr., Indianapolis: Bobbs-Merrill, 1971).

7. See Immanuel Kant, *Foundations of the Metaphysics of Morals*, trans. Lewis White Beck (1785; repr., Indianapolis: Bobbs-Merrill, 1969).

8. Perhaps this principle admits of rare exceptions, as when my sincere belief in your guilt is based on evidence sufficient to convince any rational and fair-minded person that you are indeed guilty as charged.

9. John McEnroe, quoted in Larry Schwartz, "Menace or Magician," *ESPN Classic*, August 31, 2007, http://espn.go.com/classic/000706johnmcenroe.html.

10. A. Hastorf and H. Cantril, "They Saw a Game: A Case Study," *Journal of Abnormal and Social Psychology* 49, no. 1 (January 1954): 129–34.

11. Dr. Charles F. Beck, *A View from the Tall Chair: Ten Years on the Men's Pro Tour* (Houston: D. Armstrong, 1988), 207–8.

12. Evans, *McEnroe: Taming the Talent*, 50.

13. Ibid., 111–12.

14. Arthur Ashe with Alexander McNab, *Arthur Ashe on Tennis* (New York: Knopf, 1995), 82.

15. Ashe with McNab, *Arthur Ashe on Tennis*, 82.

16. John Feinstein, *Hard Courts: Real Life on the Professional Tennis Tours* (New York: Villard, 1991), 287–88.

17. Evans, *McEnroe*, 128.

18. John McEnroe with James Kaplan, *You Cannot Be Serious* (New York: G. P. Putnam's Sons, 2002), 91, 190.

19. Ibid., 190.

20. He wrote, "My standards for myself are, as they've always been, extraordinarily high" (ibid., 15).

21. Ibid., 141–42.

22. Evans, *McEnroe*, 20, 94.

23. Ibid., 89.

Tommy Valentini

LOVE–LOVE

A Fresh Start at Finding Value and Virtue in Tennis

> But we cannot always have what we want, and we must prepare for and accept those things over which we have no control.
> —Arthur Ashe, *Days of Grace*, 1993

In the quest to find deeper meaning in sport than wins and losses, I often ask my students on the tennis court and in the classroom whether they believe that winning lies within their control. A fair percentage of them do. I usually then ask why they do not always make the choice to win if winning does, in fact, lie within their control. I explain that I have tried to win every tennis match in which I have been involved, yet I have had my fair share of losses. Clearly, if I could make the choice to win, I would always do so, and most agree that they would do the same. This choice, however, cannot be made. Far too many factors outside one's control have an influence on the outcome of a tennis match for winning to lie within one's control—the opponent, the conditions, the officials (or lack thereof), whether or not one plays one's best tennis, and luck, to name just a few.

To those students who persist in the conviction that they can control winning, I provide the hypothetical scenario of playing against Rafael Nadal. I (or any of them) could make the choice to win but would probably never do so. Nadal's skills make him a far too formidable opponent for any of us (and most other tennis players in the world). Even if I were able to produce my best tennis, I could never defeat Nadal, no matter how desperately I chose to win. A discussion surrounding this scenario usually convinces those who believe they can control winning to loosen their grasps on the claim.

In spite of the intellectual understanding that winning lies outside of one's control, western culture still values competitive results as the predominant measure of sporting success. Winning is the measure by which the success of the playing experience is judged. If one wavers at all, he usually concedes that he feels somewhat pleased with the experience as long as he played well. Even playing well, however, lies outside of one's control. If one could choose to play his best every time, why would anyone ever play poorly?

Invariably the first question parents ask children who return from matches is "Did you win?" There is less often any mention of the joy and absorption, physical improvement, and sportsmanlike interaction with opponents and teammates that playing tennis on a particular occasion provided. As a player becomes older and better, winning becomes even more firmly cemented as the barometer of success.

Pete Sampras and Andre Agassi are two of the greatest male tennis players who have ever lived. During their playing careers they were fierce rivals with contrasting playing styles and personalities that made their on-court encounters captivating and sublime. Fans and media debate whether one of these two American legends was greater than the other. On the one hand, Sampras had a slight edge in their head-to-head encounters, had more year-end #1 finishes and Grand Slam titles, and is the all-time king of Wimbledon—arguably the sport's most prestigious tournament. Agassi, on the other hand, conquered the "Terre Bateau" of Roland Garros (the French Open) in 1999 to complete the career Grand Slam, and he won the 1996 Olympic gold medal—two feats that eluded Sampras. Determining who is the greater of these two titans lies outside the scope of this chapter. The key point here is that winning represents the primary criterion for determining the better player: Sampras won more, but Agassi won them all. The beauty and mental composure with which both played and the way each used their celebrity status for philanthropic and humanitarian causes are sometimes considered, but the discussion most often centers on competitive results against each other and their contemporaries and how these results compare to the other greats in the game's history.

Holding competitive results as the primary means for measuring tennis success contributes to a winning-at-all-costs attitude. The causal connection isn't logically necessary, of course, but it is no less real for being contingent. Cheating, gamesmanship, and other unsportsmanlike behaviors become more prevalent in the pursuit of the almighty victory. Many players at all levels find value in the game only if they win. These players are then "successful" only a fraction of the times that they play. Certainly, winning is usually more enjoyable than losing, but basing success on something that lies outside of one's control leaves too much to chance. To those who love the game, tennis is too precious to be valuable some of the time. There is another approach to tennis that reduces the overemphasis on winning and focuses on values that transcend wins and losses.

Removing the focus from winning requires more than lip service. Saying that we will be less concerned with winning is one thing, but in the tense moments of competition our words are difficult to translate into action. We need a specific plan to help execute a shift in the way we define success in tennis. We need not completely remove winning from the picture; we simply need to put it in its proper place. Here I present a plan for making this philosophical change. With the theoretical basis of moral philosopher Alasdair MacIntyre, I propose that full effort, positive attitude, and the highest standard of sportsmanship can be prioritized above competitive results to make tennis an endeavor that transcends winning and positively affects lives away from the court.

MacIntyre and the Goods of Tennis

In *After Virtue,* moral philosopher Alasdair MacIntyre elucidates the concept of a virtue in terms of a practice. I base my argument here on the assumption that sport, specifically tennis, is an example of a MacIntyrean practice. MacIntyre considers a practice "any coherent and complex form of socially established cooperative human activity through which goods internal to that form of activity are realized in the course of trying to achieve those standards of excellence which are appropriate to, and partially definitive of, that form of activity, with the result that human powers to achieve excellence, and human conceptions of the ends and goods involved, are systematically extended."[1]

For MacIntyre, there are two types of goods to be achieved in every kind of practice. First, there are those external to a practice. These are considered external because they are socially connected to the practice but not necessarily inherent in it. MacIntyre describes external goods by using the example of teaching a child to play chess. To get the child interested in the game, an adult who believes that it will eventually enrich the child's life offers the child candy as motivation to play. The adult then plays against the child at a level that challenges the child but does not make it impossible for the child to win. The adult offers additional candy to the child for winning so the child will be motivated not only to play but to win. The candy serves as the external good for the hypothetical child. It motivates the child but can be obtained in ways other than playing chess.

Examples of external goods in tennis include prize money, trophies, and social recognition. In each case, the goods are not intrinsically linked to the practice of tennis. They can be obtained in some way other than playing the game. At the professional level, winning produces material and social wealth. But whether dealing with Sampras and Agassi and their status among the all-time greats, a recreational league player looking to add a trophy or a trip to nationals to her resume, or a junior competitor pursuing a top ranking or college tennis scholarship, one can see the motivating capability of external goods. They often become the main reasons for playing the game.

In addition to their lack of intrinsic connection to a given practice, MacIntyre's external goods are also distinguished by their zero-sum quality. He writes, "It is characteristic of what I have called external goods that when achieved they are always someone's individual property and possession. Moreover characteristically they are such that the more someone has of them, the less there is for other people. External goods are therefore characteristically objects of competition in which there must be losers as well as winners."[2] In tennis terms, external goods are closely linked to competitive results. The more external goods one has, such as trophies, prize money, and fame, the less they are available to others. There is only one Wimbledon ladies' singles trophy awarded each year. When Venus Williams wins it, no one else has it. There might be other ways to attain the trophy, but when someone possesses it, others cannot.[3]

MacIntyre's second type of good, goods internal to a practice, are less tangible. In contrast to external goods, they can only be cultivated by doing the practice to which they are connected. In MacIntyre's chess example, the child can obtain the external good of candy in any number of ways but cannot gain goods internal to chess without actually playing the game. The same holds true for tennis. One can gain money, fame, and tangible rewards such as trophies in multiple ways. One cannot truly gain a deeper understanding of tennis strategy, enhanced skill in hitting serves, volleys, and groundstrokes, or an appreciation for the necessity of a worthy opponent in our quest for joyful, absorbing excellence on the tennis court unless we engage in the practice of playing tennis. For MacIntyre, one must be a tennis player to recognize, understand, pursue, and judge the internal goods of tennis. The possession of such goods only comes from experiential knowledge gained by playing the game, not merely propositional knowledge gleaned from watching it played or learning about it from the outside.

Furthermore, internal goods differ from external goods in their availability. They are not limited by a zero-sum quality: "Internal goods are indeed the outcome of competition to excel, but it is characteristic of them that their achievement is a good for the whole community who participate in the practice."[4] Every competitive tennis match will produce a winner and a loser, thereby limiting access to external goods. Internal goods, on the other hand, are available to players on both sides of the score. Both players, if looking to excel, have access to internal goods.

To obtain these internal goods, however, one cannot simply play the game. It must be played a certain way. One has to engage in the practice with virtue. Herein lies the key to MacIntyre's conceptualization of virtue and to the present discussion on changing the definition of success in tennis. Although he makes clear that what follows is not his final definition of a virtue, MacIntyre asserts, "A virtue is an acquired human quality the possession and exercise of which tends to enable us to achieve those goods which are internal to practices and the lack of which effectively prevents us from achieving any such goods."[5] Virtuous practice leads to the cultivation of internal goods. Tennis that focuses solely on external goods requires no virtue.

For MacIntyre, one begins the process of cultivating internal goods by acknowledging and accepting the standards of excellence that have been established throughout the history of a particular practice. "Thus the standards themselves are not immune from criticism, but nonetheless we cannot be initiated into a practice without accepting the authority of the best standards realized so far. . . . If, on starting to play baseball, I do not accept that others know better than I when to throw a fastball and when not, I will never learn to appreciate good pitching let alone to pitch."[6] The same holds true for tennis. Learning what constitutes good tennis in terms of technique, strategy, and behavior requires one to recognize and accept, at least in the opening stages of one's involvement in the game, the best standards that have been developed to this point.

The process by which players come to recognize the standards and begin to pursue them brings practitioners into relation with one another. MacIntyre declares, "To enter into a practice is to enter into a relationship not only with contemporary practitioners, but also with those who have preceded us in the practice, particularly those whose achievements have extended the reach of the practice to its present point." For MacIntyre, learning standards of excellence and internal goods from other more experienced practitioners requires the virtues of justice, courage, and honesty. He writes, "Justice, on an Aristotelian view, is defined in terms of giving each person his or her due or desert." We need justice in the Aristotelian sense to give those tennis practitioners who have come before us and those who know the game and its goods better than us their due respect. Honesty is required in recognizing one's own limitations with regard to the standards and the internal goods that have been historically established within the practice. Last, we need to exercise courage in order to take the risks necessary to accept the standards and internal goods and to pursue them. Without the exercise of these virtues, we have no chance of meeting the practice's standards of excellence or cultivating its internal goods, rendering it "pointless except as a device for achieving external goods."[7]

External goods have their place in MacIntyre's framework. They can serve as a motivation to enter into a practice when one does not possess the experience, understanding, or virtue necessary to strive for internal goods. Virtue does not eliminate external goods, it simply provides the means by which they are reprioritized below internal goods. One can still strive to win. For MacIntyre, both internal and external goods are the results of desire to excel. While winning may be more hardwired into the competitive experience than quest for internal goods, we can still virtuously engage in tennis so as to cultivate internal goods. An extension of this claim is that one can also choose to measure success in terms of internal goods rather than the external goods that accompany winning. One can make this happen by extending the reach of the practice in a new and more virtuous direction.

MacIntyre's moral philosophical framework provides a theoretical underpinning for finding meaning in tennis beyond wins and losses.[8] He gives us the language of internal and external goods and a means for understanding virtue in our practice. Perhaps more important, he also provides hope by making room for the practice to evolve. Standards of excellence change over time as those who have successfully entered into the practice become more virtuous. For these individuals, internal rather than external goods serve as the primary motivation for doing the practice. They then virtuously shape the practice or "extend its reach" so future practitioners will have standards of excellence that promote the virtuous cultivation of internal goods.

The remainder of this chapter will delineate specific goods internal to the practice of tennis that are within one's control—full effort, positive attitude, and the highest standard of sportsmanship. Developing a deeper understanding of each of these internal goods is the first step. The second is to choose to prioritize these goods above winning and measure the success of our tennis experience based on how well the goods are cultivated. Pursuing the internal goods of full effort, positive attitude, and the highest standard of sportsmanship is a process that requires virtue. In the end, it will extend the reach of our tennis, but it will also contribute to living a meaningful and virtuous life.

Full Effort

Learning to give full effort is relevant to many sports, but it has specific meaning as a good internal to tennis. Full effort in tennis begins with preparation. Learning the techniques and strategies of the game, as well as how and when to apply them during the course of a match, requires time and discipline. Strokes must be properly learned and subsequently grooved into muscle memory. Helpful coaching combined with playing experience allows one to develop various strategies and an intuitive understanding of the right moments for their application. Off-court conditioning and strength training, getting proper rest and nutrition, and practicing mental skills such as visualization and breath control also allow one to give full effort when taking the court for competition.

Doing the work to accomplish this preparation requires the virtues of justice, honesty, and courage. Finding the right people to help improve one's game and justly giving these people their due respect as teachers of the practice is key. Honesty and truthfulness are necessary as one evaluates the extent to which one is invested in these preparatory measures. One can easily convince herself that she has prepared to the best of her ability, even when she hasn't, because of the human penchant for deceiving even oneself. Yet one must balance her understandings of her personal capacities with the analysis of those she has entrusted to help her prepare in order to evaluate, as honestly as possible, whether or not she has, in fact, prepared to the best of her ability. In the end, one must also have the courage to fully prepare to compete, knowing full well that these preparations do not ensure victory. This virtuous preparation might not lead to the external goods that accompany winning tennis matches, but it does help cultivate a portion of the internal good of giving full effort.

The most fundamental show of full effort is never giving up—doing one's best at all times in spite of circumstances. Extending full effort into a tennis match certainly includes putting forth maximum physical effort, such as hustling for every ball and making the opponent play one more shot to win a point. It also requires one to make the effort to use our mental skills and to control emotions as well as possible. The mental demands of competition can often cloud one's ability to strategize during the course of a match. Maximal effort means one has exhausted all options within the bounds of the rules and the ethic of sportsmanship in the attempt to win. Mid-match paradigm shifts are not easy and their intended results never guaranteed. Still, changing a losing strategy in the middle of a match rather than continuing to get beat while remaining within one's strategic comfort zone is a part of giving full effort. Frustration arises when one cannot summon her best tennis on a given occasion. Players can also become too anxious or excited for what they consider "big matches" or "big points." Attempting to make the proper emotional adjustments in response to frustrations and anxieties in the heat of competitive moments is yet another part of full effort.

Giving full effort during competition requires a great deal of virtue. As with preparation, one needs honesty when measuring the amount of effort given in competition. An individual is the only true judge of whether or not she has done her best to produce a complete effort. Perhaps most importantly, full effort in spite of circumstances requires courage. When we are cruising along in a match with our strokes flowing beautifully and our mind at ease, giving our full effort comes naturally. Most of us, however, have moments when we have wanted desperately to summon our best tennis yet have played poorly. No matter what we try to execute, things do not go our way. Net cords go against us, the wind picks up just as we are about to hit a crucial second serve, a string breaks in the middle of a game point, shots we have practiced time and again escape us, or the mind continually wanders to times and places that are nowhere near the moment and task at hand. We may also experience the helpless feeling of reaching the stage of a match where defeat feels imminent. Making the choice to continue to put forth full effort in these worst of tennis times requires courage.

In addition to courage, giving full effort in competition requires the virtue of respect. Although this might fall under the realm of Aristotelian justice—giving people their just due—it is important to examine how giving one's full effort is also a show of respect. First, giving full effort demonstrates self-respect. If one has trained hard and prepared to the best of his ability, he can honor and respect himself and the preparatory work he has done by trying his best. Certainly occurrences such as injury or tragedy prevent players from producing their full effort.[9] But some players at various levels do "go through the motions" or, even worse, "tank." This conduct reflects a lack of self-respect, but also a lack of respect for the opponent and the game itself. The word "competition" derives from the Latin *competitio*—"to strive with" or "to question with." If we are truly striving together with our opponents, then anything less than our full effort does them a disservice. Finally, our full effort is a sign of respectful appreciation for the opportunities that the game of tennis affords us. We are fortunate to be able to take part in a game that provides a myriad of emotions, challenges, and relationships. Full effort communicates that we value and respect the game and are practitioners who cherish the other internal goods engaging in tennis can yield. We give ourselves, our opponents, and tennis their due respect by choosing to give full effort each time we take the court.

Positive Attitude

Maintaining a positive attitude during the ups and downs of athletic competition is a challenge that some athletes never overcome. Tennis provides a unique opportunity to develop the ability of choosing to be positive. After each point, a player has a brief moment to decide how to react: one can objectively analyze what happened during the previous point, learn from it, and continue to compete, or one can react negatively. Negativity, both physical and verbal, is endemic in competitive tennis. Players often volitionally choose to verbally abuse themselves, mope around the court, or hunch over after lost points or poor play. In some cases, they will even erupt into racket-smashing tirades.

In diametric contrast, a calm, positive demeanor generally enhances performance on the tennis court and thus increases one's chances of achieving the external goods that accompany winning. Choosing to maintain a confident physical posture, focus the eyes on the racket strings, and concentrate on breathing between every point—whether it is won or lost—can curtail negative behaviors and set the stage for making the choice to be positive. When players catch themselves reacting negatively, one of the most simple and effective ways to respond positively is to smile, which can work as a reminder to enjoy and embrace the challenges and adversities that accompany competition and to remember that even though one approaches tennis with absorbing focus and intensity, it is still a game. Practitioners will not always play their best tennis or achieve the external good of victory each time they compete, but they can always choose to be positive.

Remaining positive usually produces a higher level of tennis, but it can be a powerful way for players to respect themselves as well. Players affirm their own goodness when they treat themselves positively. Each time they choose to be positive during a match, they communicate to themselves and to others that they are valued and worthy of being treated with respect. Positive self-talk and a confident physical posture during competition allow players to affirm their value in both victory and defeat, and surely this value does not depend on winning a tennis match. The more players can demonstrate the virtue of self-respect, the more they can cultivate the internal good of a positive attitude.

A similar relationship exists between maintaining a positive attitude on the tennis court and showing respect to others. Racket-smashing tirades and vulgar verbal outbursts that sometimes accompany poor play and a failure to meet expectations are disrespectful to others. One's own self is usually the intended target of these tirades, outbursts, and other forms of negative behavior. But whether or not one intends them to, displays of negative emotion demonstrate a lack of respect for opponents. When one screams at oneself, throws a racket in disgust, or verbalizes reasons she is losing or not playing her best tennis, she is taking away from what her opponent is accomplishing. A negative outburst is nothing more than an attempt to protect one's own ego. Rather than throwing a racket or screaming at herself, one might as well just look across the net and say: "If I were only playing as well as I am capable of playing, you would not have won that point, game, set, or match." However, when one makes the choice to be positive in spite of how well or poorly she is playing or what side of the score she is on, she is communicating that her opponents are valued partners in the pursuit of excellence in the practice of tennis. Indeed, the virtue of respect for others is required for the cultivation of the internal good of learning to maintain a positive attitude on the tennis court.

The point here is not to discourage those who have fallen short in such areas. Nearly all of us have, particularly in a sport like tennis, which lays bare our psyches for all the world to see. Failures aren't best understood as occasions for further self-disparagement, but rather as learning opportunities, chances to react better next time. Over time, with practice, by changing behavior, one can change his habits and even his character.

Sportsmanship

Perhaps the most important internal good that can be developed through the virtuous playing of tennis is sportsmanship. Sportsmanship is a difficult and dynamic concept to define; however, two of its key components are playing fairly and treating one's opponents the way that one would like to be treated.

Playing fairly begins, obviously, with following the rules. Tennis provides a unique set of circumstances in this regard. Most matches are not governed by chair umpires or even roving officials. Players call their own lines, lets, and rule infractions, such as double bounces and illegal touches of the net. This requires a virtuous character, since the temptation to prioritize external goods above internal goods is especially strong in cases such as these. It takes no virtue to cheat on a line call in order to increase the chance of victory. It takes honesty to avoid making an out call on a ball one saw hit the very outside of the line at a crucial stage of a match. Abiding by the rules also requires justly giving opponents their due in the form of a match contested on a level playing field. Last, following the rules of the game takes courage, for sometimes doing so means the forfeiture of a competitive advantage, risk of defeat, and a damaged ego.

Simply following the letter of the law, though, is not enough for sportsmanship to flourish. Cultivating the internal good of sportsmanship also includes upholding the sportsmanlike code of conduct of the practice of tennis. Calling one's own shots out when one is totally certain he has missed but his opponent has failed to make a call, granting an opponent a let when a slight distraction has forced her to wait longer than usual to hit a second serve, or refraining from questioning an opponent's line call even if one is certain that the wrong call has been made—none of these constitute official rules of the game. Still, they are widely practiced sportsmanlike behaviors. Upholding the sportsmanlike code of the game requires even more virtue than doing so for the written rules. There are no formal penalties for abandoning this code. In many cases, upholding it detracts from one's chances of winning a particular match. Even so, pursuing this portion of the internal good of sportsmanship helps establish standards of sportsmanship for others and requires virtue. It is an exercise in respecting the practice of tennis as well as one's opponents.

Most significant, sportsmanship means treating opponents the way one would like to be treated. Playing against someone who cheats on line calls or deliberately uses gamesmanship only takes away from enjoyment of the game. Many have also had the experience of having the joy stripped from tennis by playing with an opponent or doubles partner who followed the rules but did not treat the other player as he would like to be treated. There are no rules that mandate a friendly prematch introduction, complimenting an opponent's good shots, or offering a sincere handshake of congratulations and grateful smile at the conclusion of a match, yet players somehow know when a match has been played in the spirit of good sportsmanship and when it has not. Players who treat their opponents the way they would like to be treated are a joy to compete with. Those who place the external goods of victory above treating others as they would like to be treated strip the practice not only of joy, but also of virtue.

Sport philosopher Randolph Feezell describes a good sportsman as one who "sees his opponent as both competitor and friend, competing and cooperating at the same time."[10] Feezell suggests that people come to understand sportsmanship by playing the game and by learning from the sport's moral exemplars. In MacIntyre's terms, playing the game resembles doing the practice, and these exemplars are the people who have virtuously extended the reach of the practice. Learning to treat opponents as friends and partners with whom one competes is an internal good that requires virtue. Tennis cannot be played alone. We need to share the experience with someone for it to exist. Each time a player takes the court, he can treat his opponents as a means to achieving external goods, or he can treat them as needed friends with whom he is sharing a joyful and meaningful experience in cultivating the internal goods of the treasured game. This choice depends on the amount of virtue a player brings to the court and the extent to which he is willing to prioritize the internal goods of the game above its external goods.

Adversity and Internal Goods

One point that should be apparent here is that making the virtuous choice to prioritize the internal goods of full effort, positive attitude, and sportsmanship above the external goods that surround victory is much more difficult in the face of adversity. The adversity that prevents the cultivation of these goods internal to tennis comes in many forms. Obviously, playing poorly and losing make the pursuit of internal goods more challenging. Maintaining a positive attitude when one plays poorly requires tremendous virtue. The same holds true for continuing to produce a full effort in the face of imminent defeat. It is easy for a player to resist the temptation to make a dishonest line call in her favor when she is winning handily. The challenge drastically increases when she is deep in a deciding set, or worse yet, when she is certain that an opponent has cheated her. Being respectful to an opponent who questions line calls, cheats, makes excuses, or employs gamesmanship demands virtue well beyond what is required to be sportsmanlike to one who is fair and kind. Each time a player takes the court, the challenge and correlative opportunity of being virtuous and pursuing internal goods over external goods are ubiquitous. Despite the effect of adversity, facing and conquering this challenge lies entirely within one's control. So the primary measure of a player's success in tennis should be based on how well she meets the challenge of giving full effort with a positive attitude while exhibiting the highest standard of sportsmanship.

While one cannot always make the choice to win, culture too often mistakenly measures success primarily in terms of wins and losses. I have not suggested that players should not pursue victory. Anything less than full effort directed toward winning should be seen as lacking the virtue of respect—for oneself, his opponents, and the game. The object of the game is to win, and we should not apologize for making our most spirited attempt to do so. I have, however, asserted that if we measure our success in terms that lie within our control, our tennis will take on new meaning and importance, whatever the outcome.

Trying to change the highly socialized reward structures in organized sport is a long, difficult, and sometimes disheartening process. In a culture that demands results, celebrates winners, and has coined the locution "loser" as one of its worst terms of disapprobation, it is unlikely that a Grand Slam tournament will award the champion's trophy to the player who puts forth the most complete effort, displays the most positive attitude, or exhibits the highest standard of sportsmanship during the fortnight. The shift will have to take place in individuals who care deeply about the game, practicing virtue and reshaping the standards of excellence for future generations of tennis practitioners. Even though sweeping changes in the way in which the tennis world measures success may not be possible, we must strive for this change with full effort, a positive attitude, and a sportsmanlike spirit. By doing so, we can rest assured that our endeavor will be successful.

Tennis and Life

Though many treat their tennis with seriousness (and with what may appear to our non–tennis playing friends as overseriousness), most can recognize that tennis is a game. Yet the lessons to learn from it have the potential to change the way players live their lives. The virtuous pursuit of internal goods is one lesson that transcends the game. It helps players behave rightly on the tennis court but can also contribute to their living a life of goodness and virtue away from it.

Like tennis, life does not give the luxury of controlling its results. Being born assures all human beings of one thing: some day we will die. Even more so than the outcome of a tennis match, death lies outside of one's control. The virtuous choice to live with full effort, a positive attitude, and a spirit of sportsmanship that leads players to treat others as they would like to be treated in the face of this predetermined result can give our finite lives greater value. Feezell suggests that appealing to exemplars can help players learn to be sportsmanlike. MacIntyre asserts that people learn standards of excellence and how to pursue internal goods in a practice by learning from those outstanding practitioners who have preceded them. We can learn to transfer full effort, a positive attitude, and the spirit of sportsmanship from tennis to life in a similar fashion. No one has been more of an exemplar for this approach to tennis and life than Arthur Ashe.

From the moment he was confronted with having AIDS, Ashe immediately realized that both his condition and his death were outside of his control. He proclaims, "The two findings of 'HIV-positive' and 'AIDS' were new facts of my life that I could not evade. There was nothing I could possibly do about either one except to treat them according to the most expert medical science available to me. Neither would go away, and I had to make the best of the situation." Confronted with horribly trying circumstances, Ashe knew, as the Stoics taught, that he had a choice to make. He couldn't change his circumstances, but he could choose how best to respond to them. He could be positive and continue to live with full effort in spite of his condition, or he could dwell on the fact that he would die soon, feel sorry for himself, and discontinue living the life of deep concern for others that he had always lived. Clearly, he calmly chose the first option. "The public hysteria over AIDS was probably then at its zenith, but I would not become hysterical." In the face of his own impending death, Ashe began a foundation to help educate the world about AIDS. He writes, "Following my announcement, one of my most urgent decisions was to establish the Arthur Ashe Foundation for the Defeat of AIDS. I was conscious of the possibility that I did not have sufficient time left to mount such a project, but I became determined to move ahead with it, come what may."[11] In spite of his fast-approaching death, Ashe was committed to serving others.

In the final few years of his life, Ashe wrote *Days of Grace*. In this memoir, he demonstrates an incredibly positive attitude as his death draws near. He was able to focus on the abundance in his life. "I am a fortunate, blessed man. Aside from AIDS and heart disease, I have no problems. My stepmother, about whom I care deeply for my sake and for my dead father's, is in fine health; my wife is in fine health; my daughter radiates vitality. I have living friends in abundance. . . . I need nothing that money can buy. So why should I complain?" Not only did Ashe continue to live a life of concern for others with a positive attitude, but he exemplified the virtuous choice to pursue the internal good of living with full effort. He asserts, "I believe, too, 'that what a man discovers about the meaning of life . . . need not undergo any change as he meets death.' So I go on calmly with my life. Keeping as busy as my health allows, I press on with my modest efforts at striving and achieving."[12] Despite the adversity of an imminent death, Ashe maintained his commitment to live with full effort.

By staying positive and giving full effort in living a life of concern for others, Arthur Ashe gives an inspiring example of the powerful manner in which the virtue and internal goods of tennis can transcend the court and have a profound impact on life. Life provides many unique challenges, including death. But like Ashe, we can remain calm in the face of adversity if we choose to strive for internal goods. May we have the virtue to pursue these internal goods on the tennis court so that our tennis experiences can help us recognize and seek them in our lives outside the lines.

Notes

I would like to extend heartfelt thanks to my advisor, Nicole LaVoi, for her support of this chapter; to Ted Smith for helping me see initial connections between MacIntyre's philosophical framework and the sport of tennis, and for encouraging me to pursue them; to my coach, Steve Wilkinson, for his unwavering belief in me, his love, and for being a living example of the courage to be; and to my mentor and friend, Dan McLaughlin, for the clear insight, hard work, friendship, and care that helped this chapter come together.

1. Alasdair MacIntyre, *After Virtue: A Study in Moral Theory*, 2nd ed. (Notre Dame, IN: University of Notre Dame Press, 1984), 187.

2. Ibid., 190.

3. In March 2006, Björn Borg considered putting his five Wimbledon trophies up for auction to gain financial security. Had he followed through on his intent to sell

them, they could have been obtained by someone who has not won the tournament. Most tennis fans were relieved when John McEnroe and Andre Agassi convinced him to reconsider. It bothered most of us who love and cherish the game to think that someone who has earned these prestigious external goods would relinquish them for financial gain. It seems perverted that someone who did not cultivate the internal goods that accompanied Borg's Wimbledon title runs should possess the trophies. Still, the possibility of them changing hands for monetary compensation demonstrates the disconnect of external goods from the virtuous doing of a practice.

4. MacIntyre, *After Virtue*, 190–91.

5. Ibid., 191.

6. Ibid., 190.

7. Ibid., 194, 202, 191.

8. MacIntyre's moral philosophical framework has its limitations. The need to submit to the authority and standards of a practice in order to be initiated can be problematic. Those who set the standards might not come from an experience that looks anything like mine. They might also be people who lack virtue. This calls into question the standards of excellence to which we must submit. Furthermore, there often exist competing standards and internal goods in a given practice, or two practices (take tennis and parenthood or an academic career, for example) can come into contact with one another and have standards and goods that conflict. These are just some of the critiques leveled against MacIntyre's framework and conceptualization of virtue. I present them here to point out that MacIntyre's framework is useful yet not infallible as a theoretical framework for the present discussion.

9. See Arthur Ashe with Frank Deford, *Arthur Ashe: Portrait in Motion* (New York: Carroll & Graf, 1975), 188. In this diary from Wimbledon 1974 to Wimbledon 1975, Arthur Ashe marvels at the Australian tennis players of his era and their refusal to make excuses. He remarks, "But never will they complain about conditions or use them to alibi. If the lights were bad or the crowd was noisy or the surface was slick or whatever—they keep their mouths shut. If you have an injury, you can default; if you play, you don't have an injury. You're playing aren't you? 'You walk on the court, you have no excuses,' Roy Emerson told me once, and that is the credo." I concur with the Aussies. Full effort can and should be given each time one takes the court. If an injury is severe enough to prevent one from being able to give an honest, full effort, then one should not play. If one takes the court, there are no excuses for producing less than a full effort; doing so represents a choice that is disrespectful to oneself, the opponent, and the game.

10. Randolph Feezell, "Sportsmanship," *Journal of the Philosophy of Sport* 13 (1986): 6.

11. Arthur Ashe with Arnold Rampersad, *Days of Grace: A Memoir* (New York: Ballantine, 1993), 226, 283.

12. Ibid., 328, 327. Ashe is quoting Dr. Howard Thurman.

Robert R. Clewis

A COURT CONVERSATION

This short court conversation is a philosophical dialogue among Prussian philosopher Immanuel Kant (1724–1804), an accomplished singles player, the player's coach, and a tennis fan.

Characters

Kant, an updated version of the eighteenth-century philosopher
Kevin, a ranked player
Coach Tim, Kevin's coach
Joanna, a tennis enthusiast

Tennis and Philosophy

JOANNA and KANT are at a tennis tournament.

JOANNA: Great tournament, isn't it?
KANT: It is. Kevin played with excellence earlier today. He dismantled his opponent, making the difficult appear easy, although I am sure it is not. Do you follow tennis closely, too?
JOANNA: Oh, yeah. I come here every year. I love watching Kevin play.
KANT: Why is that?
JOANNA: I like his shot-making ability, his booming serve, his graceful slice. Sometimes he doesn't just win—he plays beautifully.
KANT: Indeed. Beauty. That is a word that I have been thinking about very much lately. You see, I am a philosopher. Philosopher by trade,

tennis fan in my spare time, as it were. I am Professor Immanuel Kant.

JOANNA: Pleased to meet you. I'm Joanna. (*They shake hands.*) I took a course in philosophy once in college. Some of the material stuck with me, but I have to admit that I've forgotten a lot. Can you remind me what philosophers do?

KANT: Philosophers try to account for and explain human experience by asking and responding to questions of a certain kind. Not scientific questions about the weather, temperature, boiling points, the movements of molecules, and the like—these are empirical matters. We analyze and discuss such things, but we don't ourselves discover them, at least not insofar as we are philosophers. We ask questions about beauty and the sublime; truth and knowledge; freedom and determinism; duties and rights; and the like. These lead to various subfields of philosophy such as aesthetics, epistemology, metaphysics, and ethics. I have written extensively about such matters, but I will not bore you with the details here.

JOANNA: Got it. What do you think of tennis?

KANT: There is a similarity between tennis and philosophy, and tennis can be used to clarify some philosophical issues, as I hope to demonstrate. Tennis involves opposition, but it also requires cooperation between the players. After all, opponents must play by the same rules, which are agreed upon by convention. Tennis players are competitive, trying to beat each other. At the professional level, accordingly, there is a chair umpire in tennis. He or she is the arbiter of disputes.

JOANNA: But there's no umpire in philosophy.

KANT: Actually, in philosophy the umpire is, or at least should be, reason. In tennis, the chair umpire is given the authority to resolve disputes and has the final word. In philosophy, your opponent is the person who disagrees with your thesis, the position that you are defending. But you also cooperate with your opponent. You both play by the rules of reason. Of course, philosophy is not primarily about winning, as if it were a debate contest, but about coming to know and defend the truth. Debate plays a role, but this "game" is primarily aimed at truth. Philosophy, in other words, is different from sophistry.

JOANNA: But tennis, too, has more than winning as a goal, since the loser of a match does not usually regret that she played. Even if I lose, I might be pleased by the fact that I played my heart out, or improved my technique or strategy, or was part of a close match.

KANT: Tennis and philosophy seem to have that in common, too.

Beauty and Artistry

JOANNA: You said philosophers talk about beauty. So what do you think about this?

KANT: In my view, there is no common denominator to beauty. We can't generalize about what makes a match beautiful. We cannot specify beforehand what makes a shot aesthetically pleasing or put that into precise concepts and words.

JOANNA: So how do we know when something is beautiful? Do we feel it?

KANT: Yes. But concepts also play a role in what I call dependent beauty, which "depends on" or is influenced by the concepts being used or applied when we look at an aesthetic object or event, in this case a tennis match. We watch tennis with certain ideas or concepts in mind. Spectators of tennis who play the game observe a match differently from onlookers who do not understand its techniques, strategies, and mental aspects. The informed fans are unlikely to find a tennis match boring, since they know what to look for. Such spectators have a good grasp of the excellence on display and what it takes to be a good player.

JOANNA: What happens when there is a disagreement between two people about whether a match or point was interesting or beautiful?

KANT: It might seem at first glance that one of them must be wrong when there is a dispute, but that is not necessarily true. Each person may be right in his or her own way. The two spectators could be talking about two different kinds of beauty: dependent beauty, which is partly based on concepts, and free beauty, which is not conceptual. Free beauty is based primarily on the visual, auditory, and other sensory aspects of the match. Dependent beauty is rooted in concepts, the game's conventions, rules, or history.

JOANNA: So what does dependent beauty feel like?

KANT: Similar to free beauty; there is still a pleasant feeling associated with it. Beauty is never only a conceptual matter. Dependent beauty incorporates and appeals to concepts more evidently or obviously than free beauty. Free beauty is based just on how things appear to the eye or at first glance, without thought or contemplation. Even though dependent beauty is based on concepts, one still cannot prove that something is beautiful.

JOANNA: Can you explain the concepts involved in a beautiful match a bit more?

KANT: Dependent beauty in tennis would see a point or match or stroke as beautiful, while reflecting on or taking into account the rules, conventions, or history of tennis. The Wimbledon match between Federer and Sampras, for instance, takes on a new dimension when we keep in mind how Federer began to dominate the men's game shortly after his win.[1] There are other concepts besides historical ones. They can be ideas of excellence or virtue. When a player hits an amazing shot, better than you or I ever can, we might think of all of the hard work the player put in so that he could hit that shot. There is even a moral quality to the action. A player can embody and thus present us with ideas of self-overcoming, responsibility, or persistence.

JOANNA: That would make the response a case of dependent beauty?

KANT: Right. The game of tennis is defined by its rules, which are conceptual in nature. These guide the movements and intentions of the players; they provide general parameters within which to operate and play. But there are other concepts besides the rules of the game, such as tennis techniques, tactics, and strategies, and the conventions associated with them. The interesting players exhibit originality and ingenuity in their choice of technique, such as Björn Borg's consistently heavy topspin or Jimmy Arias's forehand grip and stroke. Or tactics, like Jim Courier's unrelenting inside-out forehand. Or physical preparation, as in the case of Ivan Lendl. Or choice of strategy, such as switching to the serve-and-volley game, as Martina Hingis did so well. Some of these innovations changed the way tennis was played thereafter. When a player exhibits originality, intelligence, and genius or ingenuity in these areas, we enjoy it and feel aesthetic pleasure. We assess how well a player solves the intellectual and emotional problems that confront her. We desire the player to use original and interesting combinations of shots and to overcome emotional tension.

JOANNA: Can you give me some more examples?

KANT: Our aesthetic response can be affected by the dramatic conditions under which the match is played, as in Nadal's five-set victory over Federer in the 2008 Wimbledon final. Nadal became the new world #1 shortly after that, and this contributes to the significance of his victory. Or our response might take into account the match's social, moral, or political contexts. For example, we look at the 1973 match between Bobby Riggs and Billie Jean King, "The Battle of the Sexes," in light of the women's movement.[2] Similarly, Don Budge's comeback defeat of Gottfried von Cramm in a 1937 Davis Cup match takes on a greater significance if we keep in mind that von Cramm, whether he liked it or not, was identified with Nazi Germany, and Budge with the future Allied Forces.[3] When we judge in light of such historical, social, and other non-perceptual conditions, we are making a judgment that has an intellectual component. We are making a judgment of dependent beauty.

JOANNA: So, if a stroke or point can be beautiful, do you think that a tennis player is like an artist?

KANT: Yes. Although I would not argue that a tennis stroke is technically a work of art, one can consider a great player to be similar to an artist. Think of how John McEnroe would artfully carve out a drop volley with his touch at net, as if he were manipulating the ball at will. His movements were both graceful and beautiful. Add to that the fact that he did not train or lift weights as intensely as players do today, and it is easy to see his gift as innate, like the inborn ability of an artistic genius.

JOANNA: So you don't think tennis is an art form?

KANT: No, but tennis does not have to be considered an art form in order for one to have a pleasant aesthetic response to it.[4] I can have aesthetic responses to objects that are not artistic products.[5]

JOANNA: What do you have in mind?

KANT: A sunset or a mountainside or a butterfly. But even if we do not characterize tennis as an art form, there is an analogy between tennis and art, especially the performing arts like dance and drama.

Watching Kevin is sometimes like watching an artist at work. His graceful movements and strokes have something in common with those of a dancer, at least under appropriate circumstances or at certain moments.[6] And the suspense in a close match is similar to the dramatic tension and conflict in a good tragedy. To see that there is a tennis/art analogy, consider the fact that one journalist described a routine victory by McEnroe in terms of how "artistic" it was.[7] Our use of ordinary language suggests that there is an analogy between tennis and art.

JOANNA: Why is it only an analogy? Why not say that tennis *is* drama, and thus an art form?

KANT: First of all, I do not mean to devalue or diminish tennis in any way when I say that it is not art. Tennis can and does have much value, including aesthetic value, even if it is not an art form. But, to answer your question, tennis is not an instance of drama, because the tennis player is not representing anyone else. I leave aside the issue of feints to the right or left, when the player represents or portrays a player that is nearly identical to him but differs in that the represented player, the one the player wants his opponent to "see," goes in another direction.[8] In theatrical drama, an actor plays a part or role. But the athletes are themselves, plain and simple; they are not characters. When we watch *Othello,* we respond to and sympathize with Othello's—the character's—grief, not to the grief of the actor who plays him. But when Federer lost to Nadal in the Wimbledon final, we sympathized with Federer, not with a character that he was playing.

JOANNA: Okay.

KANT: Here is a second argument. Shakespeare's tragedy *Othello* has a subject matter—say, the personal effects of jealousy or the nature of deception—but tennis does not have a subject matter. A work of drama can be about tennis, but tennis cannot be about a work of drama. And it is not enough to call a match "dramatic." The fact that there are dramatic moments in tennis does not at all show that tennis is a work of theatrical drama, just as speaking of a dramatic car crash does not imply that the car crash is a piece of drama.[9]

JOANNA: That convinces me. So does the tennis/art analogy apply every time tennis is played?

KANT: No, I am speaking of extraordinary or spectacular tennis, not just any match or game. If I hit with or play against you, I doubt I will evoke any aesthetic responses—at least not positive or pleasant ones. Moreover, I doubt we would want to compare my movements to works of art.

JOANNA: I see what you mean.

KANT: It might help if I explain a connection between genius and works of art, which are created by genius. In my view, genius is defined as the ability to produce great art works. It is a talent granted by nature, a gift.[10] Note that even if you have this ability, you still have to master the conventions and rules by which one produces the work. But you do not simply follow the rules and conventions slavishly.[11] You apply them in an original and interesting way that still makes sense or is understandable to the viewers. We need to know the rules to enjoy what the artist or player is doing, and these rules are conceptual, as mentioned. When we watch and enjoy Kevin's quasi-artistry, it is not simply a sensual matter.

KANT pauses to look over at KEVIN and COACH TIM, who have heard of the renowned philosopher and have been listening. KEVIN, COACH TIM, KANT, and JOANNA introduce themselves to each other. After exchanging pleasantries, the philosophical conversation picks up again.

COACH TIM: I'd like to jump in here, if I may. When I'm watching Kevin, I usually don't care about beauty, including intellectual or dependent beauty. I'm mainly rooting for Kevin, though of course I can applaud some of his opponents' great shots and enjoy a close contest, especially if Kevin comes out with a win.

KANT: That is understandable, since as Kevin's coach you have a stake in the outcome of the match that Joanna does not.

COACH TIM: I mean, it wouldn't be much of a stretch for me to tell Kevin that I don't care how ugly or clumsily he plays as long as he wins. I might think it is desirable for him to play beautifully, but not necessary. Tennis, unlike diving or gymnastics, is not a sport that requires the player to try to move beautifully. You don't have to keep aesthetic considerations in mind to win. You don't aim for that as a player.

KANT: True, the goal of winning in tennis is separable from using aesthetic means, whereas in diving and gymnastics you have to use aesthetic means to win.[12]

COACH TIM: In tennis, you can win ugly, as Brad Gilbert says.[13]

JOANNA: At the same time, tennis can be aesthetically pleasing. Even the losing player can make great shots and play beautifully. In fact, I mainly want to see a beautiful match and fair play. I usually don't care very much about who wins.

Disinterestedness

KANT: Exactly. One could say that in those cases you adopt an impartial and disinterested perspective.

KEVIN: That might be true of some of the spectators, but I mainly care about winning when I am out there. I realize that it is good for me to have the originality and intelligence that you mentioned, but at the end of the day I also want to win.

COACH TIM: Ideally you would have both. I think you can be an ingenious player, interesting, fun to watch, and so on, and still win. There doesn't have to be a conflict here. I am happy if you play in an aesthetically pleasing way. But I do start worrying if it comes at the price of losing the match. Professor Kant, mostly I hope Kevin gets a win and advances in his half of the draw. I have a stake in the outcome, as you mentioned, and so does Kevin. We are not impartial; we want Kevin to win. I am not saying that winning is our only goal. We can still enjoy a well-fought match where the players play with courage, originality, and ingenuity. Still, remember that Federer was asked in an on-court interview after his semifinal victory if he would rather play Rafael Nadal or Andy Murray in the 2008 U.S. Open Final. Federer replied that he would prefer to win the trophy. In other words, it didn't really matter. Ultimately, he wanted to win his thirteenth Grand Slam. And he did.

JOANNA: But that's not the end of what he said. Federer added that he would prefer to play against Nadal. I guess this is because of the dramatic and historic dimensions that playing Nadal would have, after the epic 2008 Wimbledon final and the fact that Nadal was then the new #1. Perhaps Federer saw that a Nadal rematch had more aesthetic appeal than playing Murray.

KANT: On that note, let me explain disinterestedness some more. A spectator who just wants to see a good match is disinterested. Of course, this doesn't mean this spectator is *un*interested. Disinterested does not mean disconnected or detached. The disinterested spectator is not indifferent or apathetic. He or she cares about the match. After all, he is watching it and even paying to see it. But he doesn't have a stake in the outcome and is not trying to satisfy ordinary, everyday interests. The pleasure that the spectator feels is not based on personal bias or preference.

JOANNA: Unlike applauding a point simply because the player you're rooting for won that point. The disinterested spectator claps when either player wins a great point.

COACH TIM: But typically you won't find me clapping when Kevin's opponent hits a winner, unless it is a really great shot. I guess I am usually not disinterested in this sense. So I see your distinction, Professor Kant.

JOANNA: Kevin's sponsors, his parents, and his trainer would typically be interested in this sense.

KEVIN: Yes, and I am "interested," too. So is my doubles partner, and the crowd at times. The spectators sure were rooting against me when I played in New York last year. That crowd was definitely *not* disinterested. They were rooting for my opponent.

KANT: Note that some fans are disinterested and some are interested. This does not make them better or worse fans necessarily, only different, at least so long as the interested fan is still able to appreciate great play even from his player's opponent. One can imagine a fan who, by contrast, prefers his player to win at all costs, even if the player does not exhibit excellence and just coasts through on the unforced errors of his opponent. Such loyal interest would detract from the fan's ability to appreciate great play from both players. It would not allow him to see the value of beating an opponent at his best. Of course, we might respect the fan's devotion and loyalty to his player. He will always root for his player, and that is usually an admirable quality. But a partisan fan is not always the best kind, because this devotion can be taken to an extreme, beyond its proper measure. By contrast, a good tennis fan loves the game, desires to see fair play and athletic excellence, and wants to witness a good, dramatic contest.

JOANNA: When I am playing, I am interested, by your definition. I care about the results. I try my hardest to win, or at least should try my hardest. If I am Kevin, I suppose I play, at least in part, either for the money or fame or to break some record. Insofar as I am playing and have something at stake, such as improving my game or winning, I cannot be disinterested.

KANT: Correct.

COACH TIM: Isn't beauty just a matter of whatever you prefer, like having a taste for salty foods rather than for sweets or preferring the color yellow to blue? Isn't that why they call beauty a matter of taste?

KANT: It is not a judgment of mere preference, since mere preference is based on interests that can be different for each of us. A "pure aesthetic judgment" is based on a feeling that is disinterested.[14] The delight is more a mental contemplation than a bodily pleasure. Beauty comes from the harmonious play between intellect, which uses concepts, and our imagination, which produces images.

JOANNA: But how can the judgment be held to be right for everyone if it is based on just one person's feeling of pleasure?

Subjective Universality, Purposelessness, and Necessity

KANT: The fact that the pleasure is thought to apply to all of us in principle, which I call the judgment's subjective universality, is somewhat paradoxical.[15] But "subjective" does not mean that anything goes. Although the judgment is based on a person's pleasure, and so is subjective, it is nonetheless presumed to apply to or obtain for everyone. In this way, aesthetic enjoyment differs from moral satisfaction, which is based on concepts. It also differs from bodily pleasure, which is not presumed to hold for everyone.

JOANNA: So the feeling we get when watching a great match is not like approving a virtuous act. But it is not entirely random either. We all basically agree on what makes a great match. We all enjoy it.

KANT: Or at least we *should* enjoy it, if we are open-minded, impartial, and disinterested. Moreover, a beautiful match viewed for the aesthetic pleasure it gives us lacks a definite purpose for us.[16] We watch just to enjoy it and to have fun, and for no other reason.

JOANNA: So it is one thing to admire a great tennis match, and another to profit from it.

KANT: That's right, though in principle you could do both.

JOANNA: That's true. For example, I also watch to improve my game. I analyze a player's strokes and try to understand the technique better.

KANT: I would say that watching to get something out of it, to improve your game, is different from watching for the beauty, sublimity, or gracefulness of the players or match. Someone who does not play tennis, and so is not trying to improve his game, can still enjoy the gracefulness of a player's movements or feel the sublime power of a serve. Moreover, I can imagine someone analyzing the movements, techniques, and tactics so intellectually that one stops getting aesthetic enjoyment out of it. So analyzing and enjoying seem to be distinct. But I would also add that the two kinds of watching are not mutually exclusive. Many of us do both.

JOANNA: I agree.

KANT: Watching is usually not a matter of functionality or serving purposes, unless you are a coach or television commentator and you are making money or fulfilling some other personal goal. Of course, you can fulfill such goals and still enjoy the beauty of the match. In fact, some of the best commentators and coaches are so effective because they are sensitive to and pay attention to the aesthetic aspects of the game.

JOANNA: You said that everyone should feel that they have to, or must, respond in a certain way to a great match. Are universality and necessity the same thing here?

KANT: Basically. The fan who makes that judgment believes the response to be necessary and to have necessary validity.[17] When we say that the match was spectacular, we think that others should agree with our judgment. We are not just judging for ourselves. We think that we are right, not that it is merely our opinion. And our particular judgment, so long as we are disinterested, may very well be the correct one, given that we share a common psychology and biology as human beings. We have the same kinds of mental powers, understanding, imagination, reason, and so on, even if we have them to various degrees and use them in diverse ways.

COACH TIM: Professor Kant, I am not sure that I see it that way. Not everyone will agree with a particular fan's response. A person in the crowd can't reasonably expect everyone else to agree with him.

KANT: Technically you are right. The necessity feature has to do with a demand or requirement, not an expectation of what others will feel. The person making the judgment requires others to agree but can acknowledge that they might not. But I still think that frequently there is agreement. For example, consider the communal roar, the frenzy of the crowd after a long and exciting point. Almost every spectator applauds, cheers, or reacts in some positive way. That is shared agreement. But whether or not they agree is a distinct issue from the normative demand or requirement *that* they do so.

The Sublime

KEVIN: I would like to go back to a phrase you mentioned earlier, "the sublime." What do you mean by that? *(laughs)* I know of the rock band Sublime, but that's about all. Sorry.

JOANNA: Yes, I remember a teacher using that term—years ago mind you—I was confused a bit then, too.

KANT: Academics still use the word today, though not always in the sense I do. I am referring to a certain kind of experience or feeling, as with beauty. Moreover, the sublime, like experience of the beautiful, has the four features I described earlier: disinterestedness, subjective universality, purposiveness without a purpose, and necessity.

JOANNA: So the experiences of the sublime and beautiful are identical?

KANT: No. The sublime involves an intense emotional response, but beauty is more calm and peaceful, not a rush like the sublime. The sublime evokes a feeling of being small before something that overwhelms you, but you eventually get a stimulating uplift out of the impression of being overwhelmed. To feel the sublime, you must be physically safe, not in actual physical danger.

JOANNA: So you get pumped up. What brings about this response?

KANT: An object or event that is large or powerful, or at least appears to be. It is viewed as if it were infinitely extensive or forceful.[18]

KEVIN: Could you give an example?

KANT: When you say that something gives you a thrill or is breathtaking, awesome, or magnificent, you are employing words that reveal an experience of the sublime. This experience can be brought about by vast waterfalls, erupting volcanoes, a stormy ocean, an exploding supernova, looming mountains, and deep ravines. Or images and pictures of these things. Architectural structures can also evoke the sublime. Think of Saint Peter's Basilica in Rome, which is so large and extensive. Here's another example. Imagine that you are at the base of a range of mountains, say the Alps or the Rockies, and when you look at their peaks you get a feeling of freedom. Now, a mountain is not actually infinite, but if you see it in a particular way and from the right distance, *you* feel as if you were unlimited or infinite, or, in short, free. The sublime is this feeling of exhilaration, admiration, even astonishment.

JOANNA: Earlier you mentioned a sublime serve. I think tennis can be sublime. What do you think?

KANT: Yes, tennis can be beautiful, but not only that. The movements, strokes, shots, and points in tennis can be sublime.[19] When I see Goran Ivanišević or Ivo Karlović or Andy Roddick hit a booming ace, there is something pleasantly overwhelming about it.

KEVIN: But I hate returning serve against guys like that. I don't see their serves as sublime. I am just trying to break their serve.

KANT: I do not mean overwhelming for the player getting aced—I'm sure that is no fun—but for the spectators. For us, it is exhilarating. The pleasure derives from the serve's power. That is why we smile or cheer in response to it. It is awesome in the genuine sense of the word. We are awed by the power.

KEVIN: So you could say that my serve is sublime?

COACH TIM: Don't let what fans are saying go to your head.

KANT: Yes, I think we can admire the sublimity of a serve, as well as its beauty or grace.[20]

JOANNA: (*more excited*) So there might be something to what I'm saying? Your theory can be applied here, Professor Kant. We're physically safe, removed from the danger. We are confronted by power in the serve, and sometimes great size as well—as when the server is tall like Karlović. If we spectators were returning serve we would be "interested" and might even feel physically threatened by such a high-speed ball. And we would definitely lose the game. It would be the death of us, as players at least. We are usually glad we are not there on the court, in the arena. We are happy we are only watching.

KANT: Size or vastness is important here. The sublime has to do with breaking the limits, with the infinite. You could say it is the experience of the infinite before us.

KEVIN: What you say makes me think of breaking another kind of limit—tennis records. For example, Federer has broken Sampras's record of fourteen Grand Slams.

KANT: I see what you mean. Perhaps in a second sense the sublime can be found in the breaking of records, not just in breathtaking strokes and booming serves. But keep in mind that, as a ball game, a tennis match is not measured in things like seconds and kilograms.

COACH TIM: Exactly. Your opponent directly manipulates the ball and changes the outcome of the point.

KANT: The performance depends on the tactics and strategies of the opponent. Tennis is not a typical "record sport," such as weight-lifting, swimming, athletics, or skiing. There are no standardized conditions that are similar for various performances.

COACH TIM: Each tennis match is unique. The wind, the sun, the opponent, and perhaps even the ball brand vary. This makes it hard to compare performances across the board.

JOANNA: That's what I love about tennis. The record sports can sometimes dehumanize. I am not saying that they all do, only that it is a risk with them.[21] Sport can turn into number-counting and number-crunching. Where is the humanity in that?

KANT: Although tennis performances are not measured in seconds, kilos, and the like, there are records in tennis. A player can try to hit the biggest recorded serve ever, or win the most consecutive matches at Wimbledon, or win the U.S. Open the most times. In these cases, the player is testing the limits. Maybe that is part, though probably not all, of what drives some players and keeps fans coming year after year.

JOANNA: Are there other ways tennis is sublime?

KANT: In addition to the powerful strokes and the record-breaking, there is a third place where we can locate the sublime in tennis: a fan's enthusiasm.[22] Think of the observer's enthusiasm as a kind of fascinated exuberance.[23] It appears that when Joanna watches tennis she has an experience of the sublime. Her enjoyment is disinterested—she just wants to see a good match and will applaud great points and shots regardless of who hits them. She thinks that others should agree with her response and feel a similar pleasure if they are in a similar situation. So it is taken to be necessary and universal. Finally, although the movements and displays of power Joanna witnesses are based on the intentions of the players, the rules of the game, and other purposes essential to tennis, her watching is purposeless in that she is watching for the aesthetic pleasure, not personal gain.

COACH TIM: That is an intriguing idea. But it's not what we ordinarily mean by enthusiasm. We usually conceive of the enthusiast or fan as interested, rooting for one player and against the other.

KANT: Yes, I am speaking of a unique kind of experience, disinterested enthusiasm.

JOANNA: We can connect this to what we were saying earlier about disinterestedness. Imagine that you go to the opening rounds of a tournament and see relatively unknown qualifiers. They are slugging it out and hitting huge. There are long points and fast serves. Each player seems to have a deep desire to win. But you don't care about who wins. You don't even know anything about the two players. Even though you are disinterested, you feel a kind of enthusiasm when you see the powerful strokes.

KANT: Good. Here is some more background. In the sixteenth and seventeenth centuries the word "enthusiast" was used to refer to a religious enthusiast. Such a person acted in the name of his religious cause. It was a disparaging term, unlike the enthusiast I am talking about. Today we might call the religious enthusiast a fanatic.[24]

JOANNA: So what is the difference between the two kinds of enthusiasm?

KANT: Religious enthusiasm is like the ordinary, interested enthusiasm to which Coach Tim was referring. The religious enthusiast was interested in that he had a stake in the outcome of the "competition," the religious controversy. These disputes sometimes lead to violence and war, as you know. So the religious enthusiast is, despite some obvious differences, more like a sponsor or even a gambler than a fan who wants to see a good, fair match.[25]

KEVIN: I think I get it. I feel that sort of enthusiasm in the air when I enter a stadium to play a match. I love that feeling. The seats are filled, buzzing with excitement. I walk in and all eyes are on me. There is an instant of silence. Then suddenly everyone cheers and roars. I can feel that everyone is pumped up for the match. They transmit the thrill to me, and we feed off each other.

Cheating and Gamesmanship

JOANNA: If I can change subjects a bit, Professor Kant, I have a question about ethics. You make the concept of interest sound as if it is mainly about money. But personal stake in something can be more than a financial matter. Interest can also have to do with morality. Tennis can be played from good and virtuous motives. An athlete might desire to perfect herself or actualize her athletic potential. She might see her training as a way to cultivate her talents.

KEVIN: Yes, that is how it was for me when I was a kid. I didn't know enough to care about money, actually. And I wasn't old enough to care about being popular with the crowds or with the girls. I played because I was told that I was good, and I trusted the people who told me this. I believed it was wrong to waste my talent.

JOANNA: An interested athlete might play simply because she promised to do so and believes she should be true to her word.

KANT: You both make good points. In both cases, developing talents and promise-keeping, playing the sport would have moral value. The motives or grounds would be morally just. The player's heart would be in the right place.

KEVIN: But now that I am older, I sometimes don't know why I play. It is not always clear to me. Sometimes I think I still play to develop my talents. At other times, I think that I am just deceiving myself and I am just playing for the money, for the sponsors, the public adoration, or even because tennis is all I really know. Or maybe just to please my family or my coach.

COACH TIM: But as long as you go out there and play hard, according to your plan, and hopefully win, why does it matter what is motivating you, whether it is me or the money or the fame or something else? I am not saying that only winning matters. But why does what drives you to improve, whether on or off the court, matter? Some good is coming out of it, after all.

KEVIN: But I can't stand the fact that I don't know why I'm acting. That I may be lying to myself, concealing the fact that I'm mainly after fame or money.

KANT: I understand your sentiments. It can truly be difficult to distinguish the two kinds of motives. This is frustrating. Perhaps only a divine power can know for sure what is driving us and will be the ultimate judge of the morality of our actions and motives.

KEVIN: I've heard it said that sport is good for building character and that this is one reason why—besides incentives like getting exercise—we should play sports. What do you think?

KANT: I would agree to an extent. Tennis may lead to the development of fair play, sportsmanship, and a commitment to excellence. But it all depends on how one plays, of course. In tennis at the club level and even in amateur tournaments, one calls one's own lines, as you know.

JOANNA: We know it's been a while since you called your own lines, Kevin. That's okay.

KANT: This feature gives us amateurs a perfect opportunity to cheat, right? I once heard a person say that if there were a similar convention in baseball, he would cheat whenever he could.

JOANNA: Maybe, but you get used to calling your own lines.

KANT: I agree, but this person was not habituated to the notion. One should learn how to play the game of tennis in an ethical atmosphere, calling one's lines honestly and following the rules. If one plays the game the right way, it can build and develop character. But one has to play honestly for this to work. Otherwise it might actually worsen the player's character by reinforcing immoral behavior.

JOANNA: But isn't calling lines properly just a matter of custom and habit? You implied that morality consists of having the right motives. It seems to me that we call the lines correctly because of custom or habit, not moral reasons. Calling the lines doesn't seem to be either moral or immoral.

KANT: I agree that there is a difference between custom and morality. I believe you can call your lines correctly from moral motives, however. Imagine that it is break point and you are serving. Your first serve goes into the net. You toss in a second serve, and your opponent shanks the return. To your dismay, the mis-hit clips the line for a winner. You see it clearly, but you can't believe your eyes. Your opponent won the point. What might you be tempted to do?

JOANNA: Call it out.

KANT: Right, you are tempted to call the ball out, but you resist. You signal that the ball landed in. You do the right thing, even though you do not want to. Now, that is not just a matter of custom or habit. I would say that your motive was moral. You did the right thing and did not give in. You would have been blameworthy if you had.

JOANNA: I see what you mean.

KANT: Let me add that the player must do it for himself, because he thinks it is the right thing to do. In other words, he must be autonomous. He cannot do it to please others.

KEVIN: So, if a player calls the ball out because he knows his family or coach is watching him and would disapprove if they saw him do it, he is not acting from moral reasons?

KANT: Correct. It is still good that he is doing the right thing, mind you. But his action lacks moral significance because he does not have the right motivation.

JOANNA: I agree with you there.

KEVIN: I have a trickier issue. Is gamesmanship morally wrong? You know, going to the towel for a long time, drying off when you really don't need to. Or tying your shoe before a big point, or yelling at the chair umpire for a minute to distract your opponent. This is not always technically against the rules, unlike calling a ball out that you know was in.

KANT: Difficult question. I would say that whether or not something counts as gamesmanship depends on the situation. Applying the concept of gamesmanship correctly is a factual matter. Going to the towel in one situation might not be an instance of gamesmanship, but doing the same thing in another situation, or with another opponent, could be. Patrick McEnroe tells us that at the U.S. Open years ago he would hit his serve right as a plane flew by. That way his opponent could not hear when he hit the serve. That seems fair to me. Basically, whether or not the act is morally permissible depends on when and how you do it, for how long, in what way, and on your opponent's possible reaction.

KEVIN: Okay.

KANT: The second issue—and this is what you were asking about—is not what counts as gamesmanship, but whether or not gamesmanship is morally acceptable. In my view, it is wrong, even though it is not against the rules. You are seeking an unfair advantage, and you are getting the advantage without relying on your tennis skills.

COACH TIM: But isn't knowing when to go to the towel a tennis skill? That counts just as much as hitting a good forehand. You can't separate the skills from things like the timing, the pacing—the mental aspects. In fact, this is something I am trying to get Kevin to do better, to slow down play sometimes, to speed up at other times. It's very hard to learn and to teach.

KANT: I have nothing against timing and pacing the game to your advantage. I agree that this is part of the player's set of skills. But gamesmanship goes beyond this. Here is an example. If I call an injury timeout when I am not injured and do so right before my opponent has to serve to stay in the match, I would say that goes beyond fair play.

KEVIN: At the 2008 U.S. Open, Roddick accused Novak Djoković of faking injuries and calling too many timeouts. So I guess Roddick would agree with you that this is unfair.

JOANNA: One time my opponent took a bathroom break right before I had to hold serve to stay in the match. Sure enough, she broke me and I lost the match.

KANT: How did you feel?

JOANNA: After I lost, I was angry. She manipulated the situation and unfairly changed the circumstances to her advantage.

COACH TIM: Is it possible that this is because you lost the match? If you had held, you might not have thought that she was pulling a fast one on you. Or even if you thought so, you might not have cared too much. Besides, maybe you are reading too much into her actions. Maybe she simply had drunk too much water.

JOANNA: Well, as Professor Kant suggested earlier, we can't read her heart. I don't know why she acted the way she did. But you are right. Maybe if I had won, I would not have cared so much about her taking a break. It's sort of like the Roddick situation. If Roddick could beat Djoković easily, he might not care so much about the injury timeouts.

Farewells

KEVIN: Thanks for your answer, Professor Kant. I will keep it in mind; I'll try not to change the circumstances when it's not fair to do so.

COACH TIM: That doesn't mean you can't do anything at all, Kevin. There is some truth to what Professor Kant is saying, but let's talk about this some more. I want to make sure you don't lose a competitive advantage here. This is just the kind of thing we have been working on.

KANT: I certainly do not wish to interfere either. I was just telling you my position, since I was asked.

COACH TIM: That's fine. (*to KANT and JOANNA*) It was a pleasure to speak with you. I am sorry that we have to go.

JOANNA: It was an honor to meet both of you.

KEVIN: Likewise. Take care.

KANT: So long, and good luck.

KEVIN and COACH TIM exit.

JOANNA: Well, that sure was interesting, shall we say? I am a bit surprised that they actually philosophized with us.

KANT: (*clears throat*) Well, I am Professor Kant, after all.

Notes

I would like to thank Elisa Schwab Clewis and Maura Morandi for their comments.

1. Similarly, Wertz argues that the artistic value of a tennis match can be in part measured in terms of its historical conditions. See Spencer K. Wertz, "Representation and Expression in Sport and Art," *Journal of the Philosophy of Sport* 12, no. 1 (1985): 8–24.

2. Maureen Linker's chapter in this volume, "The Ridiculous Meets the Radical in the Battle of the Sexes," explores the King/Riggs match.

3. Wertz, "Representation and Expression," mentions King and Budge in this context (17).

4. For a discussion of the aesthetic dimensions of sport, including tennis, and sport's status as an art form, see Hans Ulrich Gumbrecht, *In Praise of Athletic Beauty* (Cambridge: Belknap Press of Harvard University Press, 2006), 45; Peter J. Arnold, "Aesthetic Aspects of Being in Sport: The Performer's Perspective in Contrast to That of the Spectator," *Journal of the Philosophy of Sport* 12, no. 1 (1985): 1–7; David Best, "Sport Is Not Art," *Journal of the Philosophy of Sport* 12, no. 1 (1985): 25–40; Betsy Postow, "Sport, Art, and Gender," *Journal of the Philosophy of Sport* 11, no. 1 (1984): 52–55; and Spencer K. Wertz, "Sport and the Artistic," *Philosophy* 60, no. 233 (1985): 392–93.

5. I agree with Best that we should distinguish the aesthetic qualities of sport from its status as art; see Best, "Sport Is Not Art," 34.

6. See Wertz, "Representation and Expression in Sport and Art," 12.

7. Neil Amdur describes a routine McEnroe victory over Stan Smith as "less artistic," implying that a match can be artistic. Amdur, "Borg Survives Scare: Jaeger Upset by Jaušovec," *Dallas Morning News*, June 28, 1981, B1, cited in Wertz, "Representation and Expression in Sport and Art," 12.

8. For an argument that such sport fakes or feints are representations of the same kind as those that occur in the arts, see Terence J. Roberts, "Sport and Representation: A Response to Wertz and Best," *Journal of the Philosophy of Sport* 13, no. 1 (1986): 89–94.

9. See Best, "Sport Is Not Art," 31–32, 37. I agree that sport is analogous to, but not a kind of, art; see "Sport Is Not Art," 39.

10. See also Cf. Immanuel Kant, *KU* 5:307–20, §§46–50. References to Kant are to the volume: page number of *Kants gesammelte Schriften* (KGS), edited by the German (formerly Royal Prussian) Academy of Sciences, 29 vols. (Berlin: Walter de Gruyter, 1902). "KU" is the abbreviation for *Critique of the Power of Judgment,* or *Kritik der Urteilskraft* (KGS 5) [*Critique of the Power of Judgment,* trans. Paul Guyer and Eric Matthews (Cambridge: Cambridge University Press, 2000)].

11. William James makes a similar point, namely, that without transgressing the rules there are several different ways for the person of genius to succeed. See his *Talks to Teachers on Psychology and to Students on Some of Life's Ideals* (1899; repr., New York: Dover, 1962), 3.

12. For the distinction between "purposive" sports (e.g., tennis) and "aesthetic" sports (e.g., gymnastics) in terms of means and ends, see Best, "Sport Is Not Art," 30.

13. See Brad Gilbert and Steve Jamison, *Winning Ugly: Mental Warfare in Tennis—Lessons from a Master* (New York: Fireside, 1993).

14. See Kant, *KU* 5:203–11, §§1–5.

15. See ibid., 211–19, §§6–9.

16. See ibid., 219–31, §§10–16.

17. See ibid., 236–40, §§18–22.

18. See ibid., 244–80, §§23–30.

19. Unlike me, Gumbrecht rejects the sublime in sport generally, focusing on sport's beauty. For his argument that the sublime should be reserved only for the breathtaking singularity of special sport moments or achievements, see Gumbrecht, *In Praise of Athletic Beauty*, 46–48.

20. Arnold, in "Aesthetic Aspects of Being in Sport," refers to "the cadence of the tennis serve" (5).

21. John M. Hoberman, *Mortal Engines: The Science of Performance and the Dehumanization of Sports* (New York: Free Press, 1992).

22. For Kant's remarks on enthusiasm, see *KU* 5:272 ("General remark on the exposition of aesthetic reflective judgments") and *Der Streit der Fakultäten* 7:85 (KGS 7) [*The Conflict of the Faculties*, trans. Mary Gregor and Robert Anchor, in *Religion and Rational Theology* (Cambridge: Cambridge University Press, 1996)]. On Kantian enthusiasm, see Robert R. Clewis, *The Kantian Sublime and the Revelation of Freedom* (Cambridge: Cambridge University Press, 2009), 169–99.

23. On communal enthusiasm among the spectators, see Gumbrecht, *In Praise of Athletic Beauty*, 206.

24. For religious enthusiasm in the sense of fanaticism, see John Locke's *An Essay Concerning Human Understanding* (1690; repr., New York: Oxford University Press, 1975), bk. 4, chap. 19, 697–706; Third Earl of Shaftesbury [Anthony Ashley Cooper], "A Letter concerning Enthusiasm," *Characteristics of Men, Manners, Opinions, Times* (1711; repr., Cambridge: Cambridge University Press, 1999), 4–28; and *Henry More, Enthusiasmus Triumphatus, Or, a Discourse of the Nature, Causes, Kinds, and Cure, of Enthusiasme* (London, 1656). For an overview of enthusiasm, see Robert Shaver, "Enthusiasm," in *Routledge Encyclopedia of Philosophy*, ed. Edward Craig (London: Routledge, 1998).

25. On a gambler as having something at stake, and thus interested, see Gumbrecht, *In Praise of Athletic Beauty*, 207.

STABBING SELES

Fans and Fair Play

It was chilly. That day in late April 1993 had started off clear and crisp—good weather for playing tennis. But the match had gotten a late start—after 5:00—and now she was feeling chilly as she sat down during a changeover. Nineteen-year-old Monica Seles of Yugoslavia was up against Magdalena Maleeva of Bulgaria in the quarterfinals of the Citizens Cup in Hamburg, Germany. Seles believed entering the tournament would help prepare her for the French Open in June. She had performed well coming into the quarterfinals, but the first set against Maleeva had been tough. Monica fought hard to take it 6–4. Then the second set started off badly, and Monica found herself down 0–3. She dug in and took the next four games, 4–3. She sat down during the sixty-second changeover break. She hoped she could come back and finish Maleeva off in two sets before it got too dark and they suspended the match; otherwise she would have to finish her quarterfinals the next morning and play the semifinal the same afternoon. She didn't want that.

As Monica leaned forward to wipe her face with a towel, she felt a sharp burning pain around her left shoulder blade and let out a howl that filled the stadium. She turned and saw a man in an Arthur Ashe baseball cap holding a nine-inch boning knife dripping with blood, in both hands. As he looked like he might plunge it in her again, Monica got up and stumbled onto the court. She reached behind her and when she drew back her hand it was covered in blood. A spectator reached her first, followed by a tennis trainer and Monica's brother, Zoltan. Security officials subdued the attacker and carted him out of the stands, then turned him over to the German police. Monica was transported to a local hospital, where she was cleaned, examined, and bandaged. The wound was about an inch and a half deep and just a few millimeters from her spine. Had her assailant employed just a tiny bit more strength, her spine would have been severed and she would have been permanently paralyzed.[1]

When Seles's main rival, Steffi Graf, first heard the news, her initial reaction was, "Oh God, I hope it wasn't one of my crazy fans." Sure enough, as the whole world was about to find out, the assailant was Günther Parche, a thirty-eight-year-old obsessed Graf fan who couldn't bear the thought of someone beating her and depriving her of the top spot in tennis:

> I was really upset when Monica Seles won the French Open. In 1991, or 1992 at the latest. . . . I had then definitely decided to injure Monica Seles in such a way that she would no longer be able to play tennis, or at least not for a while. I want to point out here that at no time did I intend to kill her. I did not even want to cause her a serious injury. My only concern was to injure her so that she would not be able to play for a certain time. By doing so I would have helped Steffi become number one again.[2]

Parche's perversely twisted logic is hard to hear, and though it's hardly representative of the vast majority of tennis fans, it's nevertheless instructive. For just as a diabolical literary character, even if real life never features such a person, helps us better see character flaws by embodying them so impeccably, Parche's extremism as a fan, his warped conception of sport and competition, and his scorched-earth mentality all accentuate what's wrong about the attitude in sports that winning no matter what is all that counts. The view is myopic, short-sighted, unethical, and indefensible, and although most milder instances of such a mentality don't result in stabbings, they do find expression in a myriad of other unbecoming and unsportsmanlike behaviors that dishonor and detract from the game. Much of this book focuses on tennis players themselves, professional and amateur, whereas this chapter, while doing some of that, will also direct attention to the fans and their responsibility to understand sport, the true nature and value of athletic competition, and the inner ethic of tennis.

Games and Sports

To grasp what's at stake here, I'll do some analysis into the conditions to be satisfied by games, and then extend the analysis to sports, which will provide a framework for discussing the value of sport in general and tennis in particular. Ludwig Wittgenstein (1889–1951) is famous for noting the difficulty in identifying the necessary and sufficient conditions of games, but Bernard Suits offers a concept of games that works well for present purposes in his *The Grasshopper: Games, Life, and Utopia*. He briefly defines a game as "the voluntary attempt to overcome unnecessary obstacles."[3] He writes that games involve at least four components: goals, means, rules, and a lusory attitude.[4]

Games have goals; they are goal-directed activities. The *lusory goal* is to win the game; if there's not a competition to win, there's no game. The competition might be against another person or perhaps against some established standard. Games also feature *pre-lusory goals:* specific states of affairs needed to win the game. In golf it is hitting the ball into the hole. Hitting the ball over the net is a pre-lusory goal in tennis. These two goals are not reducible to each other; one can achieve the pre-lusory goal and not win the game. For example, one can succeed in hitting the ball over the net simply by smacking it as hard as one can. Achieving the pre-lusory goal is necessary for winning the game, but it is not sufficient for doing so. The definition of the lusory goal, therefore, needs to be qualified: the lusory goal entails winning the game by achieving the pre-lusory goal through a particular means.

Means also come in lusory and pre-lusory forms. The lusory means is the way to win the game, whereas the pre-lusory means involve how to achieve the pre-lusory goals. Smashing the ball over the net as hard as one can may be the most efficient means for attaining the pre-lusory goal, but it is usually not the best way to win the game; this is why in doubles it typically makes more sense to take something off the first serve. What's sacrificed is more than made up for by the advantage that comes from a higher first-serve percentage.

What determines which lusory means are permitted is the third element of sports, namely, rules. Suits distinguishes between *rules of skill* and *constitutive rules*. Rules of skill provide the guidelines for playing well: keep your eye on the ball, extend fully on the serve, et cetera. Constitutive rules set out the conditions that must be met in playing the game. Suits argues that these are proscriptive by nature, making it harder to obtain the pre-lusory goals. They rule out the simplest way of achieving the goal and require a more complex and difficult approach. The constitutive rules of tennis, for example, prohibit a player from hitting the ball as hard as she can, since to remain in play a ball also has to fall within the lines. If no means are ruled out, the game ceases to exist; rules not only make the game difficult, they make it possible.

The fourth element of games is the lusory attitude. There needs to be some account of why a player would use a less efficient or perhaps even the most inefficient means of achieving a goal when he instead could realize it far more easily. "In anything but a game the gratuitous introduction of unnecessary obstacles to the achievement of an end is regarded as a decidedly irrational thing to do, whereas in games it appears to be an absolutely essential thing to do." His point here is a fascinating one; in normal circumstances less efficient means are only employed when more efficient ones are precluded, but in games it isn't so. There one adopts the less efficient means not because he has to but because he wants to—for no other reason than to play the game. So Suits defines playing a game as the "attempt to achieve a specific state of affairs (pre-lusory goal), using only means permitted by rules (lusory means) where the rules prohibit use of more efficient in favor of less efficient means (constitutive rules) and where such rules are accepted because they make such activity possible (lusory attitude)."[5]

Games are supposed to be challenging, and they are. Tennis most certainly is. Some tennis players, like a Chris Evert, might make it look easy, but any tennis player knows how difficult the game can be, contrary to the elitist stigma (or aristocratic virtue, depending on your perspective) attached to tennis in the minds of some as an easy sport or mere leisure activity of the upper echelons of the socioeconomic strata. In point of fact, not to put too fine a point on it, tennis makes one sweat like a pig. Television camouflages the sheer physicality and resulting wetness of tennis, as David Foster Wallace explains:

> Something else you don't get a good sense of on television: tennis is a very sweaty game. On ESPN or whatever, when you see a player walk over to the ballboy after a point and request a towel and quickly wipe off his arm and hand and toss the wet towel back to the (rather luckless) ballboy, lots of the time the towel thing isn't a stall or a meditative pause—it's because sweat is running down the inside of the player's arm in such volume that it's getting all over his hand and making the racket slippery. Especially on the sizzling North American summer junket, players sweat through their shirts early on, and sometimes also their shorts. (Sampras always wears

light-blue shorts that sweat through everyplace but his jockstrap, which looks funny and kind of endearing, like he's an incontinent child—Sampras is surprisingly childlike and cute on the court, in person, in contrast to Agassi, who's about as cute as a Port Authority whore.)[6]

So games feature goals, means, rules, and a lusory attitude, which cumulatively result in their being challenging, some more than others, of course. Tennis is a game, but it's also a sport. Sports are games, but not all games are sports. What are some of the distinctive elements of sports?[7] Well, according to Suits, they're games of skill rather than chance; sports employ specifically physical skills; they are public activities that usually have a wide following; and sports feature a kind of stability. It's the stability of sport that separates it from fads like flagpole sitting or goldfish swallowing. Suits is clear that this is not a question of longevity as much as the institutionalizing of a sport with the development of ancillary activities surrounding it, like coaching, training, research and development, educational clinics, history, the recognition of experts, and a stable body of literature.

Along with those four criteria Suits adopts, I might suggest a fifth: Sports are social activities involving competitive relationships. Such relationships paradigmatically involve individuals or teams, but they might also extend to standards established by individuals or teams in the past. So Roger Federer is not just competing against Rafael Nadal but history, as in his attempt to beat Pete Sampras's record of Slams. In a sense, Federer is involved in a competitive social relationship with Sampras even though Sampras is no longer actively playing on the tour.[8]

As a game and a sport, tennis features both value and its own internal ethic, and these inform every tennis fan as he roots for his favorite players or sits in the stands during a match. We've already gleaned some clues, but let's now see what this value and ethic more specifically look like.

The Value and Internal Morality of Sport

Externalism and *internalism* are two means by which value can be attributed to sports. Externalists say that sports don't have value in themselves; their value lies only in whether they support or reinforce other external values. Tennis is good because it involves exercise, for example, or builds self-esteem. The list of external values is extensive. Internalists, on the other hand, hold that sport has value in and of itself. Without denying that sports have external value, they argue that sport has an internal morality that supplies it with intrinsic value. Sports are a good themselves.

The most common form of internalism is *formalism,* which defines games mainly in terms of their formal structure: their constitutive rules and the goals and obstacles derived from them. Such a view reflects Suits's analysis of games as goal-oriented and rule-directed. The rules determine what counts as a legitimate move in a game and as winning the game. So, for example, one must stand behind the baseline when serving. In formalism, "fair play" is understood as "keeping the rules." One of the best-known normative concepts that flows out of formalism is the *incompatibility thesis,* which says cheaters can't win. To play the game is to keep the constitutive rules, and anyone who isn't doing so isn't playing and thus can't win a game he's not playing, appearances to the contrary notwithstanding.

Robert Simon recognizes the usefulness of formalism but nevertheless suggests that it "lacks the normative resources to address many of the moral problems that arise in connection with sport."[9] One of the notorious problems with rules is that we never have enough of them; invariably some situation arises not covered by the rules, yet still the inner ethic of the game of tennis clearly dictates what to do—such as the oft-cited case of Racketless Josie who, for no fault of her own loses all her rackets and needs to borrow one of her opponent's. There's not a formal rule here, but winning merely by default in such a case seems bad form. Formalism's inability to see as legitimate occasional purposeful and purposive violation of the rules to gain a strategic advantage (like strategic fouling in basketball) is another drawback, as is the question of rule changes. A number of years ago there was considerable debate about the service let rule. Billie Jean King, John McEnroe, and Martina Navratilova advocated eliminating the rule, arguing that lets should be treated the same as net cords during play; Andre Agassi suggested it should be ruled a fault; tennis writer Paul Fein argued that the rule should remain in place unchanged. It's hard to see how formalism can contribute to the debate about the rules when its only appeal is to the rules themselves.

For such reasons, Simon suggests that formalism is too narrow as an internal ethic, and he offers an alternative that he calls "broad internalism." He borrows his conception of broad internalism from Ronald Dworkin's criticism of legal positivism.[10] Dworkin argues that legal positivists hold too narrow a conception of the nature of law, identifying it solely with specific positive laws. He argues that in addition to specific laws there are also legal principles with normative force that judges and lawyers can appeal to in legal reasoning. Similarly, Simon argues that in addition to the constitutive rules of sport there are principles that can function with normative force that players and officials can appeal to in forming judgments when assessing tennis behavior. Such principles arise from the underlying presuppositions that are internal to the sport and supply its value.

Thomas Hurka identifies one presupposition on which to ground the internal value of sports activity: the value of achievement in obtaining a difficult goal.[11] Achieving a goal is itself an intrinsic good; when a tennis player sets out to win, a good obtains in achieving that goal. What determines the value of an achievement is a function of the difficulty of the goal. The harder the goal is to achieve, the more skill and diligence necessary to obtain it and the more intrinsic value the achievement possesses.[12] High value is attached to the achievement of extremely difficult goals requiring great skills, such as winning Wimbledon.

Before cable television and the tennis channel, the Slams were typically televised only from the round of sixteen to the finals, which could easily lend the mistaken impression that winning a Slam involved winning just those rounds. But no step of the process to get to the ultimate goal tends to be a cakewalk, and what makes the ultimate goal of winning a major tournament such an achievement is the whole hierarchy of subgoals that need to be met successfully. This is how David Foster Wallace put it: "The realities of the men's professional tennis tour bear about as much resemblance to the lush finals you see on TV as a slaughterhouse does to a well-presented cut of restaurant sirloin. For every Sampras-Agassi final we watch, there's been a week-long tournament, a pyramidical single-elimination battle among 32, 64, or 128 players, of whom the finalists are the last men standing."[13] Of course his point is that tennis fans are the benefactors of a long and arduous process, largely unseen, the mere culmination of which is the glitzy last match played before the cameras and adoring crowds. Winning that final match derives much of its value from all it took to get there, each step typically exponentially tougher than the last and often played while battling the brutal elements and a quickly approaching state of exhaustion. Tennis is hard; professional tennis insanely hard; coming out on top is nearly impossible; remaining there, among the best in the world, is herculean, requiring talent, commitment, and dedication of which most of us can only dream.

An important aspect of Hurka's conception of value in sports is that it reflects a modern view of the good that places value on the process as well as the end. It is not simply achieving a difficult end that is of value; the process of achieving the end plays a large part too. Aristotle thought any activity only has instrumental value, while its end has the ultimate value. "Where there are ends apart from the actions, it is the nature of the products to be better than the activities," he wrote.[14] But a modern conception of good activities recognizes that how one achieves goals can be as significant in determining value as the achievement itself. This certainly applies to sports.

Hurka—having identified the intrinsic good of difficult achievements—grounds the value of sport in two elements. The first involves the reasonably difficult and complex challenges posed by the rules and pre-lusory goals. Difficulty is what gives tennis its value; it must be difficult, though not unreasonably so. Hurka's second element is the pre-lusory attitude adopted by the players of the sport. Players choose the game because it *is* difficult, and this contributes significantly to its value. Hurka knows players to be animated by a variety of motives, but he hopes that all players would adopt an "amateur" attitude: playing the game for its own sake, which is integrally connected with its difficulty level. He comments,

> The elements that define this type of game playing are internally related: the prelusory goal and constitutive rules together give it a feature, namely, difficulty, and the lusory attitude chooses it because of this feature. More specifically, if difficulty is as such a good, the prelusory goal and rules give it a good-making feature and the lusory attitude chooses it because of that good-making feature. This connects the lusory attitude to an attractive view that has been held by many philosophers, namely that if something is intrinsically good, the positive attitude of loving it for the property that makes it good, that is, desiring, pursuing, and taking pleasure in it for that property is also, and separately, intrinsically good.[15]

To Hurka's two elements, a third must be added: the level of one's competition. Simon agrees: "Because sports are activities involving obstacles that are challenging for us to overcome, their logic commits the competitive athlete to competing against worthy opponents."[16] While we might occasionally desire an easy contest, one in which we blow away our opponent due to his lower skill level, we also recognize that such a contest has little intrinsic worth. The level of our competing opponent is a vital part of evaluating the difficulty of a game. One can have difficult constitutive rules and pre-lusory goals and adopt a lusory attitude, but if one is not playing a worthy opponent, one has not met the difficulty level that gives the game its intrinsic value. Andy Roddick can follow the rules of the game and have an amateur attitude, but if he is playing against an opponent with far inferior skills, such as the author of this chapter, the intrinsic value of winning the match is very low. Good players should, and usually do, want to play good players, and the best to play the best at the top of their form. That is where the value is highest.

Incidentally, adopting a broader internalist view allows one to take such values as difficulty level and the like into account in adjudicating the problems encountered in the narrower formalist ethic that focuses just on the rules. Those aspects contributing positively to achieving the difficult challenges of the game can help formulate principles apart from the constitutive rules. Broad internalism entails that one should let Racketless Josie borrow one of her opponent's; winning a game by forfeit lacks intrinsic value, for it isn't hard at all. Achieving the win is different from, and better than, just being granted it—at least if winning isn't the only important goal, and it isn't. Or consider strategic fouling; a broad internalist might allow it if it promotes the game and adds to its intrinsic value by making it reasonably more difficult.[17] And broad internalism also helps when debating rule changes. If changing a rule reasonably increases its difficulty level, adding to the intrinsic value of achieving a win, then a broad internalist perspective would argue for the change. Navratilova argues, for example, "You have to adjust [to playing let serves]. And the better athlete will adjust to it," whereas others demur, arguing that it would introduce too much luck into the point, thereby reducing the value involved in winning it.[18] Broader internalism supplies the needed resources for a debate like this to take place.

So games and sports are difficult, and they're supposed to be, and if we're right, much of the value of sport generally, and tennis particularly, comes from the challenge it poses. This invites a question: Who made tennis most challenging for Steffi Graf? Monica Seles. And vice versa. Exploding onto the scene in 1989, the grunting, giggling Seles rose to #6 in the world by year's end. From 1990 to mid-1993 she was unstoppable, winning eight Slams, including three French, three Australian, and two U.S. Opens. In 1991 she played in sixteen professional tournaments and made the final in each one, winning ten of them, and in March of that year she replaced Graf to become the youngest #1 in women's tennis history. In 1992 she became the highest paid female athlete in the world, earning 2.6 million dollars.

Her main rival, Steffi Graf, is universally acknowledged as one of the all-time greats. A litany of her achievements would be superfluous. The Seles/Graf matchup was shaping up to be one of the all-time best rivalries, perhaps on a par with Navratilova/Evert; this was tennis at its best, as it was supposed to be played, one of those once-in-a-generation delights for fans, classic matches for the ages, the best against the best, iron sharpening iron, each at the zenith of their game. The stabbing of Seles obviously hurt her, both physically and emotionally; she suffered fear, vulnerability, and depression. But the event also marred tennis, depriving it of one its greatest rivalries. And, perhaps ironically, it hurt Graf's legacy, for, invariably, counterfactual questions arise—for no fault of Graf's—such as: What if Seles had continued her whirlwind of successful matches? In his insane devotion to Graf, Parche did the worst thing he could have done to her as a champion: he deprived her of the chance to prove herself against the best. By making it easier for her, he made her task of proving her greatness harder. By eliminating the competition, he took away her chance to defeat her competition, which did violence not just to Monica but to Graf and her legacy, to tennis and its essential features of quality competition and value-conferring difficulty, and to real tennis fans everywhere who know the value of what was lost.

Fair Play as Respect for the Game

A broad internalist perspective also provides the foundation for a satisfactory concept of fair play, a notion used for evaluating the sportsmanship of individuals participating in a game.[19] In a well-known article,

Robert Butcher and Angela Schneider develop a concept of fair play as "respect for the game."[20] They consider a number of possible concepts of fair play, including "respect for the rules." They reject this as inadequate for the same reasons we rejected formalism as an adequate form of internalism. Respecting rules is one aspect of fair play, but rules by themselves are an "inadequate formulation for capturing some of our intuitions about the idea [of fair play]. For example, we sometimes want fair play to apply to situations within sport but outside of the rules of the sport." They settle on a broader conception of fair play as "respect for the game."

What does it mean to have "respect for the game"? Butcher and Schneider take their starting point from noting that sports fall under Alasdair MacIntyre's notion of a practice as "a coherent and complex form of socially established cooperative human activity through which goods internal to that form of activity are realized in the course of trying to achieve those standards of excellence which are appropriate to, and partially definitive of, that form of activity." To choose to involve oneself in a practice is to agree to adopt its standards of excellence, its rules, and its achievements as one's own: "It is to subject my own attitudes, choices, preferences, and tastes to the standards which currently partially define the practice."[21] Practices have interests, and respecting the game is to take the interests of the game seriously, to honor the game, and to make its interests one's own. This is true even if, and often when, the interests of the game go contrary to one's own desires and preferences. If the game is not going in one's favor, one must still have respect for it, because respecting the game is more important than winning. This applies to accomplished athletes as well as novices.

A number of implications emerge from this concept of fair play. It involves a Kantian-like universal normative perspective on game playing. As Butcher and Schneider comment, "Taking the interests of the game seriously means we ask ourselves whether or not some action we are contemplating would be good for the game concerned, if everyone did it."[22] Such a perspective would involve recognizing universal obligations in not only keeping rules but advancing any actions that would promote the good of the game and prohibiting actions that would harm it. Because it is universal, we can use fair play as a normative standard against the behavior of others.

This transformation of interests also provides an intrinsic motivation for participants to promote fair play. Players are motivated to play a sport for many different reasons, but motivations can be generally classified as *intrinsic* or *extrinsic*. There are a number of extrinsic motivating factors to play a sport: money, fame, glory. To be intrinsically motivated is to play the sport for its own sake: "The substance of intrinsic motivation is the internal goods of the practice."[23] Butcher and Schneider suggest that for an activity to qualify as intrinsically motivated, it must be interesting, challenging, assessable, and freely chosen. The value of intrinsic motivation is evident from studies that show that people who are intrinsically motivated to participate in an activity enjoy it qualitatively more and quantitatively longer than those who are extrinsically motivated.[24] Some have suggested that perhaps the best motivation is one that is both extrinsically and intrinsically motivated, but these same studies have shown that intrinsic motivation often (though not always) tends to decrease when extrinsic motivation is introduced.

While the elements of fair play will differ in details between different activities, five general ideal conditions can be identified for present purposes.[25] First, the players in a game should be evenly matched. Players who respect the game aim at a high level of difficulty—that is where the value of the game lies. The most difficult game will be between opponents whose skill and abilities are closest to each other's. They need not be exactly equivalent, but they should be at least approximately on the same level.

It is not enough that they merely be evenly matched. The second element of fair play is that participants should strive to play at or near their best. Players who respect the game desire to play opponents who are striving to play the best game they possibly can. It is in the interest of the game, and therefore in the interest of the player, that his opponent be playing her best. There is proportionately less value in winning against a player who is not giving her all.

This does not mean that players will not attempt to use tactics that will throw an opponent off his game. This strategy is recognized as appropriately raising the difficulty of the game, thus increasing its value, and so is not a violation of fair play. In the 1989 French Open, Michael Chang was playing Ivan Lendl in the fourth round. Lendl had taken the first two sets, and Chang came back and took the third. In the fourth set,

Chang began to experience serious leg cramps and resorted to extreme tactics to throw off Lendl's game, such as taking all the speed out of the game by playing "moon balls" and even resorting to an underhand serve, a tactic that became legendary. The result was that he won the match and seven days later became the youngest player to win that Open. Chang was not violating the principle of fair play—on the contrary, he demonstrated an acute tactical ability to rescue himself from a tight spot. But the player who abuses medical or bathroom breaks to throw off his opponent's rhythm would be violating the principle of fair play. "Tanking"— purposely not playing one's best—may not be against the constitutive rules of tennis, but it is a violation of fair play in that it does not respect the game.

A third condition of fair play is that the outcome of the match should be determined by the skills of the players, not by other extraneous factors. Of course it is impossible to avoid entirely such things as luck, weather, or other unforeseen complications. But care should be taken to keep such factors at a minimum and to maintain an environment where the game is a test of skill. The difficulty of achievement should come from within and be related to the playing of the game.

A fourth element dictates that the game should be played in accordance with the rules, by players who respect the game and understand and agree with the logic of the incompatibility thesis. To win by cheating is a valueless victory.

The final element of fair play pertains to the treatment of one's opponent. Players who respect the game respect their opponents. They do not view them so much as obstacles or enemies, as necessary components of achieving the lusory goal of winning the game. So one should do what one can to provide an environment in which one's opponent can freely compete. In the case of Racketless Josie, her opponent should lend her a racket if it's needed. Fair play also dictates that a player does not delight in a case where an opponent is not playing his best, but instead regrets that the game is not being played at its highest level. A competitor who honors the game honors his opponent's achievements. It is a sign of fair play when, at the end of a tennis match, opponents reach across the net and shake hands, sometimes even putting their arms around each other. While professionals may not always be socially involved, the sense of fair play as respect for the game also allows one to play hard against one's friends. For while this recognizes the intrinsic goods of game playing, it does not claim that games and wins are the highest good.

Fans and Fair Play

Until now I have applied the principle of fair play to the players in a game. However, the question can be asked: Do the conditions above apply to the fan of the game as well as the players? To answer this, I will address the relationship between fans and the game.

Nicholas Dixon provides a helpful rubric in understanding the motivations of fans. Fans can be divided into two basic categories: *partisan* and *purist*. The partisan fan is "a loyal supporter of a team to which she may have a personal connection or which she may have grown up to support by dint of mere familiarity."[26] The reason for the support is usually the quality of the player or team, but the relationship does not have to be personal. It can be expanded to take into account other factors. For example, a fan might support a team because of regional considerations. The Brooklyn Dodgers were famously supported by an intense fan base of Brooklyn residents who agreed that, while they were "bums," they were "our bums." One of the reasons Günther Parche was a fan of Steffi Graf was that they were both Germans. Sometimes a partisan fan may not have any kind of a relation to a player or team and may "adopt" the player or team simply because of an admiration—because of skills, abilities, or personal characteristics, such as physical appearance.

The purist fan, in contrast, "supports the team that he thinks exemplifies the highest virtues of the game, but his allegiance is flexible."[27] The purist fan will look over the field of players and teams and identify those who embody the highest qualities of the game, searching for the most skillful player with the best style who exhibits all the great qualities of sportsmanship and fair play. He is not tied into any one team or player and does not allow such irrelevant properties as personal relationships or geographical location to determine whom to support. The purist is the "neutral" fan whose desire is simply to see the best team win. Such a fan would adjust his support depending on the current qualities of the players and teams in play.

In light of the discussion above of the intrinsic goods of sport and respect for the highest qualities of the game, one might assume that the purist fan has the moral high ground, since his choice is based on the qualities of the game and not on personal or regional relationships. There is certainly something admirable to be noted here. The purist seems the true "fan of the game," but he is lacking in an important virtue: loyalty. He lacks any real allegiance to a team or player. Many would argue that loyalty is a key ingredient in being a good fan. The partisan is willing to stick with his team even when it is going through difficult times; he has a vested interest in his team and will not abandon it at a time when it may need the most support.

Loyalty should have its limits, though. While one is critical of the radical purist, who changes support at the drop of the hat, radical partisanship has its own set of problems. It can lead to supporting a player who is no longer worthy of that support. If a player is found guilty of illegal or unethical behavior—for example, if he is violent in his treatment of other players or violates the principle of fair play—then it would be time to consider withdrawing one's support. It is no longer virtuous to remain loyal to such a player. Radical partisanship can also lead to rash actions on the part of fans. In the rash actions he took in stabbing Seles, motivated by his crazed loyalty to Steffi Graf, Günther Parche is an excellent example of a radically partisan fan.

The ideal fan is a balance between these two extremes. Dixon refers to such an ideal as the "moderate partisan," who has "the tenacious loyalty of the partisan, tempered by the purist's realization that teams that violate the rules or spirit of the game do not deserve our support."[28] Like the purist, the moderate partisan can recognize the intrinsic good of the game and allow that appreciation to act as a check on his support of a player or a team.

The fan in the moderate partisan position sees the value and importance of maintaining the conditions of fair play. While the conditions would not apply in as active a sense as they might to the player, they nonetheless apply to the fans in terms of their attitudes. The partisan should adopt an attitude of fair play, because he should have respect for the game in the same sense a player would. Respecting the game entails taking the interests of the game as one's own even if they go contrary to or stand in tension with one's partisan interests. While rooting for his favored player or team, the partisan should also admire the skills and achievements of their opponents. Principled partisans want to see their favored players pushed to the limit, surmount the challenge, and rise to the occasion; illegitimate elimination of the competition deprives a player of such a chance to show his greatness. Satisfaction with a win at any cost relies on too provincial a conception of the game and too narrow a conception of the human condition. The principle of fair play provides us with a tool for judging the attitude and actions of fans. For example, one would denounce the fan who rejoices in a bad call that favors his player or who is pleased when some misfortune befalls the opponent—in her biography, Justine Henin is quoted as complaining, and understandably so, about unruly fans who aimed to undermine her game and break her concentration. Such unsportsmanlike actions and attitudes violate the principle of fair play. Such a fan is not a good fan. By loving winning too much, he isn't as big a fan as he could be; just as Augustine realized that to love something excessively or inordinately really amounts to not loving it enough, the way it was meant to be loved and rightly appreciated.

In his rabid partisanship, in his emaciated, myopic, and insipid view of competition, and in his absence of virtue, Parche damaged not only Seles in her body and mind, and not only Graf's legacy and achievements, but tennis itself. He robbed real tennis fans of what was bound to be one of the greatest rivalries ever, a most exquisite showcase of talent in tennis history. He didn't love tennis too much; he loved it too little. But in a thousand lesser ways—from booing good plays to celebrating double faults, from throwing temper tantrums to belittling or undermining true excellence—fans can fail to respect the game: its history, traditions, and inner ethic; their fellow players; and those whom they're watching perform. The question isn't just how different we are from Parche; that's too easy, especially in light of the notorious human psychological penchant for thinking ourselves better than we are. The challenge instead is to ask the extent to which we too are bad fans—and how can we be better ones?

Although Monica Seles never returned to her glory days, she did make a spectacular return, even winning another Slam title, the 1996 Australian Open. Her career record continues to be impressive: fifty-nine singles titles, including nine Slams, 178 weeks as #1, fifth highest in women's tennis. Perhaps, though, *Sports Illustrated* tennis writer John Wertheim commented on her career best when he wrote this after her retirement: "Yet, transformed from champion to tragedienne, Seles became far more popular than she was while winning all those titles. It became impossible to root against her. At first, out of sympathy. Then, because she revealed herself to be so thoroughly thoughtful, graceful, dignified. When she quietly announced her retirement last week at age 34, she exited as perhaps the most adored figure in the sport's history. As happy endings go, one could do worse."[29]

Notes

Many thanks to the philosophy club at Liberty University for a stimulating discussion of an earlier version of this chapter.

1. There are a number of sources for this narrative of Seles's stabbing and overview of her career, among them Monica Seles with Nancy Ann Richardson, *Monica: From Fear to Victory* (New York: HarperCollins, 1996); Bud Collins, *The Bud Collins History of Tennis: An Authoritative Encyclopedia and Record Book* (Washington, DC: New Chapter, 2008); Christopher Clarey, "Monica Seles: A Bubbling Career Pierced with a Knife," *New York Times*, February 15, 2008, http://www.nytimes.com/2008/02/15/sports/15iht-tennis.4.10095298.html; and Bruce Lowitt, "Disturbed Fan Stabs Top-Ranked Seles," *St. Petersburg (Florida) Times Online*, October 7, 1999, http://www.sptimes.com/News/100799/Sports/Disturbed_fan_stabs_t.shtml.

2. "Testimony of the Person Responsible," State Criminal Investigation Department (LKA) 211, Hamburg, April 30, 1993, quoted in Seles with Richardson, *Monica*, 13.

3. Bernard Suits, *The Grasshopper: Games, Life, and Utopia* (Toronto: University of Toronto Press, 1978), 41.

4. Suits derives the term "lusory" from the Latin *ludus*, "game."

5. Suits, *Grasshopper*, 39, 41.

6. David Foster Wallace, "Tennis Player Michael Joyce's Professional Artistry as a Paradigm of Certain Stuff about Choice, Freedom, Limitation, Joy, Grotesquerie, and Human Completeness," in *A Supposedly Funny Thing I'll Never Do Again* (New York: Back Bay, 1997), 225n21.

7. Bernard Suits, "The Elements of Sport," in *Ethics in Sport*, ed. William J. Morgan, 2nd ed. (Champaign, IL: Human Kinetics, 2007). Suits seems to adopt a particularist method in arriving at these essential elements of sport. When one examines what is normally called a sport, these elements emerge as the necessary and sufficient criteria.

8. Some have suggested that competition against one's own record should also be considered an element of sport. While I do not deny the intrinsic value of adopting an attitude of competing against one's self and one's own record, self-competition is not an essential element of sport, whereas competing against others is.

9. Robert L. Simon, "Internalism and Internal Values in Sport," in Morgan, *Ethics in Sport,* 37.

10. Ronald Dworkin, *Taking Rights Seriously* (Cambridge: Harvard University Press, 1977).

11. Thomas Hurka, "Games and the Good," in Morgan, *Ethics in Sport,* 21–33.

12. The relativity of difficulty needs to be taken into account. For some physically disabled persons, just tying sneakers can be extremely difficult and therefore is a goal of great value.

13. Wallace, "Tennis Player Michael Joyce's Professional Artistry," 217.

14. Aristotle, *Nicomachean Ethics,* trans. David Ross (Oxford: Oxford University Press, 1925), 1, ll. 109414–5.

15. Hurka, "Games and the Good," 27.

16. Simon, "Internalism and Internal Values in Sport," 44.

17. For example, in basketball it can be argued that since a foul shot increases the difficulty level, and hence the achievement level of the game, as it involves the exercise of a skill under pressure, awarding it to the opposing team is suitable compensation for a foul and makes the game more interesting.

18. Quoted in Paul Fein, *Tennis Confidential* (Washington, DC: Brassey's, 2002), 204.

19. The concept of sportsmanship is broader than just sports, since its meaning has been analogically extended. A person is now considered a "good sport" totally apart from participation in a particular sport. The term "fair play" will capture the attitude of sportsmanship for our purposes.

20. Robert Butcher and Angela Schneider, "Fair Play as Respect for the Game," *Journal of the Philosophy of Sport* 25, no. 1 (May 1998): 8, 6.

21. Alasdair MacIntyre, *After Virtue: A Study in Moral Theory* (Notre Dame, IN: University of Notre Dame Press, 1981), 175, 177.

22. Butcher and Schneider, "Fair Play as Respect for the Game," 11.

23. Ibid., 14.

24. R. J. Vallerand, Edward Deci, and Robert Ryan, "Intrinsic Motivation in Sport," in *Exercises and Sport Sciences Reviews,* vol. 15, ed. Kent B. Pandolf (New York: Macmillan, 1987), 398–425.

25. This list is adapted from a list by Butcher and Schneider, "Fair Play as Respect for the Game," 15. Although these "ideals" cannot always be exactly met, they are what we should strive for.

26. Nicholas Dixon, "The Ethics of Supporting Teams," *Journal of Applied Philosophy* 18, no. 2 (2001): 151.

27. Ibid.

28. Ibid., 153.

29. Jon Wertheim, "Tennis Mailbag: Saluting Seles," *SportsIllustrated.com,* February 20, 2008, http://sportsillustrated.cnn.com/2008/writers/jon_wertheim/02/20/mailbag/index.html.

Helen Ditouras

THE "KOURNIKOVA PHENOMENON"

No object is so beautiful that, under certain conditions, it will not look ugly.
—Oscar Wilde

Women and tennis, especially at the highest levels of competition, make for awkward dance partners on occasion. Tennis—"boxing without bloodshed," as Bud Collins once put it—makes one sweat, profusely, and today's conditioning regimens result in muscles, big ones. Professional sports, including tennis, sometimes have made women feel a tension between athleticism and femininity. Martina Navratilova and Steffi Graf both lamented the perception of their bodies as muscular, and Chris Evert, early in her career, admitted that she "never felt like an athlete. I was just someone who played tennis matches. I still thought of women athletes as freaks, and I used to hate myself, thinking I must not be a whole woman."[1]

Needless to say, times have changed considerably, and in many ways for the better. Now, femininity is on full display among the ranks of professional tennis players—not to mention a dazzling array of colors and styles and fashions. The young lady who has come to perhaps best epitomize this is Anna Kournikova. Rather than sensing any inconsistency or irremediable tension between sport and sex, athleticism and femininity, she unapologetically celebrated its marketing potential, and opportunities showed up on her radar screen beginning when she was quite young. After Martina Hingis embarrassed her with a double bagel (6–0, 6–0) in the 1994 junior U.S. Open, Anna blurted, "You won, but I'm prettier and more marketable than you." Such comments have, sadly for her, made her name practically become synonymous with style over substance. She has a knack for forgettable one-liners that reinforce the impression: "My breasts are really good because they don't sag. They are firm and perfect." And then there was this gem of a prediction she felt compelled to offer the world in 1998: "Ten years from now it won't be enough that we, as ladies, only play tennis. The public wants to see more. We are the possession of the public. They make us stars and let us earn money. In about ten years every woman will play topless."[2] Although she's perhaps not exactly what early feminists might have hoped for, this much can be said about her: David Foster Wallace was right when he once wrote that "great athletes usually turn out to be stunningly inarticulate about just those qualities and experiences that constitute their fascination."[3]

Perhaps Anna has grown up a bit by now, but in her single-minded and studious focus on cultivating a particular image and exploiting its marketing potential to the hilt, ultimately to the detriment of her game, she practically made her name invoke the specter of superficiality, representing an assignment of primacy to appearance over reality. Who was and is this prognosticating paragon of wisdom? Russian-born tennis star Anna Kournikova's extraordinary rise to success, despite her less than exemplary athletic achievements, has captivated critics and fans alike. Although she initially won crowds over with her outstanding performance as a junior athlete, her eventual decline in the world of tennis hardly tainted her status or popularity. Instead, as a result of the massive media attention, numerous advertising endorsements with Adidas, Charles Schwab, and Lycos (among many others), and her much-reported romance with Latin sensation Enrique Iglesias, Kournikova transformed herself into a high-profile celebrity praised for her alluring sex appeal and coveted beauty.[4] In fact, according to *People* magazine, Kournikova herself has been quoted unabashedly admitting, "I'm beautiful, famous, and gorgeous"—hardly a surprising comment from the tennis star who has been listed among that publication's "50 Most Beautiful People" for several years.[5] Moreover, in 2002, *FHM* magazine also identified Kournikova as one of the "100 Sexiest Women in the World," and in 2004, *Sports Illustrated* featured her as one of the top models in its Swimsuit Edition. Nonetheless, Kournikova's rise to fame has not been met without criticism, and some critics have scoffed at the cultural obsession with the Russian beauty. *San Diego Union-Tribune* sports journalist Tim Sullivan expressed his incredulity in an article where he commented, "She's gorgeous by the standards of professional tennis, which is like saying Tony Danza is a great actor for a guy who should be bagging groceries." In the same article, Sullivan also referred to former cyclist and author Laura Robinson who had similarly shared his views regarding Kournikova's shortcomings in her book *Black Tights: Women, Sport, and Sexuality*. Perhaps getting to the heart of the Kournikova phenomenon, Robinson wrote, "Anna Kournikova will never make it as an athlete because she puts so much time into being a sex fantasy. Good athletes train two to three times a day and have little time for anything else."[6]

If Kournikova's image as a sex symbol and beauty extraordinaire is somewhat contested, how can one explain this widespread phenomenon of Anna mania? For starters, the thriving career of tennis pro Serena Williams is an interesting point of contrast. A media darling herself, Williams is no stranger to publicity and sexual objectification. So what separates these two icons, and more importantly, why is Kournikova revered for her beauty, while Williams, also attractive, and far more successful as a tennis professional, is seldom celebrated for her "beauty" in white mainstream media? Sullivan referred to this disparity in his attempt to describe the "Kournikova phenomenon." While conducting an Internet search on Kournikova and Williams, he found forty-three Kournikova Web sites, including "Adorable Anna Kournikova" and "Anna Kournikova—the Goddess of Tennis" (among other similar titles), but his search for Williams, "the world's top-ranked player—turned up on only ten sites, none of them predicated on her appearance."[7] And why is Serena's sister, Venus, also left out of the "beauty" spotlight?

A Symposium on Beauty

Before examining contemporary standards of beauty, I'll lay a quick foundation by reviewing a few points about beauty made by Plato. Our short excursion will be useful for a few different reasons, not the least that it will serve as a reminder that not all considerations of beauty implicate us in shallowness. Plato, for one (through Socrates), argued in his *Symposium* that erotic love begins with love of particular beautiful objects and people and moves to the love of beauty itself. Eros is the desire for what we don't possess, so the lover remains ultimately unsatisfied.

What liberates us from loving only what we don't have is the transition from loving an instance of beauty—like the lovely form of a particular woman—to what's held in common by all beautiful things, whether specifically sexual or not, the ultimate Form of Beauty itself. What, therefore, might begin in something altogether earthy and animalistic can by turns transmogrify into something sublime and divine. At the culmination of this process, people can make what is good the object of desire, and such goodness can satisfy them and will continue to do so even after they have ascended from particulars to the Form of the Beautiful. Plato in this sense was an upward thinker; recognitions of beauty, he believed, reflected deeper metaphysical realities than might have been imagined—in this sense, his philosophical approach was distinctly antireductionist.

The ability to apprehend beauty and the desire to manifest it is not, on this analysis, a product of superficiality or lack of wisdom. There's something about the experience of beauty, to the contrary, that's potentially transcendent. When David Foster Wallace writes that "tennis is the most beautiful sport there is," his point is not a shallow one.[8] The Medievals thought beauty was one of the great transcendentals, which along with goodness and truth, is an overarching and undergirding bedrock reality of existence. Beauty can satisfy us at very deep levels, and it beckons us to partake in it fully. C. S. Lewis once wrote, "We do not merely want to *see* beauty, though, God knows, even that is bounty enough. We want something else which can hardly be put into words—to be united with the beauty we see, to pass into it, to receive it into ourselves, to bathe in it, to become part of it."[9] Lewis was no reductionist either; rather, he thought of beauty as wholly objective and, cultural varieties of it notwithstanding, something potentially transcultural and transtemporal.

So an elevated view of beauty is possible, but at the same time an emphasis on looks and outer appearance, if it's to the neglect of deeper truths like the content of one's character, constitutes too limited a view of beauty. It neglects the beauty that doesn't invariably disappoint and fade away, the beauty closer to the core of one's essential identity, the reality of who one is underneath temporal external appearances. This corrective, too, though, can be overdone—especially if the body is perceived as essentially bad, as it was for certain Greek thinkers. Other ideological stances, philosophical perspectives, and religious worldviews aren't nearly so harsh and seem considerably more reconciled to the corporeal aspect of our existence. Sports of course are poignant reminders of and occasionally beautiful reconciliations with our bodily natures.

Perhaps the pitfall and potential of our physical selves partially constitute the heart of the ambivalence women athletes in particular feel toward sport. While sweating copiously, they sense a pressure to be pretty that men perhaps can't begin to imagine. They want to be respected for their athletic achievements without sacrificing their femininity. They wish to compete and win, yet not sacrifice their integrity or humanity in the process. If they are thought of as pretty, they'd prefer their whole identity not be tied to that. And if their conditioning has resulted in a muscular frame, they don't want others to use that as an excuse to question their femininity—especially other women peculiarly aware already of such feelings of vulnerability.

And then there's Anna.

"Why We Love Tennis"—Sexual Objectification and Tennis Stardom

Anna Kournikova's rise to fame had plenty to do with her ability to market herself as a sexual commodity. Her appearance in 2004's *Sports Illustrated* Swimsuit Edition and her sexy cameo in Enrique Iglesias's "Escape" video marked Kournikova's crossover from being a tennis star to an emerging sex symbol. Kournikova's highly publicized rise to sexual stardom was especially noted by her famous former coach Nick Bollettieri: "I don't think all the attention she's getting is based on her as a player."[10] Kournikova has come to represent the power of sexual objectification that many young female celebrities attempt to achieve. Some feminist critics have argued that the sexual objectification of women by the media has undermined the achievements these women have worked hard to earn. And in the world of professional sports, where women are already underrepresented, the trivialization of female athletes may prove more damaging, regardless of their current media visibility. Former tennis star Billy Jean King reflects on the social importance of her infamous "Battle of the Sexes" match against male tennis pro Bobby Riggs in her intimate essay "Always on the Cusp." She notes, "The only problem for me is that I think everybody else in the world—Bobby included—had more fun with that match than I did. Men's tennis would not suffer if Bobby lost, so he had nothing to lose."[11] Here, King reveals the stakes for women in tennis prior to the pop glamorization of the profession, à la Kournikova. Feminist critic Jane English notes the challenges women in sports face and the gains that few women have been able to achieve: "The pride and self-respect gained from witnessing a woman athlete who is not only the best woman but the very best athlete is much greater."[12] The battle of the sexes led by tennis pioneers such as Billie Jean King has now been replaced with the battle of the beauties, which has undoubtedly changed the way people think about women in tennis. Having paved the path for other celebrity tennis divas, Kournikova has had to contend with fierce competition from fellow Russian beauty Maria Sharapova, among others. Having already won nineteen career titles, including three of the four Slams, Sharapova has been eager to bask in the celebrity limelight, especially in an attempt to separate herself from the Kournikova phenomenon. Regarding Kournikova, Sharapova has said, "You can't compare us. People seem to forget that Anna isn't in the picture anymore. It's Maria time now."[13]

Kournikova and Sharapova are not the only tennis pros who have profited from sexual objectification. Serena and Venus Williams have also appeared scantily clad in the *Sports Illustrated* swimsuit editions; Serena in 2003 and 2004 and Venus in 2005. Yet Serena's participation in the *Sports Illustrated* spreads seemed tame in comparison to her nude photo in the magazine *Jane*. Although the Williams sisters have been hailed more for their athletic competence than their physical beauty, their recent endorsement from one of North America's leading beauty companies, Avon, has further aligned them with the world of marketing.[14] In fact, Serena Williams made sports history in 2001 with "a five-year endorsement contract with Reebok International for $40 million—the richest such contract for any female athlete."[15]

While some feminist critics would argue that such accomplishments have leveled the playing field for women and men in the professional sports arena, others would say that relying on sexual objectification to further one's career is negligible when looking at its long-term ramifications for women in sports. Philosopher Martha Nussbaum explores the role of objectification in women's lives via commodification and representation. Although Nussbaum regards objectification (to some extent) as "morally problematic," she resists some of the clichéd metaphors verbalized by prominent feminist critic Catherine MacKinnon and adds: "All women live in sexual objectification the way fish live in water— meaning by this (MacKinnon's statement), presumably, not only that objectification surrounds women, but also that they have become such that they derive their very nourishment and sustenance from it." Nussbaum critiques MacKinnon's one-size-fits-all approach to sexual objectification and, instead, explores the differences between the commercialization of sexual objectification and objectification as a "vehicle of autonomy and self-expression for women."[16] To mark this important difference, Nussbaum refers to both *Playboy* and D. H. Lawrence's erotic classic *Lady Chatterley's Lover.* She argues that although both promote sexual objectification, *Playboy*'s crude commercialization and its sexist slant is morally objectionable; whereas Lawrence's text expands the parameters of sexual representation and may lead to autonomous possibilities for female readers.

In her analysis of *Playboy,* Nussbaum discusses three pictures of actress Nicollette Sheridan playing in the Chris Evert Pro-Celebrity Tennis Classic. In a shot of her skirt hiked up, revealing her black underpants, *Playboy*'s caption reads: "Why We Love Tennis." Nussbaum devalues Sheridan's sexual objectification by *Playboy.* She notes, "*Playboy* . . . is a bad influence on men . . . and repeatedly says to its reader, 'Whoever this woman is and whatever she has achieved, for you she is cunt, all her pretensions vanish before your sexual power. For some she is a tennis player—but you, in your mind, can dominate her and turn her into cunt.'"[17] *Playboy*'s objectification of female athletes is alive and well; in fact, twenty-three-year-old Ashley Harkleroad "bared it all" in the August 2008 edition.

In contrast, Nussbaum says of *Lady Chatterley* that the bodies of both Connie and Oliver, the lead characters, are "objectified," in other words, represented as part of the erotic energy and consumption of the novel. Lawrence's recognition of the "inequality" and "dehumanization" of women in Britain provides an important context for the objectification of these specific characters. Moreover, Connie's submission to Oliver in the novel is not indicative of male sexist consumption (as in *Playboy*), but rather part of a consensual, trusting commitment. After several tender moments of personal and sexual disclosure, the two characters fall deeply in love, despite Connie's marriage to Clifford Chatterley, an unsuspecting aristocrat confined to a wheelchair. Nussbaum writes, "Lawrence shows how a kind of sexual objectification—not, certainly, a commercial sort, and one that is profoundly opposed to the commercialization of sex—can be a vehicle of autonomy and self-expression for women, how the very surrender of autonomy in a certain sort of sex act can free energies that can be used to make the self whole and full."[18]

Nussbaum regards the commercialization of sexual objectification, as in *Playboy*, to be unethical and problematic for women and men alike. This is precisely the kind of criticism that feminists have raised regarding young female celebrities such as Kournikova and others who have permitted advertisers and the media to trivialize their numerous accomplishments in favor of a titillating, sexual representation of their physical attributes for the world of consumption. And Kournikova has satisfied this appetite for consumption by posing for such magazines as *Sports Illustrated*, *Cosmopolitan*, and *People*, in contexts that minimally showcase her talent as a world-class athlete.

What's Race Got to Do with It? Tennis at Indian Wells

In an interview with *People*, African American tennis legend Arthur Ashe was asked to comment on AIDS and the obstacles he faced as a result of his contracting the disease. Ashe detailed the cumbersome weight of his diagnosis; however, his description had little to do with his terminal illness. In a revealing moment, he explained, "Race has always been my biggest burden. Having to live as a minority in America. Even now it continues to feel like an extra weight tied around me."[19] Despite the fact that veterans like Ashe and Althea Gibson helped establish the presence of African Americans in tennis, racism still remains a palpable sociological reality in the sport. While stardom has seemed to come easily for Kournikova, the Williams sisters' equally astonishing rise to the top has not been without strife, notwithstanding their numerous accomplishments.

Venus Williams gained notoriety in the 1990s for her aggressive competitiveness and tennis expertise. Hailed as the "ghetto Cinderella," she was raised together with her sister in Compton, an area known for violence and turmoil, during the early 1980s. Her father, Richard Williams, described it as a "city where AK-47s, drugs, PCP, ice and welfare checks are more prevalent than anywhere else in the world."[20] In spite of such obstacles, the Williams sisters have spent the last two decades making tennis history—a prodigious feat for not only women in tennis but black women in particular. In the 1999 U.S. Open, Serena Williams defeated Martina Hingis and became the first African American female to win the championship since Althea Gibson did in 1958. After her victory, Williams genially referred to Gibson's landmark win: "It's really amazing for me to have an opportunity to be compared to a player as great as Althea Gibson. One of her best friends told me she [Gibson] wanted to see another African-American win a Slam before her time is up. I'm so excited I had a chance to accomplish that while she's still alive." In addition, both Williams sisters have helped cultivate black spectatorship in tennis: "With their trademark beads in their cornrowed hair and striking on-court clothes, they have made tennis hip."[21]

In 2001, a small backlash, having little to do with their quick success, emerged against the Williams sisters. New York sportscaster Sid Rosenberg was fired after referring to Venus Williams as an "animal," and saying that "she and sister Serena had a better chance of posing nude for *National Geographic* than *Playboy.*"[22] After apologizing on-air, Rosenberg was rehired by Don Imus, a shock-jock who caused controversy in 2007 when he referred to the Rutgers University women's basketball team as "nappy-headed hos." This comment incited a media storm among sportscasters, sports fans, and the public alike. The Associated Press writer Deepti Hajela analyzed the impact of Imus's comment: "The pain goes back to slavery. Whites saw blacks' natural hair as a negative attribute, a contrast to the European standard of 'ideal' beauty. As a result, even blacks started to look down on their own natural features."[23] Incidentally, the Williams sisters' cornrowed hair generated commentary during the 1998 French Open mixed-doubles match with Venus and Justin Gimelstob playing against Serena and Louis Lobo. Commentators Chris Evert and John McEnroe noticed their distinctive hairstyles during the match, and when asked to comment on them, Evert exclaimed that she was "tired of the beads."[24]

The Williams sisters unexpectedly faced an incident that surpassed the racist sentiments expressed by Rosenberg and Imus. On March 15, 2001, the Williams sisters were scheduled to play in the semifinals at Indian Wells (California). However, when Venus suddenly withdrew from her semifinal only minutes before the match, an angry crowd booed at her. Two days later, when Serena rallied against Belgium's Kim Clijsters at Indian Wells, she suffered the backlash of Venus's withdrawal. The crowd continued to boo Serena throughout the entire match. Moreover, when Venus and her father, Richard, arrived in the stadium to view the match, Richard declared that "a dozen fans in the stands used racial slurs," and that the episode was marked by "evil" on the part of the crowd. In an attempt to contextualize the response at Indian Wells, critic Nancy Spencer examines two important factors: scientific racism, in particular, the "obsession with Black athletic bodies," and "commodity racism."[25]

Spencer notes that the "construction of naturally Black sporting bodies is predicated on 'a common assumption of the innate physicality of the Black body,'" which helps "to explain the cultural fascination with Michael Jordan's physical prowess." Like Jordan, and more recently basketball superstar LeBron James, the Williams sisters have often been noted in the media for their "innate" physical superiority and aggressiveness—a noteworthy contrast to Kournikova's supposed "innate" beauty. Specifically, the sisters have been described as "muscular" with a "raw talent," which, according to Chris Evert, has made it difficult for "women who aren't Amazons" to compete against them.[26] Although as a junior athlete, Kournikova was often admired for her athletic ability, she never obtained the hyper-athletic labels the Williams sisters did. This disparity between their representations—in particular, the aggressive, animal metaphors habitually used to describe the dexterity of the Williams sisters— is an important aspect of the color-casting that has pervaded the representation of the three athletes. Such cultural dynamics as these should give one pause in accepting too quickly a standard of beauty that happens to correspond to what may well on reflection turn out to be more a product of cultural contingencies than a Platonic heaven.

According to Spencer, the second factor, commodity racism "operates to commodify Black culture in much the same way that commodity feminism works through the marketing of commodities to reflect the connection between femininity and feminism" as evident in consumer products such as "*Hanes* hose, *Nike* shoes, and *Esprit,*" where the products themselves come to "stand for, and are made equivalent to feminist goals of independence and professional success."[27]

Spencer recalls the work of literary critic Anne McClintock, whose analysis of mid-nineteenth-century advertising—in particular, the Pears soap campaign—emphasized the racist underpinnings of commodity marketing.[28] The advertisement featured two children, one black and one white; after bathing, each emerges to reveal a "whitened body," implying that the "Pears soap product has transformed the Black child's body." Moreover, McClintock describes the Victorian cult of domesticity that sought to promote domestic products such as Pears soap and others while reinforcing the ideological imperialism of the British Empire. She states, "Victorian advertising took explicit shape around the reinvention of racial difference"; thus, commodity racism "became distinct from scientific racism in 'its capacity to expand beyond the literate, propertied elite through the marketing of commodity spectacle.'"[29]

Whereas the commodity of soap once marked the racial differences between blacks and whites, according to Spencer, the marketing of hip-hop culture has come to define commodity racism for the twenty-first century. Spencer quotes Ernest Cashmore, who explores the commodification of black culture in his text *The Black Culture Industry*; regarding hip hop, he notes, "Any residual menace still lurking in African American practices and pursuits has been domesticated, leaving a Black culture capable of being adapted, refined, mass-produced and marketed. Whites not only appreciate Black culture: they buy it."[30]

Therefore, the success of Michael Jordan is worthy of noting again because his alleged "innate" ability was not the only feature that contributed to his superstardom. The commodification of black culture and, more precisely, black athletes, led to his extraordinary success. Although Tiger Woods has taken the lead in the world of athletic endorsements (at least until recently), the "commodification of Michael Jordan led Nike head Phil Knight to proclaim that Jordan was the 'greatest endorser of the 20th century.'"[31]

Moreover, the enormous popularity of hip-hop culture has also contributed to the dissemination of commodity racism, especially by the marketing of black athletes and other black celebrities. Like Venus, Serena Williams has basked in the hip-hop spotlight as evidenced by her numerous appearances in black magazines such as *Ebony* and *Jet*, and her appearance in both rapper Memphis Bleek's "Do My" video featuring Jay Z and rapper Common's hip-hop video "I Want You" in 2007.

For Spencer, the alleged lack of outstanding female talent in tennis in the early 1990s and the rise of hip-hop helped foster the necessary conditions for lucrative commodity racism. Although Venus's $40 million contract with Reebok and Serena's $12 million deal with Puma seemed groundbreaking for women in tennis, when analyzed via the discourse of commodity racism, the depiction of these accomplishments warrants scrutiny. Spencer illustrates this best in her citation of Martina Hingis's allegation that the "Williams sisters receive more endorsements because of their race." In response to this, Spencer writes that "this logic obscures the reality that people of color have historically been excluded from tennis and that White racism continues to operate in the new millennium" as demonstrated by the Indian Wells incident.[32] Hingis's comment obscures also the reality that *each* Williams sister accomplished far more on the court than Hingis ever did!

Who's the Fairest of Them All? "Beauty and the Beast of Whiteness"

I would like to return to my earlier supposition that the media's fascination with Kournikova and her beauty deserves further analysis—especially the way this is symbolic of a "Western aesthetic of beauty."[33] I have investigated the Kournikova phenomenon via the role that the media plays in sexually objectifying young, attractive female athletes such as Kournikova and the Williams sisters. I have also underscored the racial dynamics at work in the representation of both Williams sisters and the challenges they have encountered in their remarkable rise to the top in comparison to Kournikova, whose decline in the world of tennis did little to stifle her fame and notoriety.[34]

In exploring the historical connection between racism and beauty, Ama Oforiwaa Aduonum describes the damaging effects of representation on black women: "The black woman's dark skin and curly hair are directly opposed to the Western aesthetic of beauty. . . . She must have light skin and long hair, traits that continue to define a female as beautiful and desirable in the white imagination." Aduonum further explains, "Hair, and lots of it, is required both for beauty and visibility—a black woman with straight or wavy hair is considered more attractive than a woman of the same color whose hair is tightly coiled, nappy, or kinky."[35]

Her reference to hair and beauty is interesting, especially in light of the fact that the Williams sisters' trademark hairstyles have received much media attention, exemplified, for example, by a "Got Milk" ad that featured them side-by-side with their beaded braids. In an analysis of the ad, critic Donna Daniels notes, "This time the beads are white, a nice contrast to their black outfits and skin."[36] Daniels's admiration of the Williams sisters and their signature hairstyles is significant, considering that black women's hair has historically been devalued. Feminist critic bell hooks celebrates the unique beauty of black hair in her children's book *Happy to Be Nappy* in an effort to subvert the dichotomous representation of black women's hair.[37]

Although minority women and women of color have recently carved a niche in the beauty spotlight, their increasing media visibility has depended upon their conformity to white, mainstream archetypes of beauty. Jennifer Lopez, for example, first appeared as a dancer on *In Living Color*. In her early years, she wore her dark, curly hair short and cropped; she also appeared at least twenty pounds heavier than she did in later media appearances. Lopez's almost overnight makeover occurred after her success in the biopic *Selena* (1997). Upon the release of her 1999 debut album *On the 6*, a thinner, blond-highlighted and straight-haired Lopez captivated American audiences. The media frenzy that followed Lopez even surpassed the phenomenon of Kournikova, and Lopez's ethnic roots came to define her alluring appeal rather than detract from it. Despite Hollywood's growing fascination with ethnicity, Lopez had previously remained relatively invisible prior to her post–*In Living Color* makeover.

The media fascination with exotic, ethnic-looking women has not necessarily worked to the advantage of African American women, however. The "fairest of them all"—in other words, lighter-skinned women —have ranked second highest in the media's color-hierarchy of representation, whereas darker-skinned women, like Venus Williams, have ranked on the lower end. Of the sisters, Serena has been noted more for her sex appeal and beauty (as evidenced by her nude photo in *Jane*) than her darker-skinned sister, who has been praised more for her athletic ability. However, the Williamses have very similar muscular physiques and physically differ markedly only in skin tone. In any case, historically, light-skinned African American women have been coveted for their exotic beauty and have been the subject of literary and cinematic discourses.

Yet, with their exceptional beauty came, in the phrase used by Arthur Ashe, "the burden of race." According to Dr. David Pilgrim, the myth of the tragic mulatto—who suffered a sad fate because of her mixed-blood heritage, the offspring of a black mother and a white slave master—is represented at least as long ago as the 1840s, as shown in the short stories of Lydia Maria Child. "The Quadroons" (1842) and "Slavery's Pleasant Homes" (1843) each featured a female character whose real tragedy was that because she was unaware of her mother's race, she believed herself to be white and, therefore, free. According to Pilgrim, Rosalie's "heart was pure, her manners impeccable, her language polished, and her face beautiful. Her father died; her 'negro blood' discovered, she was remanded to slavery, deserted by her White lover, and died a victim of slavery and White male violence."[38]

In her essay "Beauty and the Beast of Whiteness: Teaching Race and Gender," Kim Hall examines a series of Renaissance texts in an attempt to deconstruct whiteness in relation to beauty, race, and morality.[39] Hall examines the world of Elizabethan England and the symbolic importance behind the representation of whiteness. She also examines Hollywood's role as arbiter of morality via cinematography. According to Hall, film critic Richard Dyer notes how "lighting works to associate certain film stars with whiteness in a way that marks them as morally and aesthetically superior."[40] This is especially evident in Hollywood's film noir, whose narratives of violence, corruption, and transgressive sexuality are all linked to the "blackness" of the film's antiheroes and duplicitous femme fatales.[41] Although films such as John Huston's The Maltese Falcon (1941) and Billy Wilder's Double Indemnity (1944) featured mainly white protagonists, the dichotomy of black and white was emphasized through the amoral actions of the characters in question. Several film critics, including Eric Lott, Manthia Diawara, and philosopher Dan Flory, have examined the role of race/racism in both classical film noir and postmodern noir. Flory's recent text Philosophy, Black Film, Film Noir traces the moral terrain of film noir in relation to critical race theory. According to a publisher's review, Flory's work "illuminates the ways in which categories of race have defined and continue to direct much of our vision of the moral self and what counts as appropriate moral sensibility."[42] Alongside cinema, the Renaissance literary canon has perpetuated a "Western value system that equates skin color with moral qualities."[43]

It is painfully evident that literature and cinema have each played a role in constructing a moral hierarchy on the basis of race and representation. The discourse of beauty in relation to Anna Kournikova, for example, must consequently be examined in light of its history: Kournikova has received an extraordinary amount of media adoration despite her decline as a tennis star, and subsequently, the focus on her looks is largely a function of a socially constructed picture of beauty that privileges whiteness. The backlash over Serena Williams's nude photo in *Jane*, further instantiated by the racist remarks on the popular blog *Whudat*, confirms that, in some ways, racist standards of beauty persist and hold sway—despite the inclusion of women of color in the representational spectrum and the partial step forward such inclusion represents.

Backshots and Backlashes: Serena Williams in *Jane*

"With a pair of silver Moschino pumps and flowers keeping it mysterious, Serena Williams struck a sexy little backshot," reads the caption directly above Williams's nude photo from *Jane* in *Whudat*, a popular hip-hop news and entertainment blog. *Jane*'s July 2007 issue featured seminude photos of Serena Williams, Eva Mendes, and Joss Stone, among others, and quickly captured the attention of the media.[44] Shortly after the release of *Jane*'s July issue, smaller online publications featured her nude photo, including *Whudat* and *Women's Tennis Blog*, which featured an article entitled "Serena Williams Poses Nude for *Jane* Magazine + Hits Hollywood Party Scene."[45] While the tennis blog briefly discussed the photo and recent whereabouts of Williams, the commentary that followed in *Whudat* upon the release of the photo was startlingly different. Although a few bloggers commended Williams for her sexy photo, others launched a racist attack comparing Williams, at best, to male athlete Barry Bonds, and, at worst, to an ape. On the positive side, one blogger stated, "You are proof that we as black women are absolutely beautiful and perfectly made, contrary to popular belief," validating Williams as a strong, attractive role model for African American women. On the negative side, blogger comments included "I don't care for *National Geographic* photography. I think this Bantu has a hormone problem." Sadly, there were a plethora of such condescending and demeaning remarks that relied upon grotesque racial stereotypes which we will not repeat. Moreover, in reference to Serena's alleged lack of attractiveness, one blogger stated, "Kournikova had a beautiful face, nice slim/toned body with playboy curves."[46] Again, what is interesting to note is not only the contrast between Anna Kournikova and Serena Williams, but the evocation of "beauty" to describe the blond tennis star. While the earlier African American blogger clearly alluded to Serena's beauty, she was sure to mention that her assertion was "contrary to popular belief," potentially reflecting mainstream media's repeated failure to recognize the diversity of African American women's beauty.

That last comment helps encapsulate the argument of this chapter: A color caste system exists in the world of mainstream media, and Kournikova (among several other white female celebrities) has reaped the benefits of it. In fact, in an attempt to contrast herself with the Williams sisters, Kournikova remarked: "I'm not Venus Williams. I'm not Serena Williams. I'm feminine. I don't want to look like they do. I'm not masculine like they are."[47] So, the claim that the Kournikova phenomenon exists solely because of Kournikova's undeniable beauty is somewhat erroneous. Rather, when pitted against that of fellow female tennis pros Venus and Serena Williams, two attractive stars who have also enjoyed the media spotlight but have repeatedly encountered the barriers of racism, Kournikova's stardom warrants further exploration.

The Kournikova phenomenon has become tantamount to the way our culture relishes mistaking appearance for reality; in truth, it's players like the Williams sisters whom tennis historians will remember, and the much less substantive, self-professed "marketable" Kournikova who will be largely forgotten, except as a case study in vacuity and superficiality.

Notes

1. Paul Fein, *You Can Quote Me on That* (Washington, DC: Potomac, 2005), 81.
2. Ibid., 254, 81.
3. David Foster Wallace, "How Tracy Austin Broke My Heart," in *Consider the Lobster* (New York: Back Bay, 2006), 152.
4. Kournikova was ranked #1 as a doubles player between 1992 and 2002 and subsequently won Grand Slam titles in Australia alongside Martina Hingis.
5. "The 50 Most Beautiful People in the World 1998," *People*, May 11, 1998, 121. Kournikova has appeared in *People*'s 1998, 2000, 2002, and 2003 "50 Most Beautiful People" issues.

6. Tim Sullivan, "Beauty Is as Beauty Does, and Anna K. Doesn't," *San Diego Union Tribune*, July 30, 2002, http://www.signonsandiego.com/sports/sullivan /20020730-9.

7. Ibid.

8. Wallace writes, "I submit that tennis is the most beautiful sport there is, and also the most demanding. It requires body control, hand-eye coordination, quickness, flat-out speed, endurance, and that strange mix of caution and abandon we call courage." See his "Tennis Player Michael Joyce's Professional Artistry as a Paradigm of Certain Stuff about Choice, Freedom, Limitation, Joy, Grotesquerie, and Human Completeness," in *A Supposedly Fun Thing I'll Never Do Again* (New York: Back Bay, 1997), 235.

9. C. S. Lewis, *The Weight of Glory* (New York: Macmillan, 1980), 17.

10. "The 50 Most Beautiful People in the World 1998."

11. Billie Jean King, "Always on the Cusp," in *The Right Set: A Tennis Anthology*, ed. Caryl Phillips (New York: Vintage, 1999), 174.

12. Jane English, "Sex Equality in Sports," *Philosophy and Public Affairs* 7, no. 3 (1978): 275.

13. Quoted in L. Jon Wertheim, "From Russia with Smarts," *Sports Illustrated*, July 5, 2004, http://sportsillustrated.cnn.com/vault/article/magazine/MAG1032396/ index.htm.

14. Stephanie Thompson, "Avon Targets Black Sales Reps," *Advertising Age* 74, no. 35 (2003): 16.

15. "Venus Williams Signs Richest Endorsement Contract Ever for Female Athlete," *Jet*, January 8, 2001, 51.

16. Martha Nussbaum, "Objectification," *Philosophy and Public Affairs* 24, no. 4 (1995): 251, 277. In this essay, Nussbaum explores objectification from a philosophical standpoint and examines both popular culture and literature as arbiters of objectification. However, she is careful to note that "under other specifications, objectification has features that may be either good or bad, depending on the overall context" and that some facets of objectification may be "either necessary or wonderful features of sexual life" (251). MacKinnon quoted in Nussbaum, "Objectification," 250.

17. Nussbaum, "Objectification," 253, 285. The photographs of Nicollette Sheridan were showcased in the April 1995 issue of *Playboy*.

18. Ibid., 277.

19. Arthur Ashe, "The Burden of Race," in Phillips, *Right Set*, 156.

20. David Higdon, "Venus: The Great Experiment," in Phillips, *Right Set*, 147.

21. "Serena Williams Wins at U.S. Open: First Black Female Champion since 1958," *Jet*, September 27, 1999, 51–56.

22. "Fired White Sportscaster Apologizes for Remarks about Venus and Serena Williams; Gets Rehired," *Jet*, July 9, 2001, 32.

23. Deepti Hajela, "Don Imus' 'Nappy' Remark Has Long, Hurtful History in Describing African-American Hair," Associated Press, April 12, 2007, http://www. signonsandiego.com/news/nation/20070412-1500-nappyhair.html.

24. Nancy Spencer, "Sister Act VI: Venus and Serena Williams at Indian Wells: 'Sincere Fictions' and White Racism," *Journal of Sport and Social Issues* 28, no. 2 (2004): 115–32.

25. Ibid., 116, 120, 123.

26. Ibid., 120, 121.

27. Ibid., 123.

28. Anne McClintock, "Soft-Soaping Empire: Commodity Racism and Imperial Advertising," in *Visual Culture Reader*, ed. Nicholas Mirzoeff (London: Routledge, 1998), 304–16.

29. Spencer, "Sister Act VI," 123.

30. Ibid., 124.

31. Ibid., 126.

32. Ibid., 128.

33. Ama Oforiwaa Aduonum, "*Buwumu*: Redefining Black Beauty and Emancipating the *Hottentot Venus* in the Work of Oforiwaa Aduonum," *Women's Studies* 33, no. 3 (2004): 280.

34. The subtitle of this section of the essay is drawn from Kim Hall's essay "Beauty and the Beast of Whiteness: Teaching Race and Gender," *Shakespeare Quarterly* 47, no. 4 (1996): 461–75.

35. Aduonum, "*Buwumu*," 280, 281.

36. Daniels quoted in Spencer, "Sister Act VI," 122.

37. bell hooks, *Happy to Be Nappy* (New York: Hyperion, 1999).

38. David Pilgrim, "The Tragic Mulatto Myth," *Jim Crow Museum of Racist Memorabilia* (November 2000), http://www.ferris.edu/jimcrow/mulatto/.

39. Hall examines Elizabeth Cary's *Tragedy of Mariam*, Shakespeare's *Othello*, and Aphra Behn's *Oroonoko*.

40. Dyer quoted in Hall's "Beauty and the Beast of Whiteness,"466.

41. For an interesting discussion on film noir, race, and morality, see Eric Lott's "The Whiteness of Film Noir," *American Literary History* 9, no. 3 (1997): 542–66.

42. Dan Flory, *Philosophy, Black Film, Film Noir* (University Park: Penn State University Press, 2008).

43. Hall, "Beauty and the Beast of Whiteness," 470.

44. "Serena Williams Takes It Off in *Jane* Magazine," *Whudat*, July 21, 2007, http://www.whudat.com/newsblurbs/more/serena_williams_takes_it_off_in_jane_magazine_1680721071/.

45. "Serena Williams Poses Nude for *Jane* Magazine + Hits Hollywood Party Scene," *Women's Tennis Blog*, July 24, 2007, http://www.womenstennisblog.com/2007/07/24/serena-williams-poses-nude-for-jane-magazine-hits-hollywood-party-scene.

46. "Serena Williams Takes It Off."

47. Paul Fein, *Tennis Confidential: Today's Greatest Players, Matches, and Controversies* (Washington, DC: Brassey's, 2002).

Mark R. Huston

LOSING BEAUTIFULLY

In his book *Winning Ugly,* Brad Gilbert tells a story of playing McEnroe in the Masters at Madison Square Garden. Upon losing the match, McEnroe announced in a press conference that he was "retiring." His professed reason: "When I start losing to players like him . . . I've got to reconsider what I'm doing even playing this game."[1] Apparently it was the *ugliness* of Gilbert's game that drove McEnroe to such an extreme pronouncement. Gilbert, however, was pleased as punch, wearing the "ugliness" of his win as a badge of honor.

The way I see it, if one can win ugly then surely it is possible to *lose beautifully.* These concepts—ugliness, beauty—are aesthetic ones. In the following I will explicate various aesthetic concepts, with a particular emphasis on Plato's understanding of art as craft, to gain a clearer understanding of how aesthetics relates to tennis. Unfortunately, though, to do this well there are times when this chapter gets a bit philosophically technical. Therefore, as an aid to reading, I will quickly outline it to highlight the technical areas so that you, as the reader, may skip to the sections that are of greater interest if time or inclination prohibits reading the entire piece.

I start by briefly discussing how various aesthetic concepts are sometimes applied to sports, and I soon thereafter move to a discussion of Plato's use of *techne* to give a philosophically historical basis for aesthetic appreciation of sports. Starting with the section "Aesthetics and Tennis," the chapter shifts to more recent discussions of aesthetics with an eye toward the importance of the concept of "winning" in relation to sports.

It is the following couple of sections, "Diagnosis Part 1" and "Diagnosis Part 2," where things get a bit philosophically technical. So, here is the warning: anyone who enjoyed the previous sections and desires a more in-depth discussion of aesthetics, will probably enjoy these as well; however, I recommend that readers who are at that point starting to get a bit glassy-eyed and are beginning to wonder where the tennis went skip to the section titled "Can an Ugly Win Be Beautiful?" From that point until the end of the chapter I devote much more attention specifically to tennis and how one can apply aesthetic judgments of beauty and ugliness (with a key distinction between physical and psychological ugliness) to the sport.

Aesthetics and Art

Notice the difference between the mild claim that a particular point was "nicely" played or a "good" point and the exhortation that tennis is "beautiful" or a particular player has an "ugly" game. David Foster Wallace goes so far as to say that "tennis is the most beautiful sport there is."[2] Judging something to be beautiful is an invitation for others to share the judgment, and so it goes beyond mere respect or enjoyment as expressed by "nice shot"; a point that is most obvious in relation to art judgments. If one judges a painting, sculpture, or a dance performance as beautiful, then there is an implication or expectation that others will share the verdict. However, it is always possible that others will disagree, which is why we bother to have aesthetic discussions at all; for when disagreement occurs there is a further expectation of a rational defense of the judgment in question—a defense, by the way, that is not requested for mere judgments of taste such as "I like strawberry ice cream better than vanilla." None of these points are new, but they are worth restating to show the difficulty in relating aesthetic concepts and judgments to the world of tennis.[3]

Given that aesthetic discussions usually relate to accepted fields of art, a further question to ask is whether tennis is an art at all. This discussion can take place on several different levels, one of which is whether or not sports in general should be considered art. In other words, one can debate whether the concept *art* should be (or possibly already is) expanded to include the concept *sport*. Another level is that of defending the art status of a particular sport, which C. L. R. James famously did for cricket. He argued that cricket blends dramatic spectacle, the relation between event and design, and visually beautiful elements to such a high degree that it cannot be denied the status of art.[4] While I will primarily focus on aesthetic concepts and judgments such as "beauty," I will also examine issues related to understanding art in general when needed.

Typically, discussions of aesthetics and beauty in sports relate to one of two areas: (1) the sport in general or (2) a particular player.[5] Yet when thinking about tennis and just how complicated the discussion can become, it is well worth noting some of the other areas to which a judgment of tennis beauty (or ugliness) may apply. Some of the obvious areas include tennis in general; a particular player's game/strokes/career, such as that of Rod Laver or Roger Federer; plus the sheer physical beauty of players such as Rafael Nadal or Anna Kournikova. However there are other, less obvious, areas. For example, a particular shot might be judged beautiful, either specifically or generally—Sampras's second-serve ace, after getting sick on court, to go up 8–7 in a fifth set tie-breaker against Alex Corretja (which Corretja then lost, in an ugly way, by double-faulting) or McEnroe's serve generally. An individual game, set, or match may be judged as aesthetically excellent, but note that context does play a role. The famous Borg-McEnroe 1980 Wimbledon final is one of the most beautiful matches of all time, and the fourth-set tiebreaker is one of the most beautiful individual tiebreakers of all time. Rivalries, such as Borg-McEnroe and even more so Evert-Navratilova, can also be judged as beautiful. Players, in fact, clearly understand this, which is why McEnroe was so upset when Borg retired at the age of twenty-six. While this is only a partial list, it serves to highlight the difficulties that arise when one attempts to understand the aesthetic dimensions of tennis.

Art as Craft (*Techne*)

As in most of western philosophy, discussions of art and beauty trace back to the Greeks—Plato and Aristotle in particular. Plato famously excised art from the ideal society of the Republic for metaphysical, epistemological, and psychological reasons. It would take us too far afield to go into all of the details, but some of Plato's distinctions are helpful when thinking about tennis and art. The Greek term *techne* is often translated as "craft" but also as "true art."[6] I will use the word "craft" from now on, but no matter how it's translated, it is generally understood that craft is the *general* art category, with (what we would now call) the "fine arts" as a subcategory. It is the fine arts—poetry and tragedy in particular—that get rejected from the Republic.[7] Crafts (or true art) are grounded in knowledge in a way that the fine arts are not.[8] Plato includes in the arts, in the sense of crafts, everything from practicing medicine to being a cobbler; in this sense it is clear that sports would fall into the general category of art, and so aesthetic judgments of sports are appropriate.

To emphasize Plato's point, I will highlight one of his discussions from Book 10 of the *Republic*. Book 10 contains Plato's most sustained attack on many of the fine arts, but in contrast he praises others. In the course of clarifying his various points, he relates a tripartite distinction for art creation into the "user's art, the maker's, and the imitator's."[9] It is the user who has knowledge and the maker who has true or justified belief, while the imitator has neither. The imitator would be, say, one who paints pictures or creates poems that represent the user of whatever it is under consideration. In horsemanship, by way of example, the horseman would be the user, the cobbler would be the maker (of reins, etc.), and the one who paints a picture of the horseman would be the imitator who has neither knowledge nor true or justified belief about the accoutrements of horsemanship.

Another way of putting this is that Plato seemed to think that everything has an expert, and the experts are those that can best use whatever is under consideration. In my own philosophy of art class, I have often presented an example from tennis in order to illustrate Plato's point. In the 1980s, when Connors finally decided to switch from his trusty T2000 aluminum racket to graphite, he was consulted by Wilson in the design of the Wilson ProStaff racket.[10] So, using Plato's model, Wilson is the maker with justified beliefs based on consultation with the user-expert Connors, who has knowledge of tennis and its gear. Those who take photographs or write stories about Connors would be on the lowest rung, as imitators. As far as Plato was concerned (and probably Connors as well, given his disputes with the press) the imitators only serve to take people away from understanding. The apparent moral is that one should avoid being an imitator and instead strive to be a user or at least a maker—in other words, take Plato's "advice" and go actually play some tennis.

Aesthetics and Tennis

If Plato gives us at least some grounding for considering tennis an art, there is still the general issue of just how to think about aesthetic evaluation in relation to tennis.[11] Kendall Walton discusses aesthetic value at length in a relatively recent article in which he also parallels aesthetic value and judgments in the arts with various values in other areas, such as the value of winning in sports.[12] I will use his article as a jumping-off point and means of contrast for much of the remainder of this chapter.

Making any clear sense of aesthetic value and beauty in art is an incredibly difficult process due to the wide range and long history of the concepts *aesthetic* and *beauty.* Given that an accepted work of art may be described as wonderful, marvelous, tragic, shocking, and so on, it is no surprise that Walton claims "'aesthetic value' appears to be an incredible grab bag."[13] This is not to mention the problematic assumption that aesthetic judgments are purely subjective ("beauty is in the eye of the beholder"), which, if true, makes it virtually impossible to discuss aesthetic value at all. Again, going back to Plato through Hume, Kant, Tolstoy, Clive Bell, and many others, we find recurring recognition that aesthetic judgments at least invite a discourse in a way that purely subjective matters of taste do not.

Walton skirts this problem by highlighting the institutional nature of art and art's correlative concepts. George Dickie has long trumpeted the institutional aspect of the art world, even going so far as to use it to define art.[14] While Walton does not assume Dickie's definition of art, he does point out that "aesthetic value is *institutional-bound,*" which moves aesthetic judgments outside of the purely subjective without assuming such judgments to be completely objective—just like in many other institutions certain judgments make sense within the institutional setting in a way that they may not outside of the setting.[15] For example, the pity and fear evoked by a tragic artwork, such as *Hamlet,* can be used to praise the artwork, while in real life the pity and fear evoked by tragedy are never used as points of praise or admiration.

Another point Walton emphasizes is that while the institution itself may be evaluated for its benefit to individuals and society (an extrinsic value), aesthetic judgments are intrinsic. In other words, if a work is judged as aesthetically valuable, then it is judged as good in itself. This point is often somewhat confusing because it seems clear that when one judges a work as having positive aesthetic value, such as "beautiful," it is because the work brings *pleasure* to the viewer, a seemingly extrinsic value. Often the attempt to remedy this problem devolves into near circularity because aesthetic pleasure is so commonly considered synonymous with aesthetic value. The early twentieth-century theorist Clive Bell tried to clarify things by referring to the *aesthetic emotion,* an emotion caused exclusively in relation to artworks.[16] According to Bell, the aesthetic emotion is completely independent from other emotions and worldly concerns. In this sense, the aesthetic judgment, as representing the pleasure of the aesthetic emotion, would still be intrinsically valuable because of its being sealed off from the world and relating only to art.

Another way of thinking about this issue is often expressed as the idea that judgments of beauty are disinterested; Kant thought of art beauty judgments in this manner.[17] Here one should not confuse disinterest with uninterest, which merely means lack of interest. Disinterest can be thought of as impartiality: a judge in a court case can be interested in what happens in the case but should be disinterested as to the guilt of the accused. Judgments of beauty are often understood to be disinterested, in that there is no desire tied to the object, such as any desire to possess the object. Bell did not even use the term "beauty," because he thought its meaning was too intimately tied to sexual desire. I am not necessarily endorsing any of these accounts, but only attempting to clarify how it is possible to take aesthetic pleasure in an object while maintaining that aesthetic value is intrinsic.

Walton defines aesthetic value and pleasure in terms of admiration: "aesthetic pleasure is not just pleasure taken in *my* admiration of something, but in *its* getting me to admire it." He adds that for admiration to be truly aesthetic it must be proper to take aesthetic pleasure in the object. He uses Leni Riefenstahl's *Triumph of the Will* as an example. Given that its topic is the celebration of the Nazi regime, Walton points out that it may seem "improper to admire it with pleasure."[18] This notion of admiration is very important and will be useful for the rest of this discussion as well.

Aesthetic Value, Winning, and Sports

Returning to the issue of intrinsic value and how it is often internal to an institutional setting, Walton points out that the intrinsic value in sports is *winning*. Winning a tennis match or a basketball game only has value within those respective institutions. While there are a variety of social (read: extrinsic) benefits that may come from sports, such as enhanced health or even just entertainment, the winner/loser ultimately only has meaning within, or is intrinsic to, the sport institution. Walton uses this as an analogy to aesthetic value within the art-world institution, but it is useful for present purposes to examine some of his other comments about sports and aesthetics. Furthermore, if I am correct that there is some sense that can be made of extending the category "art" to include sports, then I can make even more sense of applying aesthetic concepts to a sport such as tennis.

Walton tells us that upon accepting entrance into a sport institution (a pompous way of saying "playing a sport") "teams and players, moves, plays, and strategies, as being better or worse" are so judged "as they are more or less conducive to winning."[19] In a weird way, David Foster Wallace, in his justly famous article on Federer, echoes this point when he writes that "beauty is *not* the goal of competitive sports." Apart from the fact that I am not sure which sports would be categorized as noncompetitive, the underlying assumption of Walton (and maybe even Wallace) is the rather obvious assumption that winning is virtually the only "real" goal of sports. However, philosophers are fond of asking whether what is taken to be obvious is actually the case; perhaps one should ask that question in relation to the obviousness of winning and sports.

If part of the assumption is that we are only talking about professional sports, which, to be fair to Wallace, may be what he means by "competitive," then the obvious assumption is most likely correct—winning is the driving factor.[20] Consider, though, the concept of "sportsmanship," which appears to be intrinsic to the institution of sports (much like the concept of "winning"). Being a good sport is at times derided, but in general it is highly praised, which is why it is usually emphasized even over winning when children are taught sports. Now, Walton might argue that sportsmanship is an extrinsic value because it has to do with treating others decently and fairly in general (explaining why some people are called "good sports"). However, that is clearly a metaphorical usage that reworks the idea of sportsmanship to apply extrinsically. The same can be done with "winning," by pointing out that becoming a winner in sports prepares one for being a winner in life, or business, and so on. Again, this is clearly a metaphorical usage and should not be used as a means of denying intrinsicality to the concept of winning in sports. But if that move is not legitimate with "winning," then it is not legitimate with "sportsmanship" either—and possibly other, maybe even aesthetic, concepts as well. Another way of putting it is that while "winning," "sportsmanship," and other evaluative terms in sports may be metaphorically extended, hence, in that sense, extrinsic or instrumental, it does not follow that those same concepts are not values intrinsic to the institution of sports.

Walton does mention that games are sometimes admired for their beauty (he uses chess as an example); however, he claims that these judgments are external to the institution. His reason for this claim is that beauty (or elegance) plays no role in the evaluation of "aptness for winning."[21] Here I can pinpoint a flaw in his view: he is confusing intrinsicality with exclusivity and primacy. Walton has identified not only winning as an intrinsic value in sports, but as the only and primary value in sports against which all else must be measured. But, again, there are indeed other intrinsic values in sports that may take primacy, depending on context. When teaching a sport to children, cooperation and sportsmanship may take primacy over winning, and sportsmanship, at least, is an intrinsic value in sports. This is an important point because many people tacitly agree with Walton about winning; but now that the flaw has been exposed, it is possible to open the door and recognize other intrinsic values in sports, some of which are aesthetic.

Diagnosis

I'll attempt to diagnose the resistance to significantly extending aesthetic judgments to sports—in other words, in a way where aesthetic judgments may be understood as intrinsic to the institution of sports similarly to the role aesthetic judgments play in the art world. The diagnosis has two parts: first, the resistance to evaluating some aspect of a sport as "beautiful" specifically, and second, the general downplaying of crafts combined with the distinction between the creative and performing arts with the correlative downplaying of the performing arts. I will first examine why beauty judgments, specifically, appear problematic.

Diagnosis Part 1: Beauty and Tennis

In many ways in the world of modern art, beauty judgments have taken a backseat when evaluating works of art.[22] I would contend that this rejection of beauty as an important means of evaluation has spilled over into other areas, with the possible exception of evaluating people (models and actors), but that usage is typically much less aesthetic and much more tinged with sexual desire. So it is rare to hear or read about sports or athletes (in terms of the athlete's game) as beautiful.

Alexander Nehamas points out that this notion of sexual desire is usually linked to appearance where appearance is often associated with beauty. The problem is that appearance is considered deceptive and shallow. As Nehamas puts it, "the pleasures of appearance mislead their pursuers about nature and value."[23] Plato derided those who focus solely on appearance as "the lovers of sounds and sights," who do not understand true beauty.[24] This is the relevant point many modern theorists seem to have forgotten: Plato is telling his audience to not be so enamored with appearance that they fail to look at what lies underneath. While this may sound a lot like the cliché "don't judge a book by its cover," it points out that Plato is not rejecting beauty but explicating a fuller account of beauty and also art.

Constantine Cavarnos, along with Nehamas, analyzes Plato as endorsing a cognitive and emotional account of beauty, thus allowing desire to play an important role. The role of desire is to understand and grasp beauty and its relationship to virtue and happiness. As Cavarnos puts it, "The task of education is to train one to love and know beauty." Appearance gives an initial inroad into beauty, but it is the job of the philosopher to go beyond appearance to beauty itself. This point is echoed in Plato's distinction between real art (craft) and pseudoart (mimesis or imitation). Craft blends the rational and emotional and is grounded in underlying understanding and knowledge. Pseudoart is just a "knack" (empeiria) to produce desired effects, such as certain emotional states, and is merely procedural and experience based.[25]

I will next reiterate the reasons for this analysis. I am attempting to diagnose the reason for the resistance to applying the aesthetic concept "beauty" to sports by placing the resistance in the broader context of an overall rejection of beauty in aesthetic discourse. In addition, by invoking Plato I am attempting to show how this evaluation may be brought back in a fruitful manner, particularly in relation to tennis. It is worth bringing back David Foster Wallace here, since he was one of the few willing to discuss beauty at length in relation to tennis.

David Foster Wallace's most sustained discussion of beauty comes in his article "Federer as Religious Experience." While Wallace does claim that "a top athlete's beauty is next to impossible to describe directly," he nevertheless provides an interesting and specific categorization of the type of beauty involved in high-level sports: "kinetic beauty" is the "beauty or grace" of the body.[26] This could be called a kind of operational analysis in which not merely appearance but the interrelationship among the various abilities of an individual fulfills a given task in a fluid and creative manner. Yet Wallace's analysis of beauty does still lean toward the side of appearance and so does not quite achieve the full-fledged Platonic account of beauty I believe is appropriate and desirable for tennis.

Recall that a true art grounded in beauty blends the emotional with the rational. So a truly artistic analysis of a player, an analysis that a play or game or shot is beautiful, must establish the blend of great skill along with a demonstration of knowledge and understanding. Again, Wallace provides us with a perfect example of just such an analysis.

He describes at length a particular point between Nadal and Federer in the 2006 Wimbledon final.[27] Nadal was up 2–1 in the second set and was serving. I will not quote his wonderful description of the point, but the highlight is that Federer, using a variety of shots, finally hit a backhand winner to end the point. The interesting aspect of the point is not that Federer hit an excellent shot but that it was a "winner that Federer started setting up four or even five shots earlier."[28] Although it may be implied Wallace does not directly analyze that as beautiful, it seems to me illustrative of why Federer is considered one of the most beautiful players ever to play the game. He would not have won that point, or many others, without a full understanding of his opponent, the conditions, and his own abilities. This is exactly the blend of the rational with the other elements (such as emotional) that leads to true beauty and art according to Plato.

Suppose I now suggest that the point just discussed was "marvelous" or "excellent"; these are terms of positive evaluation and, recalling Walton, are fundamentally expressive of admiration. Admiration goes beyond mere enjoyment and often falls into the realm of awe, but still maintains pleasure and enjoyment as components.[29] Walton, in turn, describes aesthetic value as evaluation where it is proper to take aesthetic pleasure and to admire the object, so if an object is completely abhorrent then it is not a proper object of admiration—such as Reifenstahl's *Triumph of the Will*.[30] All of these points apply to tennis as well.

Diagnosis Part 2: Creative and Performing Arts

The second part of my diagnosis of the resistance to fully extending aesthetic evaluation to sports is that even if sports are considered art in some broad sense, they surely would fall under the category of craft. Except for Plato, most theorists have thought of craft as the deformed stepsister of the arts where true aesthetic evaluation has very little importance. Walton reinforces this notion in the course of discussing various parallels between sport and aesthetic value. For example, he points out that "technical facility" in the arts may "replace inspiration and insight" resulting in "art *degenerating* into craft."[31] R. G. Collingwood, though, is the most famous proponent of this position. He adamantly separated art and craft to the detriment of craft and the glorification of art; so why the animus?[32]

My goal is not to rehearse all the details and various criticisms of Collingwood's view, and so this will be brief. His primary way of separating art and craft is to focus on the means of production and the technique used. With craft, there is a specific goal and worked-out plan for achieving it: think, for example, of building a table. Art, on the other hand, has as its goal the expression of a specific emotion of the creator (the artist), which occurs in the course of tinkering with the art materials. So the poet and nonformulaic novelist tinker with words, the sculptor with clay, and so on. The main point is that the artist has no formula or plan ahead of time. While crafts can be interesting and certainly useful, according to Collingwood they cannot be art proper.

Apart from the obvious criticism that Collingwood seems to be building evaluation into his definition of art (thus begging the question), there are other issues. Plenty of recognized artworks also fall into a formula or plan. Haikus, sonnets, and impressionist paintings have a structure or plan into which the works must fit, yet denying them art status stretches credulity. So even with Walton's and Collingwood's rejection or criticism of craft, there appears to be no principled reason to exclude craft from the category of art and the realm of true aesthetic appreciation.[33]

Perhaps another element is implicitly at work here: the notion that art is creative while craft is technical and productive. Underlying this implicit idea is the distinction between the so-called creative and performing arts. The creative arts usually include paintings, sculptures, certain novels, plays and poems in written form, and so on. Performing arts include dance, acting, the performance of a play or poem, and the like. Denis Dutton rightly criticizes this distinction by pointing out that all art falls under the category of performance—that is, the performance of the creator/artist. The only real difference is whether or not its end product can be separated from the artist. In the case of a novel or painting it can, whereas in the case of dance it cannot (the dance *is* the artwork). Yet, in either case the work is the end product of the performance of the artist.[34]

Sports in general and tennis in particular, especially high-level tennis, appear to fall directly into the craft/performing-arts wheelhouse. It is like a craft primarily because of its rules and typical (although not its only or necessarily primary) end goal of winning. But, in the process of achieving that goal, there is ample room for creativity, inspiration, wonder, delight, beauty, and any other aesthetic approbation one might express toward an artwork. In this sense tennis is most like dance. While a dancer may be trying to achieve certain broad end goals, such as communicating a certain emotion or interpreting particular music, there are a variety of creative ways he may achieve it. The strokes, pace, and style also provide a variety of means from which the tennis player may choose to achieve the desired goal. And while neither the tennis player, when choosing to hit a slice backhand, nor the tap dancer, when choosing to slide, is thinking overtly about the *beauty* of the choice of move, the audience may make an aesthetic judgment of it, and rightfully so. While this may not ultimately settle whether tennis should be considered art, it does open the door enough to allow full-fledged aesthetic evaluation to be in the room and considered part of the intrinsic value of the institution of tennis.

Can an Ugly Win Be Beautiful?

S. K. Wertz agrees that, at least from the viewpoint of the audience, sports sometime provide the means for aesthetic contemplation. He subdivides sports into those where aesthetic evaluation is at best secondary, dubbing them purposive sports (he puts tennis in this category), and those where aesthetic evaluation is fundamental, calling them aesthetic sports (like gymnastics).[35] Much like Walton, though, he too hastily dismisses the importance of aesthetic evaluation in tennis. Many of these issues may be better understood by examining the aesthetic counterpart to beauty—ugliness; thus returning to my initial motivation here: winning ugly and losing beautifully.

Winning ugly, according to Walton, amounts to "winning in a manner that does not elicit admiration." Another way he puts it is that an ugly win lacks, even to those spectators rooting for the ugly winner, the "aesthetic dimension of pleasurable admiration."[36] Walton's view, unfortunately, fails to capture the range and subtlety involved in the various ways winning ugly may occur. At minimum, there appears to be a significant difference between winning ugly in a team sport, such as basketball, and in an individual sport, such as tennis. The Detroit Pistons, when winning their back-to-back championships in 1989 and 1990, were considered fairly ugly because of their extremely physical and oppressive defensive play that slowed down games and left them low scoring. This seems to be significantly different from Brad Gilbert's ugly win over McEnroe. I will focus on winning ugly in tennis without assuming that these observations necessarily generalize to other sports.

Gilbert begins his book, *Winning Ugly,* with the anecdote about playing McEnroe at the Masters. In that story McEnroe is clearly referring to the physical aspects of Gilbert's tennis game, especially his strokes, which notoriously did not resemble those of the other top ten players at that time.[37] Yet, it is striking that in Gilbert's book there is not much devoted to strokes per se; the book is in fact primarily devoted to the psychological side of the game. *Winning Ugly* is basically a manual on how to prepare psychologically and intellectually for playing and how to ward off psychological attacks from other players. That provides the impetus for an initial distinction in the world of tennis ugliness: physical versus psychological ugliness.

Physical Ugliness

I believe physical ugliness (and I am not talking about looks) can be further subdivided into at least two categories: strokes and game style. Brad Gilbert, at the higher level, would be considered to have ugly strokes; however, his game style would not necessarily be considered ugly. In chapter eight of his book, Gilbert lists several different types of game styles (or types of players, if you will). One in particular, which Gilbert dubs "the retriever," stands out as usually, and unusually, ugly.[38] The retriever runs everything down, gets it back, and lets the opponent set the pace while the retriever really sets the tempo until the opponent is worn down. Gilbert likens this style to Chinese water torture; yet the strokes of the retriever, recalling my stroke-versus-game style distinction, may be fine, or even excellent. Gilbert even goes so far as to put Borg and Evert into this category. It is players such as Michael Chang and, even more so, Andrea Yeager who are much more emblematic of this style. But it is really at the level of club play, where the retriever runs everything down, does not add pace, and often hits spins like a ping-pong player, that the ugliness is truly revealed.

This last point highlights an important element for understanding aesthetic evaluation in relation to tennis, namely, the context. Claiming that a player has ugly strokes or an ugly game is very different at the pro level than it is at the club level. I would argue that Gilbert's strokes are really only ugly when compared to those of other players at his level, not when compared, say, to mine (trust me, I am in no danger of being mistaken for a pro). So the retriever is very different at the pro level than at lower levels of play. In this sense, aesthetically evaluating tennis styles and strokes will depend on context in terms of comparison class. Of course this is common with aesthetic evaluation in other areas of art as well. When a critic praises or rejects, for instance, an outdoor sculpture such as Anish Kapoor's *Cloud Gate* (the reflective steel "bean" in Chicago's Millennium Park), it is in contrast to other known sculptures and recognized works, not in comparison to something your aunt may have done for the local fair.

Now of course a particular player may combine both types of ugly play—either always or sometimes—but it should still be recognized that they really are separate. So, yes, an ugly win can be beautiful. Gilbert, for example, was a fairly aggressive player, and even though his strokes may have been ugly, given the context, his game style usually was not. His win over McEnroe was arguably beautiful—a beautiful ugly win. It should be kept in mind that one could further subdivide strokes (a player may have a beautiful backhand and ugly forehand à la Connors), but I prefer to turn to psychological ugliness.

Psychological Ugliness

A potential rough synonym for psychological ugliness is gamesmanship. However, just as with physical play there is a further subdivision, which I will dub "legitimate versus illegitimate gamesmanship." An ugly win may come about using either of these, but the latter should be avoided by any player with basic decency. Legitimate gamesmanship, for instance, occurs when you try to take your opponent out of her comfortable game. To relate a personal example, many years ago I was playing in a tournament. Now, my game is not the handsomest; I favor a slice backhand and a fairly flat forehand, even slicing that when necessary. I was playing against the Aryan tennis dream: tall, blond, good-looking and with a classic topspin game. He won the first set, but in the second, I accidently hit a backhand with extreme back and sidespin. Not only did he fail to return the shot, but he was clearly frustrated by it. So, of course, I started hitting massive backspin off of both sides, resulting in the increasing frustration of my opponent and my eventual win.[39] While my win was surely physically ugly, it was due to the psychological breakdown of my opponent and so falls into the psychological category; however, I would claim this as an example of legitimate gamesmanship, and most tennis players would agree.

Illegitimate gamesmanship, on the other hand, can come in a variety of forms. Overt cheating is the most obvious and is not worth mentioning further, but there are other cases as well. A friend of mine who is a pro at a local club provided the following example: he played against a fellow who first would not warm up properly; he kept hitting winners during the warm up and would not let my friend hit any shots. Then, during the match, he faked an injury to take a brief break and was fine immediately after. This is a case of illegitimate gamesmanship.[40]

Obviously, moral issues are involved here, but, as Walton points out, moral and aesthetic values often interact and overlap. Take McEnroe, for example, who many would agree had one of the most beautiful physical games of all time. Now, some contesting of shots, and even a bit of yelling, especially at the pro level, probably falls into the category of legitimate gamesmanship. There were, though, times McEnroe would argue about shots that were clearly in, at length, to upset his opponent (and possibly even influence the line judges). The immorality of these actions spills over into the aesthetic evaluation. Much like Walton's point that it may be inappropriate to admire, or take aesthetic pleasure in, *Triumph of the Will*, so too is it inappropriate to admire a win by McEnroe when he acts in the manner described, no matter how pleasing the strokes, because his actions fall into the category of illegitimate gamesmanship.[41]

Beautiful Winning and Losing

From the perspective of the spectator, the fully and truly beautiful player and/or match will encompass both physical and psychological beauty. The match will evoke the "how marvelous!" response that highlights pleasurable aesthetic admiration. As a point of contrast, one may admire a player's game without the correlative pleasure—Walton calls such admiration "grudging."[42] This is the kind of respect I always had for Ivan Lendl. His game was certainly technically proficient, and I do think his backhand passing shot down the line was a beautiful stroke; overall though, his game merely evoked a grudging respect, without pleasure or joy.

These conceptual tools allow a way to make sense of the difference between grudging admiration for Lendl's game and the reason many consider the likes of Rod Laver and Federer to have two of the most beautiful overall games in men's tennis. They fully encompass the entire range of tennis beauty: physical and psychological. Take Federer: he has the full range of beautiful stokes, including the volley, which many modern players lack. He also fulfills the criterion of psychological beauty: he expresses emotion and will question shots on occasion but never passes over into the illegitimate sort that colored McEnroe's and Connors's respective careers. In fact, announcers and even other players are constantly praising Federer for this, usually by using a phrase such as "true gentleman."[43]

While Federer obviously practices beautiful winning, there still remains the question of losing beautifully. It should be fairly clear that beautiful losing will encompass many of the same features. One hindrance to understanding the full aesthetic range of a sport is the focus on professional sports, where winning dominates. However, sportsmanship, aesthetic pleasure, and the like should be considered intrinsic values. There is another clear intrinsic value in sports that gets lost in the shuffle when one focuses solely on pro sports: *enjoyment*. Sports and games, overwhelmingly, are played by amateurs where virtually nothing, but maybe pride, is riding on who wins or loses. Surely it is obtuse to suggest that the only intrinsic value in the institution of amateur sports is winning. Enjoyment, pleasure, and fun are reasons most people play sports. In fact, when a person gets too focused on winning, too competitive, it is thought that the person has lost sight of the value of playing the sport. Often, though, it is difficult for the spectator to make this evaluation, and so it is primarily from the perspective of the player that the judgment of pleasure must occur.

Remember that context is important for aesthetic evaluation. So my beautiful loss will be judged much differently from, say, a Sampras loss. When Sampras was fourteen (which is quite old at the level of competitive tennis), his tennis coach made him switch from a two-handed backhand to the more aesthetically pleasing and practically effective one-handed backhand. He also switched to more of an attacking style of play. His game, I would argue, became more beautiful and thereby more effective as a result. Yet in the course of the switch, Sampras lost many matches. These would be beautiful losses—losses that ultimately resulted in an overall better game—at the highly competitive level.[44]

At the lower level, where enjoyment has much more prominence as an intrinsic value, the judgment of a beautiful loss is different. If a player loses but plays well given her abilities, psychologically does not practice illegitimate gamesmanship, and enjoys the match, then that is a clear case of losing beautifully. When the goal of winning completely overrides any enjoyment, then it is just another loss.

Aesthetic Pleasure and Admiration

I have argued via Plato's understanding of art as craft that tennis should be considered an art. If it is an art, then aesthetic evaluation makes sense.

Through looking at Walton's discussion of aesthetic value, I have given an analysis of aesthetic concepts such as "ugliness" and "beauty" and how they relate to tennis. That analysis allows a richer understanding of notions like Brad Gilbert's winning ugly and my own losing beautifully. As a final point of interest, think about the rise of classic sports on television. Since the outcome is known, why watch? Well, why watch a movie repeatedly or look at a painting more than once? The best explanation for all of these situations is that the repeated viewings bring aesthetic pleasure and evoke aesthetic admiration. These evaluations apply to the traditional arts and sports as well; hence, even when losing, the loss can be beautiful.

Notes

I would like to thank Daryl Fisher (an excellent tennis player, coach, and my old doubles partner) for his invaluable insights and suggestions.

1. Actually, McEnroe only took a sabbatical, but the point remains. Brad Gilbert and Steve Jamison, *Winning Ugly: Mental Warfare in Tennis—Lessons From a Master* (New York: Simon & Schuster, 1993), x.

2. David Foster Wallace, *A Supposedly Fun Thing I'll Never Do Again: Essays and Arguments* (Boston: Little, Brown, 1997), 235.

3. For an interesting discussion of some of these issues see Alexander Nehamas, *Only a Promise of Happiness: The Place of Beauty in a World of Art* (Princeton, NJ: Princeton University Press, 2007); esp. chap. 3.

4. C. L. R. James, *Beyond a Boundary* (Durham, NC: Duke University Press, 1993), esp. chap. 16.

5. See ibid., for an example of (1). For an excellent example of (2) see David Foster Wallace, "Federer as Religious Experience: How One Player's Grace, Speed, Power, Precision, Kinesthetic Virtuosity, and Seriously Wicked Topspin Are Transfiguring Men's Tennis," *New York Times PLAY Magazine*, August 20, 2006, 46–51, 80, 82, 83. (I have to admit my jealousy of Wallace's titling brevity.)

6. For a good discussion of translating *techne* see Christopher Janaway, "Arts and Crafts in Plato and Collingwood," *Journal of Aesthetics and Art Criticism* 50, no. 1 (Winter 1992): 45–54. For a discussion of *techne* as "true art" see Constantine Cavarnos, "Plato's Teaching on Fine Art," *Philosophy and Phenomenological Research* 13, no. 4 (June 1953): 487–98.

7. Plato, *Republic*, trans. Paul Shorey, in *The Collected Dialogues of Plato*, ed. Edith Hamilton and Huntington Cairns (Princeton, NJ: Princeton University Press, 1961): 575–844.

8. Janaway, "Arts and Crafts," 46; Cavarnos, "Plato's Teaching," 488.

9. Plato, *Republic*, 826.

10. Of course it didn't take Connors long to switch back to the T2000 for a while; he was notoriously stubborn after all.

11. I do recognize that even though this is far from settled and that probably most modern-day philosophers of art would not agree, it does at least provide a place to start the discussion.

12. Kendall L. Walton, "How Marvelous! Toward a Theory of Aesthetic Value," *Journal of Aesthetics and Art Criticism* 51, no. 3 (Summer 1993): 499–510.

13. Ibid., 499.

14. See, for example, George Dickie, *Introduction to Aesthetics: An Analytic Approach* (Oxford: Oxford University Press, 1997).

15. Walton, "How Marvelous!" 500.

16. Bell uses the term *significant form* to indicate the essence of art, but the details would take us too far afield.

17. See Dickie, *Introduction to Aesthetics*, for a nice concise introduction to Kant's views on these matters (20–25).

18. Walton, "How Marvelous!" 506.

19. Ibid., 501.

20. Wallace, "Federer as Religious Experience," 48, emphasis added. Of course, and as I will explore later, Wallace goes on to describe at length the beauty involved in tennis.

21. Walton, "How Marvelous!" 502.

22. Nehamas, *Only a Promise of Happiness*.

23. Ibid., 19.

24. Plato, *Republic*, 715.

25. Cavarnos, "Plato's Teaching," 490, 491. Janaway, "Arts and Crafts," 47–48.

26. Wallace, "Federer as Religious Experience," 48–49.

27. There are, of course, several such points in Nadal's surprising win over Federer in the 2008 Wimbledon final.

28. Wallace, "Federer as Religious Experience," 82.

29. Walton, "How Marvelous!" 504, 508.

30. See ibid., 506, for this example. While clearly morality plays a role in this evaluation, a full discussion would take us too far afield.

31. Ibid., 503 (emphasis added).

32. For a good discussion of Collingwood's view see Janaway, "Arts and Crafts." Also see Noël Carroll, *A Philosophy of Mass Art* (Oxford: Clarendon, 1998), especially 49–70.

33. Ingrid D. Rowland makes some nice points about crafts in her article "Women Artists Win!" *New York Review of Books*, May 29, 2008, 26–29.

34. Denis Dutton, "Artistic Crimes," in *Arguing about Art: Contemporary Philosophical Debates*, ed. Alex Neill and Aaron Ridley (New York: McGraw-Hill, 1995), 21–33.

35. S. K. Wertz, "Are Sports Art Forms?" *Journal of Aesthetic Education* 13, no. 1 (January 1979): 107–9.

36. Walton, "How Marvelous!" 505.

37. Gilbert reached as high as #4 in the world and was in the top ten for five years—pretty impressive for such an "ugly" player.

38. Gilbert and Jamison, *Winning Ugly,* 82.

39. We played again a few months later, with almost exactly the same result.

40. I would like to thank Daryl Fisher for relaying this experience.

41. For good examples of ugly and possibly illegitimate psychological games-manship, see Gilbert, *Winning Ugly,* especially his examples of McEnroe (174–78) and Connors (167–71). See David Detmer's chapter in this volume, "'You Cannot Be Serious!' The Ethics of Rage in Tennis," for further moral analysis of McEnroe's on-court rage.

42. Walton, "How Marvelous!" 505.

43. Nadal, also, is getting praised in a similar fashion.

44. For a description of Sampras's switch, see Larry Schwartz, "Sampras Competes against Best—Ever," *ESPN Sports Century,* 2007, http://espn.go.com/sportscentury/features/00016453.html.

Jeanine Weekes Schroer

ARTHUR ASHE

Philosopher in Motion

"Negroes are getting more confidence. They are asking for more and more, and they are getting more and more. They are looser. They're liberal. In a way 'liberal' is a synonym for loose. And that's exactly the way Arthur plays."[1] Clark Graebner made these comments while discussing his 1968 U.S. Open semifinal match against Arthur Ashe; he goes on to further characterize the "looseness" in Ashe's style of play, a style that Graebner believed would allow him to defeat Ashe. It didn't. Nonetheless, his comments have a strange resonance; they have the ring of truth— not so much about black folk, not even necessarily about Arthur Ashe. Instead, they tell something about race in the United States. Graebner's take on race and people of color was common for his time and is probably fairly common even now. He believed that understanding Arthur Ashe as a tennis player, as a man, was best accomplished by understanding him as a "negro." Despite the unsettling nature of such a sentiment, Graebner may not have been entirely wrong.

Almost no one would argue that it is possible to understand individuals of color, especially those living in racist cultures, without any consideration of their lives as members of some race. Just as few, however, would argue that understanding a white person requires consideration of their lives as members of the white race. While race is a problem, and a defining one in the lives of people of color, it is often inconsequential, insignificant, or even invisible in the lives of members of the white race.[2] This one-way objectification typifies race relations in U.S. culture, both in Graebner's era and in this one. Arguably this conception of race, both a result and a source of racial injustice, contains a kernel of truth: for many people of color, race plays a significant role in their self-understanding and their way of being in the world. This was undoubtedly true for Arthur Ashe. Race infused more than just his political attitudes and actions; his character and personality were also constructed by his racial identity. There is a sense in which Graebner was correct: the way Ashe played tennis and the way he lived was a reflection of his racial identity. From his early tennis career under the tutelage of Dr. Walter Johnson, in which he was taught to cope with playing tennis in the Jim Crow south, to his battle with apartheid in South Africa, to raising his daughter, Camera, beautiful and black in the public eye, Ashe seemed actively engaged in a project of understanding the role race played in his life and the role his life might play in helping others understand race. This latter project will be resumed in this chapter.

This chapter will invert Graebner's lens; instead of trying to understand the man by understanding his race, it attempts to mine Ashe's life for vital insights into the social life, the politics, and the metaphysics of race. I will proceed by discussing the social, political, metaphysical, and conceptual problems that hinder serious endeavors to understand race. The remainder of the chapter will focus on Arthur Ashe and how his life both clarifies the challenges of conceptions of race and provides a guide for tackling those challenges.[3]

The Race Problem

In this world of cell phone cameras, viral videos, and instant infamy, to say that race is a touchy subject borders on wild understatement. For example, Lleyton Hewitt came under fire over remarks he made during one of his 2001 U.S. Open matches. Hewitt had a black line judge moved, referring to similarities between the judge and opponent, James Black; many interpreted this as racist.[4] These incidents force people who fear they could be the next objects of public scorn to take a defensive, reactive position toward race. They may feel they have only two options: They can become outlaws who flout "political correctness" and bask in language, viewpoints, and practices that violate taboos. Alternately, they can become model citizens, disguise any and all aspects of themselves that could be perceived as racist, avoid engagement in serious discussions of race, and indulge in platitudes—that is, "I come from a multicultural country. I'm not racial in any way at all."[5] As a result, complex and subtle critiques of the racial status quo have difficulty gaining a purchase in major public forums: consider the challenge posed by Martina Navratilova's claim that Serena and Venus Williams are treated with kid gloves because of their race or the continued lack of empathy for Richard Williams's charges of racism on the women's tennis tour.[6]

Despite society's inability to talk seriously about race—undoubtedly also because of that inability—race continues to be a significant social concern. Blacks, for example, are more likely to be poor than whites, earn nearly 40 percent less than whites, and have one-eighth the net worth of whites; blacks are also overrepresented among those arrested, prosecuted, incarcerated, and executed.[7] These disproportions demand explanation; however, an actual debate about them—one that has some hope of being progressive—would require that folks on all sides be able to sustain deep and thoughtful discourse despite defensiveness, resentment, and tears. If ever we do find ourselves able to penetrate the *social* obstacles to a serious discussion of race, we will be confronted by an astounding set of *conceptual* difficulties. The first obstacle is just to understand what it is we are really talking about when we talk about race.

The Problem with "Race"

In certain ways, it is less difficult to talk about the social injustices stemming from race than it is to talk about race itself. We have a sense of the meaning of the claim, "These folks are oppressed." There is a sense of what information is necessary to prove or disprove the claim. The concern evoked by citing the above statistics about poverty and imprisonment is that they are at least partially explained by oppression—both the legacy of violent oppression like chattel slavery as well as a continuing oppression in the form of "disadvantage[s] and injustice[s] some people suffer . . . because of [among other things] the everyday practices of a well-intentioned liberal society."[8] The people in question, in this case, are black folk; people designated as having the racial identity "black." This is where the trouble begins. Whether and how black folk are oppressed—especially whether their oppression persists through a structure hidden within liberal democracy—is a difficult question in itself; however, before we can answer that question we must answer difficult questions about just what and who we are talking about when we say "black." Fortunately, there has been an explosion of research in the metaphysics of race—inquiry aimed at explaining what kind of claims one is making about people and the world they inhabit when one attributes racial membership to them. I will proceed by sketching the major theories that attempt to explain what race really is.[9]

It is commonly believed that racial categories say something about human bodies. The idea is that the particular combination of skin color, lip and nose shape, and hair texture typically identified with black folk is not accidental. Race—as opposed to ethnicity, culture, or nationality—is supposed to capture variations in human features explained by biology. This view—"that there are heritable characteristics, possessed by members of our species, that allow us to divide them into a small set of races, in such a way that all the members of these races share certain traits and tendencies with each other that they do not share with members of any other race"—is known as *racialism*. This is, perhaps, the most widely held view of race. It is also the most problematic. Alongside any number of superficial physical traits, racialism has typically claimed that certain moral, intellectual, and even spiritual traits are determined by race. When these differences have been used as justification for things like apartheid and the Jim Crow laws that shadowed Ashe's life, then racialism becomes racism.[10]

Racialism claims that race is "real," that talk about race points to sets of genes that manifest as certain skin colors, hair textures, and so on, that make one a member of some race or another. For racialism to be true, there ought to be sets of genes or inherited traits that are genuinely unique to members of specific races. It turns out that black folk are as different from each other as they are from other racial groups and the traits that are supposed to be unique to blacks appear in other races.[11] As a result of these and other findings, as well as the role it plays in justifying racism, racialism has been widely rejected.

Those who want to think seriously about race are left with few options: many thinkers find themselves in the position of trying to understand races as real but as something other than biological essences. The main strategy for defending the race concept is racial constructivism.[12] Racial constructivists acknowledge that biological theories of race fail—either by failing to identify criteria for biological distinction or by failing to make sense of race terms—but insist that such talk captures real features of human social life. They argue that race is real because it is a successful social construction: various societies have succeeded in establishing a social order where distinctions based largely on an arbitrary set of physical traits are meaningful and significant. Constructivist views must satisfy two major requirements of a theory of race: First, such theories must explain race while correcting or eluding the racism revealed by efforts to hold on to failed biological theories of race. Second, race theories should provide some of the tools that will allow us to address racial injustice.[13] Key to satisfying both of these conditions is offering a coherent story of how race is socially constructed. There are significant disagreements among racial constructivists as to what that story is.

I will discuss two distinct constructivist strategies: *materialist constructivism* and what I will call *narrative constructivism*.[14] What distinguishes the two is a disagreement about what drives the construction. Materialists understand race as "economically driven, related to the structure of capitalism and the projects of the bourgeoisie." Narrationists will primarily "attribute [race] to culture/ideas/'discourses.'"[15] This chapter will use Arthur Ashe's life to argue that neither materialist constructivism nor narrative constructivism is a viable candidate for capturing the reality of race.

Materialist Constructivism and the Assignment Problem

Materialist accounts of race tend to focus on how superficial physical traits are used to group individuals in such a way as to mark them out for a specific set of roles in a socioeconomic structure. In his *The Racial Contract*, a thorough execution of the materialist strategy, Charles Mills argues that the separation of the world's populations into races was key to five hundred years of European imperialism and conquest, providing justification for claiming both human and nonhuman resources.[16] Such a view explains racial oppression, capturing both a meaningful conception of race and its connection to a wide range of social injustices. Black folks are those, like Ashe, whose dark skin is used to justify subjecting them to particular types of exploitation, marginalization, powerlessness, cultural imperialism, and violence.[17] Difficulties arise when we try to group people in accord with the materialist's racial categories. This chapter will refer to this as the "assignment problem."[18]

The life and experiences of Arthur Ashe provide examples of the assignment problem. Based on his superficial features, he would have been marked for racial oppression. The materialist would call him black; however, the story of his life—both the material facts and his assessment of them—presents a picture not entirely consistent with that assignment. Ashe grew up in a segregated Richmond, Virginia. Most of the public tennis courts were unavailable to him because he was black, and he was refused entry into a number of tournaments because of his race.[19] Despite this, Ashe described his life as "a succession of fortunate circumstances."[20] Ashe quietly kicked down doors that had been closed to African Americans. He showed his black face in what were formerly white spaces: tennis courts from Virginia to South Africa and everywhere between. He even excelled, winning the U.S. Open, as well as the Australian Open and Wimbledon. He was a member of six winning U.S. Davis Cup teams (four as a player and two as the coach).[21] Ashe was educated, a world traveler, a political activist, and a philanthropist. The material circumstances of his life pose a challenge to materialist accounts of race.

Though his features marked him for racial oppression, he managed, ultimately, to avoid many of the worst material burdens imposed by racial injustice. This anecdote from Ashe's own personal engagement with the question of race captures the difficulty: While discussing affirmative action with a young, privileged black man, Ashe asks him whether he would have accepted entrance into law school under the rule of affirmative action if his grades had not met the normal admission standards.[22] The young man says he would because, "As a black, I belong to a group that has been historically abused and discriminated against. I'm entitled to redress." Ashe's concern is that this young man "was born and brought up in luxury, with the best teachers and private schools from kindergarten on up. [He had] lived a charmed life." Ashe says pointedly, "Affirmative action wasn't meant for you, surely."[23] Precisely what Ashe is suggesting is that his dark skin is not, should not be, enough to qualify him for affirmative action, to qualify him as black under a materialist account of race.[24]

Billie Jean King once remarked, "I'm blacker than Arthur."[25] Some have argued that the remark was a criticism of Ashe's moderate politics, while some have called it just plain stupid.[26] Ashe interpreted this as yet another criticism of his composure, but there is reason to think the off-hand remark may have been a complex mingling of ideas about Ashe's politics, his composure, and what it means to be black. Ashe considered King a friend. He spoke with passion of the incredible contributions she made to her sport and the world, calling her "the most important tennis player, male or female . . . since World War II."[27] He spoke with sympathy about the incredible personal costs those contributions entailed. King's radical politics and the ugly and public end of a personal relationship that outed her made her anathema to sponsors. Despite that, she continued to be an advocate for women and homosexuals on and off the courts. Ashe believed that the anger that provoked King's remark about him was righteous, justified. I agree, but a righteous and justified anger about what? I cannot help but wonder if part of what motivated her to make this remark about race is a sense that part of the story of being black is a story about being oppressed. Only King can know what was on her mind at that moment. My particular interpretation could be incorrect, but the idea that Arthur Ashe when alone with Billie Jean King is not necessarily the blackest person in the room, for whatever reason, captures the assignment problem.

Materialists rely on the same superficial characteristics that racialists do in assigning people to racial categories. In doing so, they identify folks like Ashe as blacks despite the fact that they have managed to avoid a significant amount of the material consequences of racial oppression. Perhaps they should not. Part of the virtue of the materialist account is that it groups together the sufferers of racial injustice, thus providing straightforward language for talking about policies for correction and compensation. Were it to leave out the most privileged blacks—people for whom the material consequences of race were minimized or absent altogether—it would be a credit to the view. The exclusion of that segment of the population creates a representation of race that can answer questions about who deserves aid through the redistribution of goods and opportunities. It would certainly be more consistent with a position that claims that economy more than anything else defines us as members of one race or another.

Any theory will be imperfect in its assignment of racial identity, but the problem here is more significant for two reasons: First, success in the pursuit of racial justice has assured that Ashe is not simply an anomaly. Many black folks find themselves in careers where the vast majority of their colleagues are white, living in neighborhoods where the majority of their neighbors are white, even having social and private lives that are largely populated by white folks. The children of interracial couples add another layer to this complexity. These folks just do not easily fit into the confines of a system that defines race significantly by appeal to material circumstances, and their numbers are bound to expand. The second reason to suspect that the materialist account is incomplete—regardless of whether it uses economic status as a definitive measure of race and excludes those like Ashe or whether it defers to common perception and includes him—is that it seems unprepared to manage the fact that even extremely successful blacks, like Ashe, identify race as the greatest burden of their lives.[28] The burden of race for these people is not fundamentally a matter of economics; it is existential. The materialist account must, it seems, treat this significant existential burden as extraneous.

Narrative Constructivism and the Authenticity Problem

W. E. B. Du Bois's "The Conservation of Races" is a seminal work in narrative constructivism; it calls for the formation of an "American Negro Academy," whose purpose would be the development and preservation of the unique spiritual message that black people have for the world.[29] Precisely what it demands is that blacks as a people undertake the intellectual project of constructing a black racial identity. While some Narrationists believe that a properly constructed black identity simply fulfills the destiny of the black race, others have defended it on more practical grounds: "In order for a people in a hostile society to flourish as a people, their self-identity must be anchored by a conception of the good that is independent of the hostility that they wish to avoid." That narrative—a group's conception of its good—must define values, identify positive goals, specify points of historical significance, and cannot be shared by others. It fosters the trust necessary for the cooperation that will allow flourishing in the face of adversity.[30] This is a view to which Ashe was sympathetic.

In October 1973, a splendid weekend in Paris was ruined for him by a story in *The Guardian* describing the United States agreeing to support Portugal continuing to control their African colonies in exchange for continued use of their Azores bases. What saddened him most about this was the nonresponse he anticipated from blacks in the United States. "The black population in America will not blink an eye at this. There are many more blacks than Jews in the U.S., yet the Jews look out for their brothers overseas and affect our international policies—and we blacks don't, or perhaps can't."[31] Many of his racial justice projects involved promoting a positive black identity that would help blacks negotiate the hostile racial landscape they faced in the United States and in Africa.

Narrative accounts have been comprehensively criticized, but I will focus on the "authenticity problem."[32] Du Bois claims that careful study reveals that the world's history is a history of races, among them "the Negroes of Africa and America."[33] The idea that American and African blacks are unified by a common racial project has provoked severe criticism. It has been argued that nothing can serve to unite blacks worldwide while also distinguishing them from other oppressed racial groups.[34] Narrationists define race as a set of ideals that bind members of racial groups to each other to the exclusion of other racial groups. For this process to be authentic, the unifying ideals need to be substantial and the identification with these ideals—the attachment and sense of connection to them—needs to be earnest. Narrative accounts have difficulty satisfying each of these elements of authenticity. Even when Du Bois first published "The Conservation of Races" in 1897, there would have been a significant cultural gap between blacks in the United States and blacks in Africa. As time has passed, these two groups have diverged even more. The race-related difficulties faced by blacks in Chicago are quite different from those faced by blacks in Darfur. In fact, that the struggle has some connection to race might be the only commonality. However, "if what [U.S. blacks have] in common with Africa is a history of 'discrimination and insult' then this binds [them] to . . . 'yellow Asia and . . . the South Seas' also."[35] Racial injustice is not substantial enough to bind blacks to each other without also binding them to all nonwhite racial groups. It is also insufficient to foster cooperation; it does not give blacks reason to act together. Avoiding the harms of racial oppression is something one might just as well do on one's own.[36]

Developing a more substantial narrative or set of ideals is well within the grasp of any racial group. This narrative, however, must also be something with which blacks can earnestly identify. Any substantial black narrative runs the risk of alienating large portions of the group it aims to define. Again, Arthur Ashe's life offers insight into the problem. Ashe confronted the disunity of black identity on multiple occasions. He began pursuing opportunities to play tennis in South Africa in the late 1960s; his goal was to have an opportunity to see the horrors of apartheid with his own eyes. After doing so, he became an envoy for blacks living under apartheid. Not everyone agreed with his methods. South African students heckled him during a speaking engagement at Howard University; they called him an Uncle Tom and a Judas. Ashe countered the students' accusations by asking why they believed that the honorable response to apartheid was to "hide" in school in the United States.[37] Similar charges were leveled when he played the South African Open in Johannesburg.[38] In this instance, both sides better articulated their concerns. His onetime visits, they argued, made no real change. They believed that only economic isolation—boycotts—would end apartheid. Ashe's presence, they insisted, supported the status quo and, thus, hurt blacks. Ashe, in his defense, offered the history of seemingly small actions taken by seemingly inconsequential persons making an extraordinary impact. His example to the South Africans was Rosa Parks. He pleaded with them to recognize all the ways change might come and the key role their patient persistence would play in that change. He left South Africa believing they remained unconvinced. This circumstance is especially revealing of the difficulties that attend the absence of a unifying black narrative. Precisely what Ashe struggled to do was offer a story of his actions that would allow black South Africans to perceive him as an ally. Differences in the histories of their two struggles—the struggle for civil rights in the United States and the struggle to end apartheid in South Africa—made identifying this common ground very difficult.

On another occasion, Ashe felt that disunity as he battled internally with a decision to prevent his daughter from being filmed playing with a white doll on national television. Aware of public expectations that he actively advocate for justice for blacks, Ashe found himself worrying that he would be perceived as allowing his daughter to embrace white standards of beauty, anxiously anticipating the backlash, and resentful of the whole situation. In the end, he stopped his daughter from playing with the doll, but he was not happy about it. "I am angry with myself because I have just acted out of pure practicality, not out of morality. The moral act would have been to let Camera have her fun. . . . Instead, I tampered with her innocence."[39] Again, Ashe found himself aware of an ideological disunity between himself and some other elements of the black community. Though Narrationists are better able to answer the challenge that Ashe's particular racial burdens pose for race theories than are Materialists, they cannot do so without risking alienating someone they would rather include.

A Loose Negro

The fundamental challenge facing constructivism can be stated quite simply, "There is nothing in the world that can do all that we ask 'race' to do for us."[40] We need it to capture what it is about the dark-skinned peoples of the world that explains why they consistently suffer the worst material circumstances and reap the least of the society's benefits. We also need it to tell nonwhites how to hold up their heads, what they stand for, who they are, how to live, and how to thrive. We want it to do all this as some discrete metaphysical entity that is apparent and easily described. Unfortunately, race eludes us, because it is not what we thought it was. The fundamental lesson revealed by the constructivist dilemma—Are Materialists correct, despite the assignment failures, or are Narrationists correct, despite the problem of inauthenticity?—is that race is no *one* thing. We must acknowledge the way that something rightly called "race" has shaped the history of nations and altered the economic and social lives of millions of people, white and nonwhite. We must also realize that people must subjectively engage race; people must figure out how to live race, that is, how to be black. These two projects will not be unified in virtue of finding that they track some common metaphysical reality. What unites them is that both are about identifying, defining, and managing a peculiar set of constraints: the obligation to wrestle with the ghost that is race.

One of the undersold strengths of constructivism is its recognition that race is dynamic. Most constructivist theories engage with the idea that race has changed over time and will continue to do so. The dilemma between materialist and narrative constructivism reveals that race also shifts between two different perspectives. The first takes a wide view, seeing how people are parts of a large and complex social system that is capable of affecting nearly every aspect of their lives. The second takes a narrower view, acknowledging the personal project of seeing and making a life for oneself.[41] To get what we need from race, we need to accept it for what it is, all that it is. We need to stay on our toes and be prepared to move. In what remains of this chapter, I will argue that in his life, Arthur Ashe incorporated the strengths of both materialist and narrative constructivist approaches to race while avoiding many of their pitfalls. He allowed himself the freedom to traverse the divide in race.

Ashe's antiapartheid activism showed this deftness of foot. Central to the materialist account of race is an awareness of race as an external force that shapes our lives without our permission. Superficial features are the basis for racial assignments, but being perceived as a member of one race or another has profound consequences. These realities of race—the way racism controls lives and changes souls—were brought home to Ashe during his early visits to South Africa during apartheid. He was playing the South African Open in Johannesburg, and a teenage boy followed him everywhere. Ashe finally asked the boy why he was following him. The boy said, "You are the first truly free black man I have ever seen."[42] In that moment, Ashe found what was for him the fundamental injustice of apartheid: it programmed and destined young blacks for a lifetime of servitude. The harsh realities of race in South Africa under apartheid would remake this boy in ways Ashe found intolerable. Ashe never lost sight of these serious material consequences of race. Apartheid did more than make those boys serve; it made them servants.

Ashe first applied for a visa to play in the South African Open in 1969 and was refused. He applied again in 1970 and was refused again. When he applied again in 1973, he was granted the visa. It just so happens that South Africa was also readmitted to the Davis Cup competition by the International Lawn Tennis Federation that year. Ashe articulated what almost anyone might have thought, "A more cynical man than I might think that I was a quid pro quo." In this situation, Ashe saw the big picture; it turns out that his admission to South Africa had been a bullet point in the president of the South African Lawn Tennis Association's argument to readmit South Africa to the Davis Cup. Ashe assessed the situation like this:

They're ahead; they've already hooked something very big with me as part of the bait. . . . It can work both ways though. There is a concept in international trade called comparative advantage. Two nations will trade with each other if each believes it can gain. My going to South Africa is a trade. They've already gained something out of me, and I'll gain something too. If nothing else, my presence signals a pause in apartheid. In the sweep of history, a pause maybe for only five minutes—but maybe next time ten. I am banking on a trait of human nature that concessions are won with great cost, that, indeed, small concessions incline toward larger ones.[43]

Ashe was able to place his decision to play the South African Open into its incredibly complex context. His presence would be a tool for South Africa, a bargaining point. He would stand as a shallow display of the egalitarianism that was woefully lacking in their government and a stark reminder of the profound injustice of that government. Apartheid would cease, for only a moment, but that moment would give a fourteen-year-old black South African boy the opportunity to see what a free black man looks like. In this watershed moment, the course of that boy's life would turn; inspired, this boy would play tennis, and tennis would set him free. The boy Ashe inspired that day was Mark Mathabane, author of *Kaffir Boy*, an autobiographical account of his childhood under South African apartheid. Mathabane was able to escape South Africa with the assistance of Ashe and a scholarship earned by playing tennis.[44]

Though the South African government was using Ashe, he would advance his own project as well. He would be part of the hammer that would smash apartheid. The interplay of Ashe as another black man restricted by a system of a worldwide white supremacy and Ashe the activist is impossible to see without engaging both the materialist and the narrative accounts of race. Narrationists recognize that people must subjectively engage race—they must confront the ghost—while materialists identify the socioeconomic conditions that shape that engagement. Our struggle with race cannot always put us on a noncontroversial path. This was a challenge Ashe was always prepared to face.

Ashe's early life was formed by a host of friends and family members who prepared him for navigating race's uneven territories. Ashe's coach, Dr. Walter Johnson, always understood that he was not just training Ashe to play tennis; he was training him to be a black man playing a white sport with white players. The Junior Development team—the mostly black players at the tennis camp Dr. Johnson ran from his home—had some very specific rules: self-control, honor, discipline. On the court, they would be models of sportsmanship: considerate of other players, respectful of judges, and tantrum-free. Johnson even taught his team to play anything that was less than two inches out of bounds. As a result, Ashe would never be guilty of the laziness, sense of entitlement, or emotional instability that is often attributed to blacks.

Ashe was, in fact, known for his "towering calm." As a black man, he would be expected to be the least disciplined, the most irascible; instead, he was a study in calm. His opponents found it maddening. Johnson's teachings, however, were not simply about winning. They were about access. Johnson knew that tournament organizers would use any excuse to exclude his Junior Development team. If they were models of good sportsmanship and behavior, they might have a few more opportunities to compete. This was early training for a lifetime project of seeing the structural features of race without losing oneself in them. Johnson's first students had not yet learned this lesson. When they competed in the U.S. Lawn Tennis Association's national Interscholastic Championships, they were "scared to death," "slaughtered," and "humiliated."[45] A simple material restriction—preventing these young men from regularly playing in tournaments with whites—had more than material consequences. Their fear reflected a narrative that goes along with such restrictions, that says that they are inferior, that their failure is inevitable. Ashe saw that combating this narrative was just as necessary as combating the socioeconomic circumstances that created it: "When you must limit your idols, surely you must limit all the dreams and aspirations, and you remain, perforce, a limited man."[46]

As important as the tennis skills that Ashe picked up from Johnson was the lesson to be his own person. This is a daunting endeavor when pursued within the context of oppression. For example, Clark Graebner questioned Ashe's "majestic cool": "Would he have been that way if he had been white? . . . He has had to master the restraint of his emotions on the court. In fact, I think he works too hard at trying to keep his cool. . . . It's not human to be that cool. He is penned in. Feelings need an outlet. I hope he is not going to lose his cool by trying to keep his cool." In stark contrast to his worry that Ashe was penned in, Graebner also found Ashe "loose."

> He's carefree, lackadaisical, forgetful. His mind wanders. I've never seen Arthur really discipline himself. . . . He doesn't gut out a lot of points where

he has to work real hard, probably because he is concerned about his image. He doesn't want to appear to be a grubber. He comes out on the court and he's tight for a while, then he hits a few good shots and he feels the power to surge ahead. He gets looser and more liberal with the shots he tries, and pretty soon he is hitting shots everywhere. He does not play percentage tennis. Nobody in his right mind, really, would try those little dink shots he tries as often as he does. . . . He plays to shoot his wad.[47]

Graebner was of course wrong about Ashe's discipline, but Ashe admits to being "reckless" on the tennis courts, to trying difficult shots to thwart boredom—both his own and that of his fans.[48] Penned in, but reckless. Cool, but out of his mind. Superficially, Ashe was a bundle of contradictions; more contradictions are found in Ashe's politics.

Some have described Ashe's politics as "moderate"; in direct contrast to the politics of contemporaries like Billie Jean King, that may have seemed true. After all, he was decidedly against militant black activism and staunchly advocated self-discipline over affirmative action.[49] However, he was also arrested on multiple occasions for protesting; the last time was just a few months before his death.[50] Ashe's politics—like his tennis—are better described as diverging wildly. He shifted between his commitment to relatively conservative values like self-reliance and personal responsibility and much more radical agitation against a variety of antiblack racisms—from apartheid to the treatment of black refugees. This string of contradictions—like the statistics cited near the opening of this chapter—requires explanation, and I think the answer can be found in Ashe's looseness.

For folks like Ashe, race is inescapable. He described the problem this way:

I am a prisoner of the past. . . . [Segregation] left me a marked man, forever aware of a shadow of contempt that lays across my identity and my sense of self-esteem. Subtly the shadow falls on my reputation, the way I know I am perceived; the mere memory of it darkens my most sunny days. I believe that the same is true for almost every African-American of the slightest sensitivity and intelligence. Again, I don't want to overstate the case. I think of myself as extremely self-confident. I know objectively that it is almost impossible for someone to be as successful as I have been as an athlete and lack self-assurance. Still I know that the shadow is always there; only death will free me, and blacks like me, from its pall.[51]

Here Ashe is managing yet another contradiction: his own clear self-image—a talented and fortunate man—and the shadow image projected on him by racism. This burden weighed on every decision—political and personal—shaped every aspect of his character, but it was *his* character, nonetheless. This is what Graebner did not understand about Ashe's calm or his recklessness: racism, even when unsuccessful, changes who you are, but it cannot claim you unless you let it. Ashe was altered by his engagement with racism, but he was not lost to it. When he coached the Davis Cup team from 1981 to 1986, one of the greatest sources of tension between him and star player John McEnroe was McEnroe's proclivity for profane outbursts during the matches.[52] McEnroe's tantrums did not hinder his play, but it was not a simple difference in style either. For Ashe, it was a matter of honor and respect. The discipline, restraint, and self-reflection that served him on the court were not just parts of a performance he put on to win matches or even to maintain access. They also were more than just what racism had made him. Ultimately, that was who he *chose* to be. Ashe was not "penned in." He was Ashe.

Navigating the minefield of race requires, in a word, grace; by his persistence, his insistence on respecting his choice, Ashe modeled that grace. He looked at the systematic oppression of blacks around the world and saw himself in them. He felt the shame, self-doubt, and uncertainty of being marked by race, but he did not succumb. He insisted, for himself and others in his position, on pride and individual initiative. He believed that despite the many obstacles they face, blacks must stand on their own feet. The genuine looseness in Ashe was his flexibility, his willingness and ability to see beyond himself without losing himself. He could see the larger social structure, oppression, and its effect on him and still recognize and maintain his sense of self, his spirit. He took ownership of the personal and political contradictions that being a black man entailed. He modeled courage, strength, and integrity to millions of people, whether they were fans of tennis or not. He always believed he was obliged to try to be more than just a tennis champion; through his grace, he elevated himself and tennis, making being a tennis champion so much more.

You've Got to Push

I will conclude by further characterizing the unique metaphysical position on race that Ashe's life reveals. Racism is undeniably real. People are denied access to housing, education, employment, and a host of other social goods because they are identified as members of various racial groups. They are told explicitly and implicitly that their needs are less important and that they have less moral and legal standing than whites. These denials and restrictions—and the threat of them—shape how these folks make their way in the world. They may struggle against stereotypes, reject racial identification, protest against racial injustice, or cleave to those with whom they share racial identity traits. All of that is real. It all must be tended to if we hope to live in a just society. The questions that arise in tending to all the effects of racism seem to point to common concepts: race concepts. The challenge undertaken in this chapter is to pry open these concepts. When you look inside "black," however, you will find no biological components that definitively connect all the folks who are called black by someone. You also will not find a continent, nation, principle, project, economic status, education level, or cultural ideal that unites all those who are called black by someone.

The flaws of materialist and narrative constructivism reveal that race concepts inevitably point back to projects like racial justice and authenticity. Materialists identify race in ways that examine and rectify the socioeconomic consequences of racism. Narrationists identify race in ways that try to engage authentically with life within a body marked with the traits and features of race. Race, itself, is empty; only the projects are real. Over time, more and more people will see race for what it is: a set of projects whose ultimate goal is to witness the end of race, an end to both the socioeconomic injustices of white supremacy and the personal identities and attitudes developed to manage those injustices. In the meantime, we must engage earnestly and enthusiastically with those projects, giving ourselves the leeway—the looseness—to slide our definitions as necessary. I will give Ashe the last word. He was commenting on the pursuit of racial justice, but it applies just as aptly to this race project: "Progress and improvement do not come in big hunks, they come in little pieces. . . . You've got to push. You've got to act as though you expect it to come tomorrow. But when you know it's not going to come, don't give up. . . . We'll advance."[53]

Notes

I would like to thank Steve Patterson for getting me involved in this project; it has been intellectually stimulating and inspiring in ways that I did not anticipate. I am also grateful to Robert Schroer for comments that helped me work out my ideas.

1. John McPhee, *Levels of the Game* (New York: Farrar, Straus and Giroux, 1979), 93–94.

2. I do not mean to suggest that no one thinks about the racial ramifications of whiteness; my point is that for many people's ordinary lived experience race only matters for people of color.

3. My discussion of race, especially of issues of authenticity, will tend to focus on answering these questions for and about African Americans to the exclusion of other people of African descent and other people of color; it also focuses on characterizing and clarifying race in the United States to the exclusion of other nations. While I think the kind of project undertaken here could be equally useful for other racial groups in other nations, ultimately, the details are likely to be different. Certain groups would have to make issues of language difference and language loss more central in their story, while others would need to make religion and cultural identity more central to theirs.

4. See Associated Press, "Hewitt under Fire," *CNN/Sports Illustrated,* August 31, 2001, http://sportsillustrated.cnn.com/tennis/2001/us_open/news/2001/08/31/hewitt_recap/; and "Hewitt—Blake Racial Incident," October 13, 2001; online video clip, YouTube, http://www.youtube.com/watch?v=6dUGXtiMNqk.

5. This was Lleyton Hewitt's defense of his behavior during his 2001 U.S. Open match with James Blake. The worry here is that he presumes that the fact that he comes from a multiracial country is evidence that he could not be racist. See "BBC Sport: Hewitt Caught in Race Row," *BBC Sports,* September 1, 2001, http://news.bbc.co.uk/sport2/hi/in_depth/2001/us_open_tennis/1520183.stm.

6. My contention here is that the most public discourse on race—that available on television and some major newspapers—lacks sophistication, avoids complexity, and often does more harm than good. Not all discourse on race, however, suffers from these weaknesses. See Joel Stein, Jennie James, and Amanda Bower, "The Power Game," *Time,* September 3, 2001, 54–61, for a discussion of Navratilova's remarks, and this recent article on Williams, Associated Press, "Women's Tour CEO Reacts to Richard Williams' Remarks on Racism," *CBS Sports,* March 20, 2008, http://www.sportsline.com/tennis/story/10725357. It is not my contention that Richard Williams is subtle in his opinions about race. I cannot help but worry—alongside authors like Ralph Wiley in his *Why Black People Tend to Shout* (New York: Penguin, 1992)—that part of the reason for his outrageousness is that there is little willingness to carefully examine the role racism may play in the bizarre treatment to which the Williams family has been subject over the years.

7. Eduardo Bonilla-Silva, *Racism without Racists: Color-Blind Racism and the Persistence of Inequality in the United States,* 2nd ed. (New York: Rowman & Littlefield, 2006), 2.

8. Iris Marion Young, *Justice and the Politics of Difference* (Princeton, NJ: Princeton University Press, 1990), 41. This is just one particularly pithy characterization of oppression; in reality it is a complex phenomenon that has been carefully considered by a number of thinkers: see Sandra L. Bartky, *Femininity and Domination: Studies in the Phenomenology of Oppression* (New York: Routledge, 1990); Ann E. Cudd, *Analyzing Oppression* (New York: Oxford University Press, 2006); and Marilyn Frye, *The Politics of Reality: Essays in Feminist Theory* (Trumansburg, NY: Crossing Press, 1983).

9. Very complete discussions of the variety of theories of race can be found in Ron Mallon, "'Race': Normative, Not Metaphysical or Semantic," *Ethics* 116, no. 3 (2006): 525–51; Charles W. Mills, "'But What Are You Really?': The Metaphysics of Race," in his *Blackness Visible: Essays on Philosophy and Race* (Ithaca, NY: Cornell University Press, 1998); as well as Paul Taylor, *Race: A Philosophical Introduction* (Malden, MA: Polity Press, 2004).

10. Kwame Anthony Appiah, "Racisms," in *Anatomy of Racism*, ed. David Theo Goldberg (Minneapolis: University of Minnesota Press, 1990), 4–5.

Appiah actually distinguishes between two different types of racism: Extrinsic racism occurs when people use their racialist views to justify giving different moral standing to different racial groups. Intrinsic racists apply different moral standards to different racial groups regardless of whether or not they can identify essential moral differences between those groups. Intrinsic racists are, in Appiah's view, implicated in a more significant moral failure than are extrinsic racists (ibid., 5–6).

11. To be more specific, there is at least as much genetic variation within racial groups as there is between them, and the genes (traits) that are supposed to be unique to particular racial groups turn out to be distributed outside those groups. The Web page "Race: The Power of an Illusion"—maintained in concert with the documentary of the same name—includes an exercise in sorting people that both anecdotally and more substantially demonstrates the dispersal of various traits across racial boundaries; see Larry Adelman, "Race: The Power of an Illusion—Sorting People," *PBS.org*, http://www.pbs.org/race/002_SortingPeople/002_00-home.htm.

12. Racial population naturalism—another option for those who reject racialism—attempts to establish a biological foundation for race. It continues to reject the idea that we will eventually identify sets of genes present only in particular races. Instead it argues that races are biological groups resulting from periods of reproductive isolation. Thus, when I say that some woman is black, I am claiming that she is a member of a group that is (or was) reproductively isolated from other groups that I would identify as white or Asian, for example. While racial population naturalism offers a viable biological alternative account of race—one whose criteria have a hope of being met—it faces two major challenges. First, there is serious doubt as to whether human populations were ever reproductively isolated enough to create biological distinction; even if there was sufficient isolation, it is doubtful that such isolation has persisted into contemporary society. The second challenge concerns whether the biological populations produced by reproductive isolation correspond to the populations

currently identified as racial groups. In other words, there may be a racial group (or more than one) resulting from the reproductive isolation of sub-Saharan Africans, but this may have little or nothing to do with the group of folks that we call "black" right now.

13. At the very least, we need to be able to coherently discuss groups who have suffered or continue to suffer injustice by virtue of having been misidentified as members of racial groups.

14. What I'm calling narrative constructivism is more often called idealist constructivism, and describes views suggested and defended by W. E. B. Du Bois, Lawrence Thomas, and Lucius Outlaw.

15. The quotations can be found in Mills, "But What Are You Really?" 48–49. I will be using the slightly awkward construction "Narrationist"—with a capital "N"—through the remainder of the chapter to refer to narrative constructivists and the less awkward construction "Materialists" to refer to material constructivists.

16. Charles Mills, *The Racial Contract* (Ithaca, NY: Cornell University Press, 1997). This particular materialist constructivist account of race has been widely criticized. Whether Mills's account of constructivism is accurate or not is irrelevant to this argument.

17. Young, *Justice and the Politics of Difference*, 48–63.

18. There are other reasons to worry about materialist constructivism. In its eagerness to explain the social structure that oppresses people of color, it may dehumanize them. I worry that viewing the problem of race as fundamentally a socioeconomic one risks making people into mere cogs in a machine, that this perspective is profoundly disempowering. I focus on the assignment problem, because I consider it an internal critique. While most materialist constructivists do not share my concern that their position is dehumanizing, they will be worried if it turns out that materialist constructivism does not accurately map the groups of people who are oppressed by virtue of race.

19. Arthur Ashe and Arnold Rampersad, *Days of Grace: A Memoir* (New York: Knopf, 1993), 137, as well as McPhee, *Levels of the Game*, 45.

20. McPhee, *Levels of the Game*, 125.

21. "Sport and Tennis—Career History," *The Official Site of Arthur Ashe.org: The Tennis Legend*, 2007, http://www.arthurashe.org/site/#sportlhistory.

22. I reject some of the parameters of Ashe's thought experiment here. I believe the criticism that affirmative action serves to advance unqualified or underqualified people leans heavily on racist and sexist beliefs that populations served by affirmative action—for example, blacks and women—could not be qualified for certain jobs or as qualified as their white and male counterparts. This disagreement does not undermine the important point I think Ashe does make.

23. This series of quotations are all from Ashe and Rampersad, *Days of Grace*, 152.

24. In the interest of full disclosure, I admit Ashe regularly discouraged talented blacks from relying on affirmative action because of his personal commitment to self-reliance and rather classically conservative criticisms of affirmative action as degrad-

ing to those it is intended to help. However, Ashe also did not hesitate to offer personal and material assistance to blacks in need. I think this suggests that part of what motivated him was the recognition that understanding race requires a finer brush than what strictly material analysis provides.

25. Ashe and Rampersad, *Days of Grace,* 236.

26. The political assessment occurs in Tina Gianoulis, "Arthur Ashe," *St. James Encyclopedia of Pop Culture* (Detroit: Gale Group, 2002), available online at http://findarticles.com/p/articles/mi_g1epc/is_/ai_2419200039. The less constructive criticism can be found in Jeff Rowan, "Obama, Palin, and the 'Witness Protection Program,'" *Political Waves,* September 10, 2008,   http://jeffrowan111.tblog.com/post/1970016893.

27. Ashe and Rampersad, *Days of Grace,* 235–36.

28. Ibid., 126. Most materialist constructivist accounts allow that ideals or discourse plays some role in race; my concern is about the very small degree of significance placed on these more abstract aspects of race.

29. W. E. B. Du Bois, "The Conservation of Races," in *Identities: Race, Class, Gender, and Nationality,* ed. Linda Mendieta Alcoff and Eduardo Mendieta Alcoff (Malden, MA: Blackwell, 2003), 46–47.

30. Laurence Thomas, "Group Autonomy and Narrative Identity: Blacks and Jews," in *Race and Racism,* ed. Bernard Boxill (New York: Oxford University Press, 2001), 361–66.

31. Arthur Ashe and Frank Deford, *Arthur Ashe: Portrait in Motion,* first Carroll & Graf ed. (1975; repr., New York: Carroll & Graf, 1993), 105.

32. In fact, the critique and defense of "Conservation of Races" has become a small cottage industry. See Anthony Appiah, "The Uncompleted Argument: Du Bois and the Illusion of Race," in "Race, Writing, and Difference," ed. Henry Louis Gates Jr., special issue, *Critical Inquiry* 2, no. 1 (1985): 21–37; Lucius Outlaw, "'Conserve' Races?" in *W. E. B. Du Bois on Race and Culture,* ed. Bernard W. Bell, Emily R. Grosholz, and James B. Stewart (New York: Routledge, 1996): 15–37; Lucius Outlaw, "On W. E. B. Du Bois's 'The Conservation of Races,'" in *Overcoming Racism and Sexism,* ed. Linda A. Bell and David Blumenfeld (Lanham, MD: Rowman & Littlefield, 1995); Robert Gooding-Williams, "Outlaw, Appiah, and Du Bois's 'The Conservation of Races,'" in Bell, Grosholz, and Stewart, *W. E. B. Du Bois on Race and Culture,* 39–56.

33. Du Bois, "Conservation of Races," 44.

34. Appiah, "Uncompleted Argument," 73–74. Appiah's contention is, in fact, that in the absence of a legitimate ideal through which all blacks can be united, Du Bois falls back on a racialist account that explains the connection between blacks in terms of "common blood."

35. Ibid., 74.

36. See Thomas, "Group Autonomy and Narrative Identity," 361.

37. Ashe and Rampersad, *Days of Grace,* 104–7.

38. Ashe and Deford, *Arthur Ashe,* 126.

39. Ashe and Rampersad, *Days of Grace*, 130.

40. Appiah, "Uncompleted Argument," 75.

41. It is important to acknowledge that historically, we have found it much more difficult to see race as a complex social system. We are much more inclined to see race from the perspective of individuals. No doubt, part of the explanation of this tendency is that seeing race from the perspective of individuals can often serve to preserve the status quo, for example, making housing discrimination about one or two bad apples and ignoring its connection to white flight and urban decay.

42. Ashe, *Days of Grace*, 105.

43. Ashe and Deford, *Arthur Ashe*, 107.

44. Mark Mathabane, *Kaffir Boy: The True Story of a Black Youth's Coming of Age in Apartheid South Africa* (New York: Simon & Schuster, 1998).

45. McPhee, *Levels of the Game*, 7, 27.

46. Ashe and Deford, *Arthur Ashe*, 108.

47. McPhee, *Levels of the Game*, 7, 99, 93.

48. Ashe and Rampersad, *Days of Grace*, 35.

49. His opinions on black militantism can be found in McPhee, *Levels of the Game*, 144. His rejection of affirmative action occurs, among other places, in Ashe and Rampersad, *Days of Grace*, 147–53.

50. See Ashe and Rampersad, *Days of Grace*, 110; and Bob Carter, "Ashe's Impact Reached Far beyond the Court," *SportCentury Biography*, 2007, http://espn .go.com/classic/biography/s/Ashe_Arthur.html.

51. Ashe and Rampersad, *Days of Grace*, 127–28.

52. Ibid., 60–100.

53. McPhee, *Levels of the Game*, 145.

Maureen Linker

THE RIDICULOUS MEETS THE RADICAL IN THE BATTLE OF THE SEXES

Various lists of the twentieth century's most significant sports moments as well as the century's most important athletes invariably include "The Battle of the Sexes" and Billie Jean King. The *Sporting News* in a 1999 list of the five most important sporting events of the twentieth century places the Billie Jean King–Bobby Riggs tennis match second only to Jackie Robinson's entrée into major league baseball. These roundups of the previous hundred years in sports also include Jesse Owens's famous victories at the Munich Olympics and the Joe Louis rematch against Max Schmeling in 1938. What all of these legendary athletes and their victories share is demonstrated proof that the best of American meritocracy can rise above social ills like racism, fascism, and sexism. Yet much of the rhetoric around the success of athletes like Jackie Robinson, Jesse Owens, and Joe Louis is serious, sober, and respectful. Robinson is often noted in sports literature for the calm demeanor he perfected, his ability to gracefully withstand public criticism and humiliation, and his thoughtful intelligence and measured pride. The specific sporting events in which Robinson, Owens, and Louis participated have been documented with care and diligence in the historical literature, noting the significance and the high-stakes nature of their social and political implications.

Yet when it comes to the Battle of the Sexes and the athletes involved, both the event itself and much of the subsequent rhetoric that followed proved to be a comedic spectacle that lacked the seriousness of these earlier watershed sporting moments. Why, if it counts as one of the most significant moments in both American social and sports history, was it such a public show of silliness and over-the-top theatrics? Why, in essence, was it publicly acceptable to joke about sexism in the culture, with both participants exploiting stereotypes with glee, when earlier sports struggles with racism or fascism were painful, somber subjects?

In this chapter, I will explore the differences between cultural perceptions of race and gender and the ensuing challenges these social categories present by comparing the case of Jackie Robinson to that of Billie Jean King. I will argue that the challenge that African American men pose to athletics has evoked greater fears of "the angry black man" stereotype in white men while gender challenges in sports, particularly in an individualized sport like tennis, raise less competitive threats to male conceptions of strength and competency. For that reason, a fifty-five-year-old male tennis player can behave like a court jester challenging a twenty-nine-year-old female tennis star to a public battle of the sexes, and the event can become comical entertainment that both challenges while it reaffirms existing gender divisions. King and Riggs were in many ways the right people for the right issue at the right time. Riggs's earlier match against Australian tennis champion Margaret Court failed to garner the same level of interest as his Battle of the Sexes with King, in large part because Court treated the match like a straightforward sporting challenge rather than a piece of public theater. That is also the reason she lost the match against Riggs.

In this chapter, first, I will briefly discuss sports as a site of relevant social resistance despite criticisms of sports as politically arcane and socially insignificant. Second, I will draw out the differences between race narratives for an athlete like Jackie Robinson as compared with gender narratives around Billie Jean King and the Battle of the Sexes. While both the athletes and the events in which they participated had significant social consequences, humor played a central role in the success and the public interest in the Battle of the Sexes while seriousness, calm, and dignity were the central features of Robinson's success. I will draw upon the notions of "playfulness" and "world traveling" as outlined by feminist philosopher Maria Lugones in her work on challenging social injustice; it was not merely Billie Jean King's athletic ability that won her the decisive victory on September 20, 1973, but her instincts as a competitor, who recognized that Riggs's use of humor and stereotyping was an effort at control. King rose to the challenge, even if she was not the huckster and jester Riggs was. She played the part of the showman because she knew it would be required to wrest control from Riggs and ultimately make the match be about tennis. Finally, again drawing on Lugones's work I will comment on the "loving perception" that King had for Riggs, leading eventually to an understanding and shared humanity between the two players as opposed to a simple dichotomy between good and evil or morally right and morally wrong.

Does Sports Matter?

Consider the following words from Noam Chomsky in his documentary film *Manufacturing Consent*:

> Take, say, sports—that's another crucial example of the indoctrination system, in my view. For one thing because it—you know, it offers people something to pay attention to that is of no importance. That keeps them from worrying about things that matter to their lives that they might have some idea of doing something about. And in fact it's striking to see the intelligence that's used by ordinary people in [discussions of] sports [as opposed to political and social issues]. I mean, you listen to radio stations where people call in—they have the most exotic information and understanding about all kind of arcane issues. And the press undoubtedly does a lot with this. You know, I remember in high school, already I was pretty old. I suddenly asked myself at one point, why do I care if my high school team wins the football game? I mean, I don't know anybody on the team, you know? I mean, they have nothing to do with me, I mean, why am I cheering for my team? It doesn't mean anything—it doesn't make sense. But the point is, it does make sense: it's a way of building up irrational attitudes of submission to authority, and group cohesion behind leadership elements—in fact, it's training in irrational jingoism. That's also a feature of competitive sports. I think if you look closely at these things, I think, typically, they do have functions, and that's why energy is devoted to supporting them and creating a basis for them and advertisers are willing to pay for them and so on.

Chomsky's comments regarding professional sports capture some of the frustration some intellectuals have with the priority of sports in our culture. Sports pages in newspapers, reports on radio and television news, and merchandising all contribute to the centrality of sports in our culture. And as Chomsky highlights, sports is used in American culture as a diversion from the harsh realities of the world. The "arcane" and "exotic" information that Chomsky refers to here is vastly different from the kind of information most Americans have about foreign affairs, global economics, and worldwide social inequalities. The intelligence and analysis many people invest in sports most likely outweighs their investigation and analysis of the broader world.

Chomsky also argues that sports is "of no real importance" and is something that does not really matter to most people's lives. Of course, most sports fans would likely disagree, arguing that sports matter just as art, music, and other forms of entertainment do and that they provide a glimpse into significant aspects of the human experience. As a friend of mine once commented, "Sports are like movies or plays except no one knows the ending. The script hasn't been written beforehand, and we all have to wait and see what the outcome will be." That sense of witnessing an unfolding drama of beauty, skill, and competition is very meaningful for many spectators, and Chomsky's dismissal may reflect more of his own personal disinterest and unfamiliarity with sports. Certainly his comment—"Why do I care if my high school team wins the football game? I mean, I don't know anybody on the team, you know"—conveys the disconnection he had with the athletes in his youth. If he had known the players, would that have changed his attitude? There is a sense for many fans that they do know the players. Fans pay attention to sports stories, to personal information about athletes, and to the communities that athletes come from. As sports writer David Zirin has pointed out, the very passion that people invest in sports can transform it from a mindless escape into a site of social resistance. Zirin refers to the role that Jackie Robinson played in focusing the nation's attention on civil rights and the Billie Jean King–Bobby Riggs tennis match as pivotal in the struggle for women's rights. Zirin argues that sports are neither to be defended nor vilified; rather, sports need to be understood so that we can separate the "disgusting from the beautiful, and the ridiculous from the radical."[1]

I take Zirin's point to be that sports provide complex and relevant data for understanding social issues. While Chomsky oversimply dismisses them as mindless diversion, sports can play a role in changing social attitudes just as they can reaffirm existing social attitudes. For that reason, analysis of sports, particularly sporting events that draw attention to issues like racism or sexism, should be taken seriously by scholars and theorists of social issues. I will take the view, then, that sports can be more than "irrational jingoism" by examining how sexism in sports was shown to be both ridiculous and radical in the Battle of the Sexes.

The Seriousness of Race and the Silliness of Sex

Jackie Robinson was a man of restraint, courage, intelligence, calm, and altruism. In fact, much of the literature around his career emphasizes his ability to hold back from confronting the assaults on his race, character, and humanity: "'I'm looking for a ball player with guts enough not to fight back,' [Branch] Rickey is said to have told Robinson during their first meeting. Jackie's wife, Rachel Robinson, remembered well Jackie's equanimity, his reliance on reasonable argument, his restraint, his calm and his willingness to act on behalf of another."[2] Not that Robinson wasn't a man with a healthy sense of moral outrage; rather, he is described as one who held back his frustration with injustice for a larger purpose, for the ultimate goal of integrating the sport of baseball. Many credit his efforts as a major contribution to the emerging civil rights movement in the United States. For that reason, as well as his exceptional athletic ability, Robinson is considered among the most influential Americans of the twentieth century. In fact, in recent cultural analysis, comparisons have been made between Robinson's gracious demeanor and Barack Obama's historic presidential campaign. Both men, it is argued, achieved success because of their ability to withhold their reactivity and perform gracefully under pressure. Branch Rickey, the Brooklyn Dodgers general manager from 1943 to 1950 and the man who signed Robinson, knew that if an African American man was to be successful in sports he had to have the "guts not to fight back." Rickey reasoned that white fans would never come to feel at ease with a black man who was surly, angry, ostentatious, or boastful (for many African Americans, the later career of Mohammad Ali challenged this expectation of how a black athlete should act and was celebrated as furthering the efforts to break down racist double standards). Robinson embodied the kind of quiet, restrained, intelligent dignity that was needed to challenge prevailing racist attitudes in the emerging civil rights movement.

Alternatively, Billie Jean King's decisive win (6–4, 6–3, 6–3) in three straight sets against Bobby Riggs in 1973, while considered a substantial contribution to the emerging feminist movement, was still framed within the context of a comical circus with sexism on display as theater. One story put it: "With the possible exception of a nude tag-team wrestling match pitting Burt Reynolds and Norman Mailer against Gloria Steinem and Germaine Greer, it is scarcely conceivable that any other single athletic event could burlesque the issue of sexism so outrageously."[3]

As one sports article at the time described Riggs's earlier challenge, against Margaret Court: "The gracious Australian ace made the mistake of picking up Bobby's challenge, and the result was this year's Mother's Day massacre. Bobby rattled her by presenting her with a bouquet of roses before the match started. He neutralized her normally sharp attack with frustrating spins and lobs. Court did not merely lose, she disintegrated. Final score: 6–2, 6–1."[4]

At the time of the match, Court was at the top of her game, having won twenty-seven of the twenty-eight tournaments she had played that year. King explained later that she believed Court was enticed by the money, a guaranteed $10,000, although Court has always denied that charge. Court, according to King, said the match would be like taking a stroll in the park. However, because it was played during the height of the women's movement and promoted by Riggs's endless chauvinistic ranting, it took on political overtones that made it bigger than any women's match had ever been. Court, who hated women's liberation and embraced everything gracious and traditional in tennis, had unwittingly walked into a circus carrying the banner of women's rights.[5]

Court's prior success in legitimate tennis arenas could in no way prepare her psychologically for what she faced on that Mother's Day in 1973. Journalists had come from thousands of miles away, and CBS televised the match nationally. Court remembered it as a nightmare. "It was a mistake that I ever did it. . . . I'd never been in anything like that before. It was show biz, and here I was coming off the sedate courts of Wimbledon and the U.S. Open. I never got into it. I thought what in heaven's name am I doing out here?"[6]

After his win against Court, Riggs eyed his ideal opponent in Billie Jean King. King, unlike Court, identified as a feminist advocate and had worked for several years to address prize-money disparities in men and women's tennis championships. By 1972, King had become the first female athlete to earn more than $100,000 in prize money and was named *Sports Illustrated*'s Sportswoman of the Year. That same year, Congress passed and President Nixon signed into law Title IX, the measure that prohibited sex discrimination in education, including disbursement of federal money for athletic programs.

King feared that refusing to play Riggs after Court's loss would not just derail the progress of women's tennis but threaten a host of other gains women had made, including Title IX. So she agreed to participate in the Battle of the Sexes in the Houston Astrodome. The match would prove to be a made-for-prime-time, best-of-five-sets, $100,000 winner-take-all. And once King agreed to play, she knew she had to do whatever she could to win.

What made King different from Court was that she willingly took on the banner of women's liberation and knew that a win could lend momentum to the emerging women's movement. While King was serious about the game and about the match, she exhibited what feminist philosopher Maria Lugones describes as the "playful world traveling" essential for those on the margins challenging prevailing social injustice.[7] When an individual or group seeks to challenge aspects of its world, Lugones argues, one strategy for success is a willingness to be "playful," meaning that the individual or group is open to surprise, to self construction, and to existing creatively and not dogmatically or passively.

King was traveling into a particular kind of world in the Battle of the Sexes. This was high-stakes tennis, played against a man, in a hugely public forum that had overtly political overtones. Court's earlier loss against Riggs could be attributed in part to the fact that she was unwilling to "world travel" in any "playful" sense. She assumed the game against Riggs was going to be a match like the others she had played before. She remained fixed, dogmatic, and decidedly unplayful in the unfolding circus. King, on the other hand, embraced these unknown elements and, rather than hold fast to playing the game as she knew it, was willing to be open and creative, with few expectations about the rules and the norms of competency.

Riggs began mounting his sexist attacks in the press with claims like "Women belong in the bedroom and the kitchen, in that order." He posed for sexually aggressive ads for Hai Karate cologne and then in costume as George Washington and Henry VIII for Houston newspapers. He wore a "Sugar Daddy" jacket in many photographs and happily denigrated the women's movement in press interviews before the match. It was clear to King that playing under pressure was the real challenge of the match, and the pressure was not about athletic ability but about psychological resilience. She said at the time: "When I finally saw the film of the match between Riggs and Margaret Court and I watched him present her with those roses and Margaret curtsy, I yelled 'Margaret, you idiot, you played right into his hands!' If that was me, I would have grabbed him and kissed him. He's not going to jive me. If he gets too dirty, I can get tough too."[8]

Both Robinson and King had to demonstrate psychological resilience in the face of public bias, but in Robinson's case, the pressure was to not react to the overt violence aimed his way from the public bigotry. King required the psychological resilience to react very demonstrably to Riggs's showmanship and publicly match his over-the-top humor. Just as restraint was not necessarily in Robinson's nature but had to be cultivated in the face of social resistance, King was not necessarily a natural in the role of clown, but she cultivated the appropriate persona as a form of social protest. King saw the relationship among humor, power, and gender dynamics. In an article that appeared before the match, a reporter noted: "King told Riggs that she didn't care if he showed up for the match in a jock strap. So he had pictures made of himself clad only in a supporter. If it has contributed nothing substantial to the history of sexism in the 1970s, the Riggs-King repartee has at least lent some much-needed humor. Billie Jean cannot resist getting into the spirit occasionally. She calls him 'Roberta' and mocks his duck-footed waddle. 'I'm pigeon-toed,' she says, 'so maybe this match should be billed as the duck v. the pigeon.'"[9]

Anthropologist Mary Douglas has argued in her essay "Jokes" that "humor confronts and changes existing power/control dynamics and for that reason all humor is subversive."[10] Simply put, if you can laugh at your enemy, then you are in a position of power.[11] Social humor exposes defects, weaknesses, and contradictions in cultural biases and is hence negative in its critique but positive and even palliative in providing an escape valve for anxieties and aggression.[12]

The day before the match, Riggs contemplated the outcome: "I'm taking so many vitamins I must have a glass stomach. Billie Jean's banking that I'm not in shape and not serious enough and she may be right. But I saw the girls at Wimbledon and they were so bad it confused me. I know I can play my game. The question is can she play up to her ability under the pressure. Can she stay loose, hit out, be great on the tough points and win?"[13]

As mentioned, playing under pressure was the true challenge of the match, and the pressure was more about psychological resilience than about athletic ability. King's willingness to take on the pressure in a playful, non-arrogant way meant that she could ultimately travel into this world of high-stakes public spectacle and transcend its borders to reach the common ground of playing competitive tennis. According to one sports reporter at the match: "Riggs' fate probably flashed before him sometime during the fourth game of the opening set. Serving at 15-all, he hit every shot in his arsenal yet King kept coming on. Back and forth they went, huffing and running on both sides for about nine exchanges. Then King hit a backhand wide and Riggs waddled across the sideline, breathed heavily, and smiled down at the floor. The psych was over and he knew it. Now it was tennis only, and he was in against a champion 26 years his junior."[14]

Returning again to the contrast between Robinson's calm and somber restraint and King's humorous and broad theatrics, it is apparent how public attitudes about race operate at a different level from attitudes about gender. Racism, as many identity theorists have pointed out, occurs mostly in the public sphere as "us" against "them," as compared with sexism and its prominence in the private sphere of home and family. Whites have historically had the racist privilege of choosing not to associate with African Americans in a variety of public places, including businesses, schools, political institutions, and religious institutions. On the other hand, most men have to encounter women as mothers, sisters, wives, and daughters. With gender, there is an intimacy that is not necessarily shared with race relations. Though racism and sexism are both volatile and demeaning, sexism does not pit man against man but man against woman. Racism has a more aggressive, violent, competitive edge, since it is intertwined with traditional conceptions of masculinity. This is not to say that there are not clearly violent aspects to sexism, but the violence is often perpetrated within the private sphere and involves efforts made by men to exercise control over women. Retaliation against sexism has not held the same threat for white men that retaliation against racism holds.

For this reason, it is much harder to imagine the kind of joking and theatrics that occurred during the Battle of the Sexes happening in any similar way with Robinson's introduction into major league baseball. For instance, spectators on the day of the King-Riggs match wore buttons that said "Bobby Riggs—bleah!" or "Male Chauvinist Pig" or even "Down with Women's Lib." King herself sent Riggs a pig named "Larrimore Hustle" (Larrimore was Riggs's middle name), symbolizing his repugnant sexist attitudes. Riggs countered by entering the Houston Astrodome on the evening of the match in a gold rickshaw pulled by eight scantily clad female models identified as "Bobby's Bosom Buddies." King matched this move by entering the arena on a divan carried by five burly, scantily clad men. Fans, the media, and the athletes themselves wore their social attitudes proudly and playfully, a fact that seems almost unimaginable from the point of view of racial conflicts in sports. The derision Robinson faced on the field, in the press, and among fans shared none of the playfulness of the Battle of the Sexes and required him to stoically withstand serious physical and emotional threats.

To be clear, however, I am not suggesting that sexist expressions in the culture do not come in overt aggressive or even violent forms. Both racism and sexism in the public sphere convey a fear, an anger, and an aggression that can have quite serious consequences for the targeted individuals. Rather, the conclusion intended here is that the underlying seriousness of racist overtones in the case of Robinson was due in part to the challenges within male-to-male competition. In the case of Riggs and King, the humor involved conveys the cultural acceptability of male jokes around female incompetency—typical fodder for comedians, film and television plots, and even family stories.

The Emergence of Loving Perception

The match between King and Riggs also typifies another aspect of Maria Lugones's recommendation for successfully challenging social injustice. Lugones adds to the notion of "playfulness" a conception of "loving, world traveling." As Lugones says, "By traveling to someone else's world we can understand what it is to be them and to be ourselves in their eyes. Thus we become fully subjects to each other."[15] By "world" Lugones is referring not to actual borders or physical boundaries but to the limits of conceptual schemes that make up our belief systems. When our values conflict with another individual's it is as if we occupy different worlds. A difference in values can mean a difference in what we believe exists and what we can know. By adopting a perspective of "loving, world traveling," one opens herself epistemically and metaphysically to a different kind of reality. Why might other individuals hold the beliefs that they do? What kinds of experiences could lead them to their beliefs? Asking these kinds of questions is very different from assuming another person is just wrong or, even worse, morally repugnant.

This emergence of "loving perception" as compared with arrogant dogmatism is evident in the relationship that developed between King and Riggs in subsequent years. Cokie Roberts asked King in a recent interview, "What was your relationship with Riggs like after the match?" King replied, "I adored him. We stayed in touch. I kept telling him, 'It's not about winning a match. It's about making history, making a difference.' The last conversation we had on the phone, the day before he passed away in 1995, he said, 'We did make a difference, didn't we?' I thought, 'He finally got it.' It was so sweet. Then I told him I loved him, and he said he loved me. I really enjoyed him because he was such a showman, but the world didn't really appreciate him as a player, and I did. I think he underestimated me because he didn't realize how much I knew about him."[16]

This shift from Riggs as arrogant, idiotic, male chauvinist pig to a loving, endearing, key player in the success of King and her colleagues is one of the triumphs of liberatory social movements. Rather than functioning as moments in history for "special interest" groups, they become opportunities for all of us to experience our shared struggle for worth and dignity. While Riggs may have done more for women's tennis than any other man, King may have done more for Riggs than anyone else in giving him a lasting legacy.

King was always committed to seeing the shared humanity in herself and Riggs. She sought to know him and, to an extent, identify with him, so that they could eventually share in her victory. She insists "it's not about winning a match but making a difference," and in framing the event that way, she transforms the Battle of the Sexes into a show that she and Riggs put on together, equal partners in challenging existing assumptions about women's inferiority. Thus, King complicates the relationship she had with Riggs for the better. The match then is not simply a superior player against an inferior one or a morally repugnant character against a morally virtuous one, but a complex interplay of individuals in the midst of social transformation, each having a significant role to play. King restored Riggs's humanity even as he set out to undermine hers. In so doing she presents an alternative to the dichotomy of winners and losers that often marks masculine competition. In fact Rosie Casals, who told *Sports Illustrated* at the time of the match "that there is no reason women should have to justify themselves to an old, obnoxious, has-been like Riggs who can't hear, can't see and is an idiot besides," later said, "Bobby Riggs did more for women's tennis than anybody."[17]

What did The Battle of the Sexes ultimately prove? In assessing its impact, I close with King's own words: "I knew that as an athlete my victory over a man twenty-six years my senior was no great feat. Yet if I had done nothing sensational in beating Riggs, I had shown thousands of people who had never taken an interest in women's sports that women were skillful, entertaining, and capable of coming through in the clutch. The match legitimized women's tennis. It was the culmination of an era."[18]

Notes

1. David Zirin, *What's My Name, Fool: Sports and Resistance in the United States* (New York: Haymarket, 2005), 21, 22.

2. John Kelly, "Integrating America: Jackie Robinson, Critical Events, and Baseball Black and White," *International Journal of the History of Sport* 22, no. 6 (November 2005): 1021.

3. "How Bobby Runs and Talks, Talks, Talks," editorial, *Time*, September 10, 1973, 3–4.

4. Curry Kirkpatrick, "Mother's Day Ms. Match," *Sports Illustrated*, May 21, 1973, 40–45.

5. Billie Jean King and Cynthia Starr, *We Have Come a Long Way: The Story of Women's Tennis* (New York: McGraw Hill, 1988), 144, 146.

6. Ibid., 148.

7. Maria Lugones, "Playfulness, World Traveling, and Loving Perception," *Hypatia* 2, no. 2 (Summer 1987): 3–19.

8. "How Bobby Runs."

9. Kirkpatrick, "Mother's Day Ms. Match."

10. Mary Douglas, "Jokes," in *Rethinking Popular Culture: Contemporary Perspectives in Cultural Studies*, ed. Chandra Mukerji and Michael Schudson (Berkeley: University of California Press, 1991), 292.

11. Regina Barreca, ed., *New Perspectives on Women and Comedy* (Amsterdam: Overseas Publishing Association Press, 1992), 5.

12. Joanne Gilbert, *Performing Marginality* (Detroit, MI: Wayne State University Press, 2003).

13. "How Bobby Runs."

14. Kirkpatrick, "Mother's Day Ms. Match."

15. Lugones, "Playfulness," 17.

16. Cokie Roberts, "Interview with Billie Jean King," *USA Weekend,* April 8, 2008, 2.

17. King and Starr, *We Have Come a Long Way,* 143.

18. Ibid.

David Baggett and Neil Delaney Jr.

FRIENDSHIP, RIVALRY, AND EXCELLENCE

You gotta live it to feel it, you didn't you wouldn't get it.
—Eminem

Friendship today is a concept that has undergone a fair bit of degradation. It used to be a highly exalted notion. It was thought by many ancients to represent the highest form of love. It was touted as a school of virtue, and as something relatively rare. More recently, casual acquaintances are liable to call each other friends, or even online acquaintances in the form of a plethora of Facebook "friends" and the like. So friendship is well worth exploring, and doing so in the context of discussing tennis affords the extra advantage of identifying some of the challenges posed to friendship at the highest levels of competitive sport.

In tennis, what intensifies the competition is that the game is played directly between the participants. I hit my backhand to your forehand, and your drop shot requires me to run. And at each step along the way, we find a zero-sum game; your earned point means my lost point, and my winning game means a lost game for you. This adversarial structure may not always conduce to friendship. The problem, in a sense, is exacerbated in the case of the Williams sisters. Just imagine facing your own sister (repeatedly!) in the finals of Grand Slams—and the sort of cognitive dissonance such an encounter is likely to induce. Winning the trophy means depriving your sister of it; little wonder this is one of the reasons why this legendary rivalry ranks near the top of the all-time most dramatic to watch unfold, and every such matchup is bittersweet for the ambivalent participants, by their own admission.[1]

Even though tennis is a sport, many of us on occasion have taken it too far, happy to win by nearly any means available, growing disgusted at ourselves for a lost opportunity or bad execution. Sometimes we even allow a tension to develop with the player on the other side of the court, whom we, in our worst moments, think of not merely as a fellow player or perhaps even friend, but the enemy, the obstinate opposition. Just as it's tempting in a dispute or dialogue to demonize those on the other side, to be not content merely with expressing disagreement, likewise in tennis too, and sports in general: it's easy to fall into the trap of thinking of the conflict as more than it is. We can lose perspective, and rather than just a snapshot of who happens to win on a particular day, a tennis match or other competition is reconceived as practically a death match, a struggle for domination, a chance not just to win a set or match but to vanquish a foe. We see this in rabid political partisanship, conflicts between avid proponents of divergent worldviews, as well as on the tennis court. This means that there's an important issue here indeed. How can rivals (or, for that matter, disputants, interlocutors, dialogue partners, debate participants, and the like), either on the tennis court or off, be friends?[2]

Friendships of Pleasure

The history of thought has featured several important philosophers and writers probing the question of what friendship is all about—ranging from Plato to Augustine, Aristotle to Cicero, Montaigne to Emerson. What makes someone more than an acquaintance, a genuine friend? Must a friendship have for one of its basic ingredients warm feelings, or will grudging respect do? Are friendships vital for human flourishing? Are there different sorts of friendships? To get a handle on some of these questions, let's begin with what Aristotle, Plato's most famous student and one of the most important analysts of friendship, thought was an important sort of friendship, namely, one of pleasure or enjoyment.[3]

Suppose you and a hypothetical tennis partner just have a really good time playing tennis with each other. Foremost in your mind, imagine, isn't the improvement of your game or the moral fiber of your opponent but rather simply the enjoyment and pleasure you derive from playing tennis with this person. Knowing that she seems to be enjoying it as well may even enhance your own pleasure. What really drives such a friendship, more than anything, is this shared enjoyment from time spent together playing tennis. Aristotle would say of such a friendship—and he wouldn't deny that it is a kind of friendship—that what each person most cares about in the friendship is something other than the other person; rather, the pleasure time spent with that person produces is the driving concern. If a different person could equally well provide the same quantity or quality of enjoyment, the partner in question could be easily replaced; moreover, a friendship of pleasure functions irrespective of the caliber of the other person's character. Perhaps the person is one of integrity and great character, perhaps not; but a friendship of pleasure doesn't require it; such an issue isn't on the radar screen, isn't relevant. Nor are the friendship and its benefits at root due to this integrity, real or imagined, and nothing in the friendship intentionally aims at producing such character. This makes such a friendship a (mere) friendship of pleasure.

Pleasure is not intrinsically bad; in fact, it's probably inherently good. This is not to say, however, that every enjoyment or search for pleasure is morally respectable. Deriving pleasure from a friendship is not necessarily bad. As friendships go, however, such a model does leave something to be desired. In terms of a real-life example from the world of tennis, it would be altogether presumptuous to reduce any friendship on the tour merely to the level of a pleasure friendship. So let's be circumspect here and engage in a thought experiment involving two of our childhood favorites, known for having a great friendship. Björn Borg and Vitas Gerulaitas were dear friends. They spent a great deal of time together, enjoying one another's company immensely, playing tennis regularly, despite their rather different personality types. Before his premature and tragic death, Gerulaitas, in addition to being one of the best tennis players in the world (reputed to hardly ever miss a shot in practice), was notorious for his ebullience and ability to have fun. Whether their friendship was actually a mere friendship of pleasure is beside the point; we're entitled to harbor huge doubts that it was, and so let's not say otherwise. But just suppose that the basis of the friendship were merely the enjoyment they derived from one another's company. Again, this supposition may well be entirely contrary to fact, but if it were true, then such a friendship would have been a mere friendship of pleasure by Aristotle's account. It was a fact that these two were something of rivals, playing some classic matches (that Borg won); so, perhaps counterfactually speaking, if they were friends in the sense of a friendship of pleasure, they were obviously able to function as such friends despite their rivalry and its attendant challenges.

Friendships of Usefulness

A friendship of usefulness or utility is the second form Aristotle explores. Suppose two tennis players develop a friendship because each derives a benefit from practicing with the other. Their games are sufficiently suited to one another's, and the quality of their play is adequately complementary, that they serve as ideal practice partners for each other. Their friendship never goes much beyond the mutual benefit they derive from their shared interest in improving their games, but they get along well and come to regard each other as friends. Aristotle would characterize this as a friendship, to be sure, but a friendship at the level of utility or usefulness. Each is in it for the usefulness the friendship serves. Such a friendship of utility isn't a bad thing, but note that each person is primarily in it not exactly because of the other person considered in her entirety but because of a specific thing that happens to be true about her, namely, that her tennis game conduces to an effective playing and practice partner. In the absence of such a trait, presumably, the relationship probably would not endure.[4]

Friendships of usefulness introduce an interesting twist when one considers rivalries. For friendship and rivalry may be thought mutually exclusive at the highest levels of competitive tennis for the following reason: in a game sometimes decided by millimeters and milliseconds, the slightest psychological advantage can make the difference between winning and losing. If a friendship makes one more susceptible to letting up, feeling bad for winning, sacrificing an advantage, forfeiting a killer instinct, that might make all the difference. Winning at the highest levels requires a kind of ruthlessness, a single-minded focus, a nearly unquenchable thirst for domination, not exactly the stuff of warm fuzzy feelings. When there are two opponents and only one prize, the one who blinks will probably lose. This is perhaps why the friendship between Pete Sampras and Jim Courier cooled as they approached the top of their games and why regarding the 2001 French Open semifinal between Justine Henin and Kim Clijsters, Henin's biographer says "there was no space for friendship any more, there was too much at stake."[5] Sampras admits to benefiting from the persona that grew up around him on the tour as someone a bit untouchable and unapproachable, which he didn't mind reinforcing.

In philosophy, say, I don't rightly construe my friend's publishing a paper as an occasion for feeling diminished, because his or her publishing a paper isn't inconsistent with my publishing my own. (Consider the joint authorship of this very chapter!) I should be happy for my friend; indeed, I can choose to perceive her achievement in a way that enhances us both. It can be something of a source of pride for me that my friend is faring so well professionally. This is an altogether appropriate occasion to rejoice with those who rejoice. But in tennis there's an added challenge. For my rival and I are going for the very same goal. My winning means her losing. The analogy with academics, to be consistent, would be that my friend and I are each going for the same dream job, and only one of us can get it. I may be happy for my friend if she gets it, but her getting it precludes me from doing so. Imagine now that such a dynamic were operative not just on some such rare occasion, but all the time. This is the situation in tennis between two top rivals. When one thinks of the magnitude of winning a major, the way it forever changes one's life, one really sees the height of the stakes.

At the same time, there's something paradoxical about rivalries that perhaps carves out an important space for a friendship of usefulness; this is the interesting twist we promised. A great player benefits from other great players. Such rivalries provide a chance to display true excellence, a quality of play that may not otherwise find expression. Nadal pushes Federer to play better on clay than Federer would otherwise have to (for three years in a row, only Nadal was able to beat Federer at Roland Garros); Agassi pushed Sampras to add new elements to his game to meet the former's challenge. Perhaps the most notorious example of all here is the way that Steffi Graf's legacy itself was hurt, obviously through no fault of her own, by her crazed fan's attack on her main rival, Monica Seles. As Mark Foreman's chapter in this volume details, this tragedy hurt not only the game, tennis fans, and most obviously Seles herself, but Graf's own legacy. Rivalries thus understood aren't just consistent with friendships of usefulness; the great rivalries provide the truest test of tennis greatness.

For now, though, let's shift gears and find in tennis history an altogether different example of a friendship of usefulness, not between two rivals per se, but between two legends whose paths overlapped in a fascinating way. Let's consider the complex relationship between Arthur Ashe, to whom this book is dedicated, and John McEnroe. Ashe served as captain of the Davis Cup team through many of the years McEnroe played. As McEnroe's coach, Ashe shouldered the job of reining in Mac, which made for some awfully tense moments. By nature Ashe was a study in equanimity, whereas McEnroe is notoriously irascible. Their diametrically opposed reactions to volatile situations vividly manifested themselves on numerous occasions, one of which we will recount: In a Davis Cup doubles match against Clerc and Vilas, various displays of gamesmanship, delaying tactics, and needling remarks were getting to McEnroe. The Argentinians were rattling him, and the obscenities and verbal jabs between Clerc and McEnroe between points were escalating. After Ashe tried settling Mac down, reminding him that he was representing the United States, Mac seemed temporarily better, until Clerc "looked at him sweetly and lisped, provocatively, 'You're so nice!'" To which McEnroe retorted, "Go f—— yourself!" Ashe was incensed; here's his account of what happened next: "I was stunned. I stormed onto the court, and John and I exchanged some bitter words for a few seconds. This time I thought I might punch John. I have never punched anyone in my life, but I was truly on the brink of hitting him. I had never been so angry in my life. I couldn't trust myself not to strangle him. Of course, if I had, any jury would have acquitted me."[6]

Ashe admitted that as captain and player they were like total strangers. "I wasn't happy about the situation, but I had no stomach for fake camaraderie or ersatz shows of friendship."[7] So far, this makes it sound as if they weren't friends at all, especially when we remember Mac's aversion to authority, which Ashe had come to represent as a coach willing on occasion to stand up to him. But that wouldn't begin to capture the complexity of their relationship, for a genuine friendship did in reality emerge between these two men. McEnroe didn't want Ashe to remain entirely quiet on the sidelines during a match, and Ashe greatly appreciated the talent, loyalty, and excitement Mac brought to Davis Cup. In various ways they did find each other useful, and this was the basis of some semblance of friendship. The friendship was less rooted in pleasure than usefulness, though Ashe did delight in watching Mac's on-court brilliance.

Even that analysis, though, doesn't do justice to their complicated friendship. McEnroe came to grow fond of and deeply respect Ashe, and Ashe, surprisingly, came to respect Mac as well, even if he didn't respect some of his antics and explosions. Even regarding Mac's rage, though, Ashe offered a nuanced analysis that many readers may find surprising. It's tempting for us to think that Mac was the vicious one and Ashe the virtuous one; Mac never held his anger in check, Ashe always did. But appearances can be deceiving. Ashe explained that Neil Amdur's analysis of him may have been right: that Ashe held his emotions so tightly in check due to a certain amount of repression. "Neil traced my repression back to the death of my grandfather and mother in the span of one year during my childhood, and especially my father's grief when my mother died when I was seven." Seeing adult family members openly sobbing and mourning frightened the young Ashe, and to protect himself, he may well have built an "emotional wall." "Each time McEnroe loses control on the court in a Davis Cup match," Amdur writes, "it forces Ashe to deal with the most delicate frames in his psyche."[8]

Ashe came to think that this may have been right, which tempered his judgment of McEnroe. He elaborated:

> I suspect now that McEnroe and I were not so far apart, after all. Far from seeing John as an alien, I think I may have known him, probably without being fully aware of my feelings, as a reflection of an intimate part of myself. This sense of McEnroe as embodying feelings I could only repress, or as a kind of darker angel to my own tightly restrained spirit, may explain why I always hesitated to interfere with his rages even when he was excessive, although I sometimes had to do so. Now I wonder whether I had not always been aware, at some level, that John was expressing my own rage, my own anger, for me, as I never could express it; and I perhaps was even grateful to him for doing so, although his behavior was, on another level, totally unacceptable.

Theirs was a complex relationship, not easily reducible to a preset category. If it's at least best characterized as a friendship of utility, it certainly glimmered with aspects of more. "I developed a deep affection for McEnroe, and also a genuine respect for his character and integrity that defused my outrage at behavior often so different from my own," Ashe wrote. He added, "What bound me to McEnroe was not simply his rage but also his selflessness in making sacrifices to play for our country, and his artistry on the tennis court. I couldn't resist that combination. I began to see him as a brother. He was, in some ways, an incorrigible brother; but our fights were indeed, in my mind, 'intrafamilial.'"[9]

Ashe's depiction of the relationship as practically familial is telling. A relative is someone we're stuck with, someone we're more unconditionally committed to than a friend whose company we might prefer and whose reciprocity is required. A bond formed between these two tennis greats, one that was deep and complex, welding together two men who were in many ways complete opposites, yet at a deeper level kindred spirits. Ashe recognized the virtue in Mac, despite his very public failures, and he saw that virtue can sometimes be less about behavior than the struggle required to behave rightly, a bigger challenge for some than for others. In the Tennis Hall of Fame in Newport, Rhode Island, is a water color of Arthur Ashe. John McEnroe donated it to the museum.

Ashe's concern about Mac's behavior and his recognition of virtuous aspects of Mac's character reveal that their friendship to some degree and in certain ways shaded into Aristotle's third and highest form of friendship.

Friendships of Virtue

For Aristotle, friendships of both pleasure and usefulness pale in comparison with the highest form of friendship, friendship in the fullest sense. Such friendships exist between friends who are more than just useful to or pleasurable for one another—these are for people of virtue. Virtues for Aristotle are stable character traits achieved by hitting the right mark between the lines, as it were, avoiding both the excesses and deficiencies that make for vice. Through the right achievement of moderation, one achieves the virtue of courage, for example, rather than fall to either cowardice (which is the deficiency) or rashness (the excess). In friendships grounded in virtue, the friend's character and integrity enhance the pleasure and usefulness of the friendship. The friends care about each other's character and enjoy each other for each's own sake and in virtue of each's own goodness, rather than just some benefit the friendship accords. And friends of the highest type genuinely wish good things for each other as well.[10]

A friendship in this sense in the context of tennis might obtain between two individuals who, say, grow to respect one another for their sportsmanship and excellence of play. The enjoyment and usefulness derived from playing one another are a direct function of recognizing such underlying character that manifests in tennis. The opponents mutually recognize in each other the way they consistently hit the right note, balancing competitive fire with a respect for the opposition, a desire to win with respect for the game, a desire for excellence with an appreciation of an opponent's superior play. A friendship rooted in virtue like this will be largely free from jealousy; in contrast, a virtuous friend will root for another, not merely and certainly not primarily to win, but to win virtuously. A virtue-friend's winning a tournament, even if it's at her virtuous friend's expense, won't be perceived by the friend as detracting from her; the victory can be a victory for both parties in the deepest sense. Rather than diminishing the losing friend, it enhances both friends, for mutual growth in virtue is possible even if only one can win the tournament. All of this sounds perhaps a bit overly ideal in the crucible of a real-world, world-class rivalry, but supposing it is, it still can constitute something of an ideal of which to be aware, even if one never fully actualized.

So can two tennis rivals remain friends? According to Aristotle, they surely can. What's most clearly at stake is not just a victory but the sort of people the friends are. Win or lose, the friends can share in growth of character and virtue, for such things aren't a scarce resource available for only one. Such rivals can still care passionately about winning and can try their best to beat each other, but they can come to recognize, perhaps in fits and starts, that winning, though important, is not the only or most important thing there is.

For one salient example of a virtuous friendship between two great tennis rivals, let's turn our attention to Martina Navratilova and Chris Evert, whose rivalry and friendship inspired a whole book, entitled *The Rivals*. Ashe presciently anticipated the possibility of such a book when he wrote that "someone could write a book about, for instance, the rivalry between Chris Evert and Martina Navratilova, which was not only glorious and protracted—both were superb players—but also fraught with so many rich overtones deriving from their very different personalities and histories."[11] Navratilova and Evert, by their own admission, are flawed people, like everyone else, and Evert in particular has taken pains to emphasize that she was never quite the innocent princess many early on presumed her to be. We use their example of a virtuous friendship not unrealistically but rather as a recognition of how, in the crucible of real life, a career-long struggle for tennis dominance, altogether contrasting styles of play and public personas, along with an unusual range of life's normal vicissitudes, these two extraordinary women came to care deeply for one another and each other's well-being. And in the process they formed an authentic and lasting friendship that, in many ways, serves as a model worthy of emulation. In the penultimate paragraph of her book about their great rivalry and friendship, Johnette Howard writes, "They are proof that conviction counts, and that by telling the truth, you carve out room for more truth around you. Evert and Navratilova's shared odyssey underscored that if you live honorably, time can leaven the ups and downs, the heartbreaks and the thrills."[12]

What makes the virtuous friendship between Navratilova and Evert all the more impressive are some of the reasons friendship among the top tier of professional female tennis players was especially difficult in their era. Citing an interview of Steffi Graf, Arthur Ashe elaborated on this dynamic—while pointing out that on one level women were more sociable than men on the tour, in terms of union and associational activity, and while qualifying his point that the dynamic of which Graf speaks didn't hold so true at the amateur level. "Aggressively seeking dominance and almost careless about the possible consequences, men tend to challenge one another with macho posturing. Women, on the other hand [at the amateur level], seem to take exquisite care not to offend one another and jeopardize their friendships. Frequently, they may even play beneath their top level of skill in order to preserve peace. Not so on the women's tour, according to Graf and several other commentators."[13]

What Graf pointed to in her interview with *Tennis* magazine was an almost poisoned atmosphere among the women players, resulting in her best friends being men on the tour. "The rivalry among women tennis players is overwhelming," she said.[14] In considering why this dynamic of antisocial competition prevailed among the top women players, Ashe found Laura Tracy's analysis insightful in her book *The Secret between Us: Competition among Women*. Tracy refers to the "secret" as this: while women have been socialized by the ideal of femininity to deny that they are competitive and to resist being openly competitive, they have no choice but to be competitive for jobs, possessions, and the like. But the denial of the reality of competition can force women to act subversively and destructively, especially against other women, as they make their way through life. Competition, Ashe summarizes, becomes a clandestine and often self-destructive activity, one that preys on and exacerbates the elements of vulnerability in a woman.

Tracy writes—remember this was several decades ago—that women have been taught that competition is immoral, that they've been socialized against full participation in our economy and our history. They have been taught to be secret competitors, and their secret has kept them subordinated members of our society. Most of them recognize competition only when it's practiced by another woman. Even worse, many of them often don't realize they are in a competition until they have lost it. Unlike men, then, women don't have the masculine ideal of win-at-any-cost guiding them; rather, they can't make competition impersonal the way men can, and thus they tend to be haunted by fears not simply that they will seem selfish or greedy but that they actually will be that way.

In the realm of professional tennis, competition is the very essence of the activity, and especially with all that's at stake, the context generated is quite different from the rest of the world (well, there's always politics). Where the killer instinct, fierce independence, will to win, willingness to stand alone, and tenacious belief in oneself, not to mention assertiveness and aggressiveness, are what's needed for the highest levels of success, women conditioned by the ideals of femininity (as construed classically) understandably feel huge tensions. Ashe concluded that women were faced by "many more subtle and complex obstacles than have faced their male counterparts on the professional tour," obstacles forged by cultural dynamics owing to understandings of gender and a presumed tension between fierce competition and the ideals of femininity. If some of Tracy's analysis today seems a bit dated, we can hope that's a mark of some societal improvement in this area of gender relations. In Graf's interview, despite the paucity of friendships among the professional women on the tour (at that time), she cited, as Ashe put it, "both Martina and Chris as shining examples of friendship, courtesy, and respect extended to her in the otherwise rather bleak social world of women's tennis, as Graf experienced it."[15]

C. S. Lewis on Friendship

As a scholar trained in both literature and philosophy, C. S. Lewis hoped for a resurgence of the ancient view of friendship as the most fully human of all love and the crown of life. He recognized that friendship is now often thought of as eliminable, an optional diversion. It's true, he thought, that friendship, like art, philosophy, or tennis, is something we can do without, but it's one of the things that can help make life worth living too.

One of friendship's most important distinguishing features, he argued, is that, whereas lovers are face to face, absorbed in each other, friends are absorbed in some common interest.[16] He thought that some shared activity is a prerequisite for friendship, whether it be a common profession, common studies, perhaps even a shared recreation—like tennis. Friends are side by side; their eyes look ahead, focused on a shared passion. This means, among other things, that merely seeking friends tends to be futile, for friendships are about something. Friendship is a journey that requires a destination: "If, at the outset, we had attended more to [our friend] and less to the thing our Friendship is 'about,' we should not have come to know or love him so well. You will not find the warrior, the poet, the philosopher, or the Christian by staring in his eyes as if he were your mistress: better fight beside him, read with him, argue with him, pray with him."[17]

Friendship in this sense of a shared venture and perspective certainly seems consistent with a great rivalry. Indeed, considering the likelihood that the challenge of staying the world's #1 player or sustaining a winning streak at Wimbledon is something that can only be understood by those few others with similar experience, rivals in this sense would seem able to share in experiences of which nearly everyone else can't help but remain irremediably ignorant. After Sampras's last major final, he and Agassi agreed to stay in contact "just in life." "We agreed," Sampras writes, "that it would be a shame, after all we'd been through together, to lose touch. Besides, we had a lot of things in common, including two kids each. We'd been players since the age of seven. We had a lot of history, a lot of life—a certain kind of life—in common."[18]

René Stauffer's biography of Federer also details in a chapter on Tiger Woods and Pete Sampras how Federer has more recently formed a friendship with them both.[19] Of course what all three hold in common is a complete domination of play against the competition in their respective spheres and eras. This makes for the possibility of a unique bond. Since Federer's and Sampras's careers just barely overlapped, and Federer and Tiger aren't in the same sport, there are few of the tensions that can accompany a shared dominance in a field.

Lewis also recognized that, though friendship can be a school of virtue, it can also be one of vice. "It makes good men better and bad men worse," and in a variety of ways. For example, friendships require a certain deafness to those outside the circle, but the partial deafness that's noble and necessary "encourages the wholesale deafness which is arrogant and inhuman." The initial humility felt at being part of a group of friends can easily transition into corporate pride and sense of superiority, "a little self-elected (and therefore absurd) aristocracy, basking in the moonshine of our collective self-approval."[20]

This brings us to the last account of friendship we will consider, provided by a philosopher who wished to turn on its head the notion that the purpose of friendship at its best or in its highest form was to inculcate virtue, construed classically. What Lewis would vociferously reject, this thinker enthusiastically embraced.

The Overman

Rife with aphorism and subject to varying interpretation, Friedrich Nietzsche's writings can be hard to decipher. Like many prodigies in tennis, Nietzsche too was a prodigy, though of the mind, becoming a chaired professor by the tender age of twenty-four. Not easily domesticated or romanticized, his writings are challenging and iconoclastic, typically an effort to turn on their heads a number of Christian teachings and morals. His goal was to effect a grand reversal of ethics, a "transvaluation of values," according to which many traditional Judeo-Christian virtues (such as humility and, importantly, pity) would be seen as vices, while restoring value to such ancient virtues as pride. Among the virtues he wished to extol were strength, courage, and conquest. What were discussed earlier as the "feminine virtues" would have revolted him, insofar as they were seen as enervating. Most charitably construed, his antipathy was a result of his aversion to the way women are typically socialized and conditioned, requiring them to renounce conquest and achievement or, at most, to pursue such goals subversively.

In *The Genealogy of Morality* and elsewhere, Nietzsche suggests that in the "master morality" heroic figures or natural nobles actively rather than passively define themselves by, as it were, looking in the mirror and approving of what they see—strength, martial prowess, intelligence, et cetera. This leads them to distinguish the good (themselves) from the bad or plain, those lesser persons who fail to exhibit the attributes the masters observe primarily in themselves. But there is something more to the story, for the natural nobles are also able to recognize one another and regard each other with, if not warmth, a suitable respect.

Perhaps it's not too big a stretch to argue that Nietzsche, to whom art mattered a great deal (and tennis certainly has its aesthetic elements, as several chapters in this book emphasize), would have seen the tennis greats as a cut above, potential "overmen," heroic figures, rare individuals of tremendous achievement and prowess. Great tennis rivals of such caliber, he would think, could come to regard each other, after many epic athletic battles, as comrades to a greater or lesser degree. These men and women to some extent look at their rivals and see something worthy of approval, just as they approve of themselves. This, it could be thought, is a valuable aspect of individual competition. Sometimes these rivalries turn into warm friendships; other times, as in the case of McEnroe and Lendl, all that emerges from the rivalry is a sort of grudging respect, coupled with straightforward dislike.

Friendship for Nietzsche was less about warm feelings and more about relationships that spurred individuals on to yet greater forms of excellence, achievement, and creativity. The best friend is also the best enemy, inspiring one's best. Friends, he was wont to say, show their mutual devotion by clashing head-on. Life in the modern state withers the will of great souls, so there aren't many such heroic figures anymore; finding one is rare. The possibility of a friendship between two of them is rarer still.

Perhaps the greatest irony of all in Nietzsche's analysis is that such "star friendships" between overmen are best illustrated by pointing not to a pair of friends but a single individual.[21] For unlike Aristotle's goal of an activity of reason that is able to be shared between virtuous friends,

Nietzsche would say that the overman ultimately must strive for complete self-definition and independence. The star player might need the other star in order to play his very best, but his goal is ultimately to stand alone, at the top of the heap. He strives to be the winner who has vanquished every other foe—the lone ranger willing to renounce even those friendships with the other heroic figures in order to emerge victorious and achieve the highest level of creativity and make the biggest impact. Who might our example be?

To our thinking, there's one player who best of all in the realm of tennis represents the paradigm of a Nietzschean overman: Jimmy Connors. By his own admission, Connors was not a team player, in part accounting for his aversion to Davis Cup. When he did get involved, he resented the greater attention paid to his teammate McEnroe. He refused to ever admit that Mac was better, even after his infamous drubbing at Mac's hands in 1984 at Wimbledon. Connors was renowned for keeping his game face on before, during, and after matches, even in the locker room. For him his opponents weren't collaborators but competitors who threatened his bread and butter. Of Connors, Borg wrote in his autobiography that they were not really friends. Connors was the consummate showman, did nothing to forfeit a psychological advantage, fought for every point, saw tennis as an absolutely zero-sum game.

Arthur Ashe had this to say of Connors, indicative of the effect the man produced:

> Connors' effervescence, the stellar quality of his magnetism and drive, lifted everyone. . . . Connors wore an air of such arrogance that he regularly intimidated his opponents even before he had hit a ball. Then he proceeded to smack the ball with a force that bordered on vindictiveness. His two-handed backhand shot was among the most damaging strokes ever seen in tennis. . . . Jimmy's return of serve was unbridled aggression. . . . His heart was always in it, and his readiness to fight never left him. . . . Looking back from the early 1990s, with Connors still playing well, I see that he was the greatest male tennis player, bar none, in the two and a half decades since the Open era began in 1968. No top player lasted longer as a major attraction or so thoroughly captured the admiration and sympathy of the public for the same length of time. Only Billie Jean King, with her mixture of dedicated feminism, general gifts of leadership, and athletic brilliance, has been more important among all tennis players since World War II.[22]

Some readers may find dubious our application of the Nietzschean over-man idea and the correlative notion of the star friend to a tennis player. But if any player could be chosen, we'd be hard-pressed to find a more suitable candidate, a player whose fight not just to get to the top but to stay there nearly defies description where the inner impulse to dominate is concerned. If the title does properly apply, in some measure or sense, Connors was the best sort of friend to his rivals, by Nietzschean stan-dards: not a warm and fuzzy fellow, but one who always pushed them to their limits, never gave up, made them play their best to beat him, and offered them too a chance for greatness. As Nietzsche wrote, perhaps aptly with respect to Connors and his rivals especially, "Let us then be-lieve in our star friendship even if we should be compelled to be earth enemies."[23] In *Thus Spake Zarathustra*, Nietzsche actually offers the paradoxical argument that the best friend may indeed also be an enemy.[24] Looked at from a certain respectable perspective, perhaps Connors would appreciate this sort of tribute paid on his behalf to his (few!) rivals.

Tensions and Other Unresolved Problems

Rather than ending this chapter by telling you whom we think was right and wrong, we will leave it to readers to come to their own conclusions. We have seen a variety of perspectives on the nature of friendship, and a number of ways to construe the connection between friendship and ri-vals. What remains unclear is how best to understand the tension that emerges within the context of a friendship between rivals when they're competing for the same prize. Whether the tension takes a back seat to the superior goal of a higher shared purpose or can be eliminated by compartmentalizing the competition and the friendship or by women es-chewing ideals of femininity or men adopting them is an important ques-tion. Along these lines, one might ask whether the tension is an ineliminable aspect of friendship and rightly celebrated or is lamented but thought inevitable and something that must be simply lived with. In any case, it's clear that the tension's existence can serve to make us think about what a true friendship is really all about. It's mildly amusing that an essay (and book) on tennis ends with a reflection on the importance of tension!

Notes

1. In another sense, the love the Williams sisters have for each other goes beyond friendship, of course. As sisters who seem genuinely close, they probably have a much deeper bond than many friends do. This, however, is not always the case. Siblings are not necessarily friends, and, not uncommonly, friends can be far closer emotionally than siblings. Sibling relationship is (typically) rooted in a biological deliverance, not a volitional preference the way friendship is (although volition may have much to do with loving a sibling); thus the saying, "We can choose our friends, but we're stuck with our relatives." It seems more likely that a "mere" friendship between rivals would cool or snap than that a sibling rivalry would ruin the relationship, since clear thinking immediately reveals the primacy of, say, a sibling relationship over even, say, a Grand Slam; but stranger things have been known to happen. Family relationships ideally feature *agape* (unconditional) love, not merely friendship, or *phileo* love, but hopefully *phileo* love as well. A third type of love is *eros*, romantic love; *agape*, *eros*, and *phileo* love are not mutually exclusive. Hopefully a marriage features all three. We need not settle here whether they are collectively exhaustive.

2. It's probably attributable to the erosion of the notion of friendship that "friendly" has come to mean niceness, affability, et cetera, rather than the thicker and richer traits associated with genuine friendship; but if we were to defer to such watered-down and common colloquialisms, we could say that part of the goal of this chapter is, more minimally, to ask how rivals (opponents, conflicting partisans, et cetera) can remain at least on "friendly" terms despite the conflict.

3. Alasdair MacIntyre criticizes Aristotle's analysis of friendship on this ground: "His catalogue of types of friend presupposes that we can always ask the questions, On what is this friendship based? For the sake of what does it exist? There is therefore no room left for the type of human relationship of which it would miss the point totally to ask on what it is based, for the sake of which it existed. Such relationships can be very different." Alasdair MacIntyre, *A Short History of Ethics* (Notre Dame, IN: Notre Dame University Press, 2007), 80.

4. My [Neil's] old hitting partner, Paul Koscielski, was ranked #1 at the University of Texas, Austin and also played professionally but found hitting with me good for his game; I never really regarded him as either friend or enemy!

5. Mark Ryan, *Justine Henin: From Tragedy to Triumph* (New York: St. Martin's, 2008), 39.

6. Arthur Ashe and Arnold Rampersad, *Days of Grace: A Memoir* (New York: Ballantine, 1993), 86.

7. Ibid., 88.

8. Ibid., 89.

9. Ibid., 89, 90.

10. For an eminently useful resource on Aristotle and friendship, see Lorraine Smith Pangle's *Aristotle and the Philosophy of Friendship* (Cambridge: Cambridge University Press, 2003).

11. Ibid., 263.

12. Johnette Howard, *The Rivals: Chris Evert vs. Martina Navratilova, Their Epic Duels and Extraordinary Friendship* (New York: Broadway, 2005), 271.

13. Ashe and Rampersad, *Days of Grace*, 260.

14. Ibid.

15. Ibid., 263.

16. Here's a passage from Lewis instructive in this regard: "Friendship arises out of mere Companionship when two or more of the companions discover that they have in common some insight or interest or even taste which the others do not share and which, till that moment, each believed to be his own unique treasure (or burden). The typical expression of opening Friendship would be something like, 'What? You too? I thought I was the only one.' We can imagine that among those early hunters and warriors single individuals—one in a century? One in a thousand years?—saw what others did not; saw that the deer was beautiful as well as edible, that hunting was fun as well as necessary, dreamed that his gods might be not only powerful but holy. But as long as each of these percipient persons dies without finding a kindred soul, nothing (I suspect) will come of it; art or sport or spiritual religion will not be born. It is when two such persons discover one another . . . they share their vision—it is then that Friendship is born. And instantly they stand together in an immense solitude." C. S. Lewis, *The Four Loves* (New York: Harcourt Brace Jovanovich, 1960), 96–97.

17. Ibid., 104. Lewis's observation that friends look at projects side by side as opposed to pure romantic lovers, who may gaze at each other, seems especially useful when considering a doubles partnership like that between Mac and Peter Fleming. One can only imagine the almost martial solidarity that those two felt as they played Davis Cup in front of hostile crowds. Indeed, they did to some extent resemble comrades in arms, which seems to be a friendly amendment to the basic Lewisian model.

18. Pete Sampras, with Peter Bodo, *A Champion's Mind: Lessons from a Life in Tennis* (New York: Random House, 2008), 273.

19. René Stauffer, *The Roger Federer Story: Quest for Perfection* (New York: New Chapter, 2006), 169–74.

20. Lewis, *Four Loves*, 117, 122.

21. For powerful resources on Nietzsche and friendship, read Ruth Abbey's "Circles, Ladders and Stars: Nietzsche on Friendship," in *The Challenge to Friendship in Modernity*, ed. Preston King and Heather Devere (London: Frank Cass, 2000), 50–72. In addition, we would direct you to Peter Berkowitz's *Nietzsche: The Ethics of an Immoralist* (Cambridge: Harvard University Press, 1995), esp. 171–75. Also see Daniel Conway's *Nietzsche's* On the Genealogy of Morals (London: Continuum, 2008) and Brian Leiter's *Routledge Philosophy Guidebook to Nietzsche on Morality* (New York: Routledge, 2002).

22. Ashe and Rampersad, *Days of Grace*, 82.

23. See Friedrich Nietzsche, *The Gay Science* (New York: Random House, 1974), section 279.

24. Friedrich Nietzsche, *Thus Spake Zarathustra* (New York: Dover, 1999), part 1, chap. 14.

THE PLAYERS

David Baggett is professor of philosophy at Liberty University. He's the editor or coeditor of six books, most recently *Did the Resurrection Happen? A Dialogue with Gary Habermas and Antony Flew* (InterVarsity Press, 2009). His next book, *Good God: The Theistic Foundations of Morality*, with Jerry Walls, is forthcoming (Oxford University Press). Despite his portly appearance, he assures us that in reality, down deep under the surface, there resides quite an agile tennis player.

Robert R. Clewis is assistant professor of philosophy at Gwynedd-Mercy College, Pennsylvania. Robert's book, *The Kantian Sublime and the Revelation of Freedom* (Cambridge University Press, 2009) examines Kant's theory of spectatorship and enthusiasm. He recently published a chapter, "A Spielbergian Ethics of the Family in *Saving Private Ryan* and *The Color Purple*," in *Steven Spielberg and Philosophy* (University Press of Kentucky, 2008). Robert is a USTA sectionally ranked tennis player, a tennis enthusiast, an assistant coach, and even a Kantian. He could play all of these roles well, if only he didn't suffer from an identity crisis.

Neil Delaney currently teaches philosophy at Ohio State University, having taught previously at Georgetown, Arizona State, and the University of Nevada, Las Vegas. He works primarily in moral philosophy. His articles and reviews have appeared in numerous scholarly journals, including the *American Philosophical Quarterly, Philosophical Studies,* and *Notre Dame Philosophical Reviews,* and in anthologies in English and German. As a junior player he was four-time First Team All-State, re-

ceived an All-American Honorable Mention, and garnered over sixty titles in singles and doubles. He was also highly ranked in the Westerns and
played on the JV team at Stanford University. Delaney has never won a
sportsmanship award at any level of competition for anything.

David Detmer is professor of philosophy at Purdue University Calumet.
He is the author of three books: *Sartre Explained* (Open Court, 2008),
Challenging Postmodernism: Philosophy and the Politics of Truth (2003),
and *Freedom as a Value* (Humanity Books, 1988), as well as essays on a
wide variety of philosophical topics. Formerly a notorious hothead, he
has calmed down in recent years and has not been ejected for arguing a
point since the 1998 World Congress of Philosophy.

Helen Ditouras is currently assistant professor of English at Schoolcraft
College in Livonia, Michigan. Her academic interests include popular
culture, feminist theory, and film and philosophy. Although she never
played tennis for her high school, Helen played female and mixed doubles on her high school badminton team for three years and is eager to
resume the sport. Though a fan of tennis, she currently lives happily with
her husband and son, whose love most definitely means considerably
more than nothing.

Mark Foreman is professor of philosophy and religion at Liberty University. Author of *Christianity and Bioethics: Confronting Clinical Issues*
(College Press, 1999) and at work on an introductory text in philosophy,
Mark is interested in ethics, bioethics, and philosophy of religion. He
recently finished his doctorate at the University of Virginia, where his
initiative to turn The Lawn into one big grass tennis court was consistently thwarted.

Mark R. Huston is currently assistant professor of philosophy at Schoolcraft College in Livonia, Michigan. His philosophical interests are in the
areas of mind, epistemology, aesthetics, and film. He also started playing
tennis when he was eight years old (ping-pong at six), played #1 singles
for a year on his high school tennis team, and currently plays about two
times each summer. Hopefully, that number will increase.

Kevin Kinghorn is philosophy tutor at Wycliffe Hall, University of Oxford, and associate professor of philosophy at Asbury Theological Seminary. He is the author of *The Decision of Faith: Can Christian Beliefs Be Freely Chosen?* (T&T Clark, 2005), as well as various articles in ethics and philosophy, including a contributing essay for *Basketball and Philosophy*. His office in Oxford, England, overlooks a row of picturesque lawn-tennis courts, which he delights in frequenting during the three weeks of the year when it's not raining.

Maureen Linker is associate professor of philosophy and women's and gender studies at the University of Michigan-Dearborn. Maureen specializes in epistemology, metaphysics, and feminist theory. Her articles have appeared in journals including *Social Theory and Practice, Journal of the National Women's Studies Association,* and *Social Epistemology* and in books such as *Science and Culture; Virtue, Order, Mind; Women Succeeding in the Sciences;* and *ReReading the Canon: Feminist Interpretations of Quine.* Maureen remembers how her mother saved up one summer to afford tennis lessons for her then twelve-year-old daughter, no small feat in Brooklyn during the 1970s; and she still fondly remembers her first tennis teacher, Steve Cranberry, and the tension/excitement surrounding the King/Riggs matchup. To err is human, but Maureen hastens to add that to put the blame on someone else is doubles.

Jeanine Weekes Schroer is assistant professor of philosophy at Arkansas State University. Her teaching and research interests revolve around feminist theory, critical race theory, and ethics; her recent publications examine the cognitive challenges that social oppression poses for authentic moral agency. She spends much of her spare time hiking Arkansas' woods, fishing its rivers, and talking philosophy with her excellent partner and her very excellent cat. Her interest in tennis, developed at her father's knee, is mainly in watching Wimbledon. She continues to be mesmerized by its very crisp white costumes, by how much of the transformation of Western culture ends up on those courts, and, of course, by the flash of that vibrant yellow ball.

Tommy Valentini is a doctoral candidate in the School of Kinesiology at the University of Minnesota, where he studies sportsmanship and moral development through sport. He is also the head men's tennis coach at Gustavus Adolphus College (NCAA III). Valentini played varsity tennis at Gustavus, where he was an Arthur Ashe Sportsmanship Award winner and an Academic All-American while captaining the team to an ITA National Indoor Championship and three consecutive NCAA Division III final fours. Tommy served two seasons as the assistant women's tennis coach at the University of Nebraska-Lincoln (NCAA I). At Emory University's Candler School of Theology he wrote a master's thesis entitled "Not Winning at All Costs: An Analysis of the American Religious Culture of Sport." While at Emory, he served two seasons as assistant women's tennis coach, helping the team win two NCAA Division III national championships. A lifelong Minnesotan, Tommy finds that his lefty slice serve bites best in blizzard conditions.

David Foster Wallace, who died in 2008 and is greatly missed, is considered one of the best authors to have come out of the latter part of the twentieth century. His fiction is often ranked in the pantheon along with the works of William Gaddis, Thomas Pynchon, and others. He also wrote several excellent essays on tennis. There are two in his first collection of essays, *A Supposedly Fun Thing I'll Never Do Again,* others that have yet to be included in a collection, and an absolutely hilarious/devastating review of Tracy Austin's autobiography in his collection *Consider the Lobster*—and possibly the best of all is included here in this volume. If you have already read Wallace, then you know what to expect; if you have not read him before, you are in for a treat.

INDEX